Study Skills for Chinese Students

Mike Courtney & Xiangping Du

有中文:
关键词和
小贴士

Los Angeles | London | New Delhi
Singapore | Washington DC

Los Angeles | London | New Delhi
Singapore | Washington DC

SAGE Publications Ltd
1 Oliver's Yard
55 City Road
London EC1Y 1SP

SAGE Publications Inc.
2455 Teller Road
Thousand Oaks, California 91320

SAGE Publications India Pvt Ltd
B 1/I 1 Mohan Cooperative Industrial Area
Mathura Road
New Delhi 110 044

SAGE Publications Asia-Pacific Pte Ltd
3 Church Street
#10-04 Samsung Hub
Singapore 049483

Editor: Matthew Waters
Assistant editor: Nina Smith
Production editor: Sarah Cooke
Marketing manager: Catherine Slinn
Cover design: Shaun Mercier
Typeset by: C&M Digitals (P) Ltd, Chennai, India
Printed and bound by CPI Group (UK), Ltd,
Croydon, CR0 4YY

Library of Congress Control Number: 2014936623

British Library Cataloguing in Publication data

A catalogue record for this book is available from
the British Library

ISBN 978–1–4462–9448–2
ISBN 978–1–4462–9450–5 (pbk)

Contents

About the authors

Dr Mike Courtney is an academic skills tutor at the University of Hertfordshire, UK. He has taught in China, Hong Kong, Malaysia, the Middle East and the UK. He has researched the influence of culture and language on learning styles and academic skill development. He currently teaches in the UK and in Hong Kong, in the area of academic skills development and Open Learning.

Dr Xiangping Du is an academic skills tutor at the University of Hertfordshire, UK, supporting students in a wide range of academic skills areas. She studied in both a Chinese and English Higher Education environment, and understands the different academic expectations from her own experience both as a student and as a tutor. Her research in investigating Chinese students' perception of motivation towards, and identification with, the English language enhanced her understanding of the academic challenges Chinese students face when they come to study in an English context.

Preface

This book is written for Chinese students studying in the UK. It will give you strategies for successful study which will help you get the best marks and the best results from your studies. The book can be used as a convenient reference book for all the things that you will be required to do to successfully get your qualification.

It is important to realise that all students have similar issues, and that all students can benefit from study skills advice. We have written this book especially for Chinese students because we have taught Chinese students in China and in the West for many years, and we have observed some important differences between learning and teaching styles in China, and learning and teaching styles in the UK. We have also written parts of this book in Chinese to help Chinese students fully understand the advice we have given.

You don't need to read the book from the beginning to the end. The book is written to provide you with a complete study skills course, so reading the whole book will be a good idea. However, you can use the table of contents and the index to find particular topics that you need help with – it might be how to write reports, for example. There are five main chapters, and in each chapter you will find essential information which will help you study successfully. The information is general because each Higher Education institution will have its own specific requirements. However, there are enough similarities for us to feel that any Chinese student coming to the UK to study, whatever the subject, will be able to benefit from reading this book.

We consulted many academics and students in different Higher Education institutions when we wrote this book. Therefore, we know that particular institutions – universities and colleges – have their own specific requirements. For example, there might be differences in the way that tutors in some institutions want you to write essays and reports. There might be different referencing systems, for example. It is important therefore that you check carefully with your tutors about their specific requirements and that you follow their specific guidelines. However, the basic 'study skills' we have included in this book will be similar to all Higher Education institutions in the UK, and will help you produce the kind of work that all tutors will want to see, using 'good practice'.

We have written the book in what we hope is a very easy style to read and understand. The chapters inevitably get more detailed as you go through the book, but we hope that each chapter will be easily understandable by itself. To help you, Xiangping has also written to you personally, in each chapter, about her own experience of studying in the UK. She successfully completed a master's degree and a PhD here, so she knows 'first hand' what you will experience here. Xiangping has also put some 'study tips' in Chinese to help you fully understand each chapter.

You will hear too from some of our Chinese students about their own experiences studying in the UK.

We have also provided a convenient translation of some of the more important key words from each chapter, as well as a simple 'test' at the end of each chapter (with answers) so that you can be sure that you have understood some important points. Each chapter also provides you with some helpful activities and opportunities to think about what you have read. You don't have to complete these activities, but we think they will help you to develop your personal study skill ability.

How to use this book

You can use this book in two ways. Firstly, if you need to know specific information about essays for example, you don't have to read everything in this book from beginning to end. Use the table of contents or the index and go directly to what you need to know. Another way to use the book – and if you have time, probably the best way – is to read it completely, and complete the exercises and reflective notes. This will ensure that you cover everything and you learn the basic academic skills you will need in Higher Education in the UK.

We have given you lots of examples of general 'good practice' that would apply to any Higher Educational institution in the UK. We have also given you some useful activities to help you remember what you have read. In addition we have put a simple 'test yourself' section at the end of each chapter so that you can check to see if you correctly understood some of the most important ideas from the chapter. The answers to these self-test questions can be found in the Appendix.

Tutor, programme and module

There are some differences in the words that are used for teachers and courses in the UK and China. We have used the word 'tutor' to mean your teacher since this is the most common word for a teacher in UK Higher Education. We have also used the word 'module' to mean your 'subject', and degree or diploma 'programme' to mean your course. In China, a course is a programme and a subject is a module.

Higher Education institutions

Chinese students coming to the UK will be going to UK universities for degree programmes, but also to colleges for other types of programmes. We have therefore sometimes used the words 'institution' and 'Higher Education institution' to mean either universities or colleges.

We have used the word 'skills' to indicate the different kinds of abilities which you will need for your academic work.

Surname

In English, your family name is called your 'surname'. When we have given examples of what scholars have said, we have used the term 'Surname' to indicate the scholar. This is the usual way to show a scholar's name in the text – we don't normally use first names in academic writing.

The reflection box

THINK

Each chapter contains some questions which we would like you to reflect on and think about. Reflection is a very important part of UK education and we explain how to write reflectively in Chapters 3 and 4. Reflection means to think about what you have done, and to think about how you can do it better, and how what you are doing now will help you in the future. We would like you to make some notes to answer the THINK questions in each chapter. You can write these notes in the 'Reflection box' at the end of each chapter. This will help you focus on the chapter content. You can review your notes later to remind yourself about how you can improve.

Guide to icons

Study tips

Example

Reflection box

Think point

Activity

Test yourself

Summary of chapter contents

Chapter 1

Different cultures: Living and studying in a new country: This chapter contains some essential information for Chinese students coming to the UK to study. The chapter provides you with information to help you feel comfortable living and studying in the UK.

Chapter 2

Essential academic English skills: Because your English language skill is the most important skill to ensure that you develop effectively the other skills in this book, we have devoted this chapter to essential information and revision for the academic English you will need to use in your reading, your researching and your writing, as well as communicating effectively with your tutors and other students.

Chapter 3

Essential academic study skills: This chapter introduces you to the special study skills you will need to develop in order to study and learn effectively in the UK academic environment. You will need to use your improved understanding of academic English and academic skills to become effective in the processes of UK Higher Education.

Chapter 4

Assignments, assessment and feedback: This chapter gives you essential information about the main types of academic products that you will be expected to produce to achieve module learning outcomes, against which you will be assessed. The chapter therefore contains more detailed information about the kinds of assessment you will meet in the UK, and how you can best use feedback from your tutors to improve your academic performance.

Chapter 5

Research and dissertations: This chapter gives you further detailed information about the research aspect of Higher Education study in the UK. This chapter brings together all the study skills covered so far to help you develop one of the most important skills in Higher Education – the research skill. This is an important skill to develop because it is required not only to produce successful assignments, but also for longer individual research projects such as dissertations. The ability to research well is important for finding good secondary data for assignments, as well as carrying out primary research projects requiring your own original research.

Appendix

Answers to 'Test yourself' sections, activities and reflection writing space.

Acknowledgements

We would like to acknowledge the valuable contributions of our colleagues in the Hertfordshire Business School Centre for Academic Skills Enhancement (CASE) in the writing of this book. We also have to sincerely thank the Editorial team at SAGE, and the many anonymous reviewers of the book, for their expert and insightful comments and suggestions, which have helped us to shape the final text. Any deficiencies, errors or omissions are entirely our own responsibility.

We also need to sincerely thank all of our hard-working Chinese students for their invaluable help and comments in relation to the issues covered in this book. We must thank, in particular, Xiao Zhou (Ava) and Aoke Zhang (Cici) for the written reflections about their student experiences in the UK. Lastly, thanks to all our students who gave consent for us to use their photographs in this book.

We hope this book helps you to achieve success and happiness in your UK studies!

Mike and Xiangping

Student Endorsements

'*Study Skills for Chinese Students* really helps me to understand how to study successfully in the UK. I like the personal stories of some of the students, and Xiangping's tips in Chinese are really helpful and give me confidence.' *Aoke Zhang*

'This book gives us all the information that we need for all our assignments and reports. It has good examples and explains things very well for me. When I came to study in the UK, everything was very different from studying in China. This book is so valuable to me because it shows me how to do everything and explains why doing essays and reports in the UK are different from in China.' *Jennifer Li*

'This book is very easy to read and understand. The tips in Chinese help me make sense of English texts. I also find the examples are very useful to demonstrate 'good' and 'bad' ways of writing. I wish I had this book when I first started studying in the UK. I would strongly recommend all Chinese students studying in the UK to get hold of the book and I am sure it will make a big positive difference to their academic studies and success!' *Sean Song*

'This book is different from other study books I have used. I like the photographs and stories from real students, and I like the examples and the Chinese translations. They are very clear and helpful, and I can learn how to write good assignments and reports. The book is very detailed and covers everything that we need to know.' *Huang Zhu*

'I really like the clear and detailed explanations of the UK academic ideas and assessments. There are lots of good examples on how to structure answers and how to write and reference academically to avoid plagiarism.' *Keith Tong*

1

Introduction: Living and studying in the UK

Being successful

Congratulations! You have made a very good decision to study abroad in the UK. This book will help you to study successfully so you should read it and keep it with you while you study.

Studying in the UK is a very exciting and valuable experience for you. We know that it is very important to you, and your family, that you are very successful in your studies, and very happy with your life in the UK. Being successful while you are in the UK can mean many things:

1. Getting a good qualification.
2. Feeling happy with yourself and the new experiences you will have in the UK.
3. Improving your English language skills.
4. Gaining a wider knowledge of the world, and UK society in particular.
5. Being independent for the first time since you left China.
6. Making new friends and finding out about their countries and their lives.
7. Preparing yourself well for a good career, either back in China, or internationally.

So success can mean many things, but all of these things can come from using this book to make sure that your studies achieve the results that you want.

Chapter 1: Xiangping's study tips

Read Xiangping's tips about settling down well in the UK, managing your time well, and things that you might find strange at first about UK culture. 在来英国之前先做一些功课，了解英国的基本文化和礼仪，以及中西文化的基本差异，尤其是基本的吃、穿、住、行，以免被一些不同的行为吓倒。比如：

- 和英国人见面时，不光是是握手，他们见面**打招呼**的方式可能是一个很热情的拥抱，或者一个法式的拥抱外加亲吻你的双颊。如果这么做的是位是男士，请不要误认为他对你有什么想法或者企图，这可能只是他和你打招呼的方式。

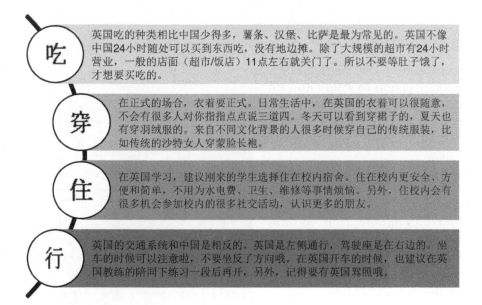

FIGURE 1.1

- **广交朋友**：尤其是与不同于自己文化背景的人交朋友，多听、多问、多说、你的眼界和见解会越来越广。尽量不要和中国人凑堆，否则你的英语很难提高。加入校内外的社团组织，增加交友学习的机会。
- **合理安排和利用时间**，做好自己的日程安排。

  o 课前：做一位"有准备的人"。俗语讲：机遇偏爱有准备的人。一定要提前预习老师要讲授的课程：查阅课程的课件，以及老师指定的阅读资料：相关书籍、文献、案例、新闻等

- o 课上：一定要认真听讲，做详细的笔记。有不明白或者不认同的观点，可以随时向老师提问，这不仅会有利于自己的学习，并且会让老师对你印象深刻
- o 课后：复习学习过的知识，阅读老师推荐的，以及其他相关的书籍和材料。理论联系实际，思考这些阅读资料与课堂学习的知识之间的关联和应用

- **任何事情都不要等到"最后一刻钟"**。有作业的时候，一定要提前开始搜索资料，计划，然后组织。提前把作业写完，给自己留出时间修改检查。因为作为国际学生，英语不是自己的母语，所以写作可谓是一项艰巨的任务，一定要给自己足够的时间准备和写作。
- **有成年人的自立和自主**，对自己负责。因为在英国的学习中，老师把大学生像成年人一样对待，所以很少老师会像对待小学生一样，检查你课堂上听懂了吗，课后阅读了么，作业做完了没。如果需要任何的帮助，你都要要自己积极主动寻找。
- 积极参加**预备周**学校或者学院组织的所有的活动和预备课程，这会是你了解学校的设施设备、组织机构、以及教授你课程的老师团队的良好的机会。
- 记住教你每门课程的老师的姓名以及职位。如果你老师的名字显示为：Dr Mary King，如果在很正式的场合你要介绍她给他人，可以说Dr King。日常学习生活中，你只需要叫他们的名 (Mary)就好了，不需要加**姓** (King)。不可以称呼他们为Dr Mary，或者King。
- 做一名能让老师记住你的好学生：上课尽量靠前坐，积极回答老师提出的问题。课后也尽量与老师交流，让老师在众多的学生中也同样记住你，**留下好的第一印象**
- 利用老师的 **Office Hour** – 老师每周至少会有一天或者两天安排几个小时的时间在自己的办公室里接见学生，你可以利用这个时间去和老师打招呼，反馈你的学习经历，探讨学习中的任何问题。
- 如果你学习、生活中遇到任何的问题，**一定要和你的老师交流**。不要等到太晚了才告知你老师。比如，你的家里发生了重要的事情，需要你回国1周处理，你一定要和老师打声招呼，最好是面对面交流，如果没有时间，至少也邮件解释一下，或者找其他的代课老师转达。
- **和来自不同文化和国度的同学交流**。利用这个机会，多了解他们，他们的文化和风俗。如果你依旧和中国同学聚在一起，你的英语会提高么？你对跨文化的了解会增强么？那又和在国内学习有什么区别？

The United Kingdom: A multicultural society

What exactly is the UK? It means the 'United Kingdom', but why 'United' and what is a 'Kingdom'? You might be confused by what exactly the 'UK' means. UK is a short form (or acronym) for the 'United Kingdom', which is also called Britain. Its full name is the 'United Kingdom of Great Britain and Northern Ireland', which indicates that it is a sovereign state consisting of two main islands: Great Britain and the north-eastern part of the island of Ireland. This is different from China, which is considered to be one country. Even though they are part of these two islands, England, Wales, Scotland and Ireland have all been regarded for centuries as nations, with their own languages and cultures, and this is still the correct way to refer to them. So we can talk about the English nation, the Scottish nation, the Welsh nation and the Irish nation. Each of these nations has had kings or queens to rule them in the past. This is why we still use the word 'Kingdom'.

What does 'British' mean?

You will hear this word quite often when you are in the UK. You might hear people say that they are British, or that they prefer British food for example. It is the established term for anything which relates to the UK. So if you have a British passport, you are a 'British citizen'. Sometimes, the word 'British' is shortened to the word 'Brits' to refer to British citizens.

The UK is a multicultural society with people from many different nations, ethnic groups, cultures, and religions. In the UK, the word 'foreigner' is not a polite word to describe people from outside the UK. People can be referred to by their country of origin – so you are Chinese, but not a 'foreigner'. It is government policy to treat all citizens fairly and equally under the law, regardless of their country of origin.

The UK is regarded as a monolingual English-speaking society, and the main originator of the English language. The English language is the only official language used in central government. It is one of the most widely spoken languages globally, particularly in business, and is also one of the most popular foreign languages learned and used in the world. The global use of the English language brings many international students to the UK, and China provides one of the largest groups of international students in the UK.

The European Union

The UK and Republic of Ireland are also members of the European Union (EU), which is an international organisation (not a state). It has its own laws which member countries must obey. Citizens of all the member countries have the right to settle in any member state. You will find many European citizens living and working in the UK.

THINK 1.1

What differences do you think you will find between your education experience in China and your new study home in the UK? Write some notes in the reflection box at the end of this chapter.

The UK Higher Education system

In the UK, many students go on to 'higher' education from 'secondary' education. As in China, good final exam results are essential for all British students who want to go on to further study. However, students also enter Higher Education from many other different routes. Since learning is regarded as a lifelong process, many adults enter Higher Education after years spent in other careers, often enrolling on 'distance' modules which are largely taught online, with minimal actual contact with tutors. In UK Higher Education, there is a great diversity of qualifications and study programmes. You will meet students from many different social, cultural and political backgrounds. You will also meet students engaged in many different types of degree programmes, such as direct entrants to particular programme years, on 'top-up' degrees, as well as European students on 'double-degree' programmes from European universities. This diversity is an important characteristic of the UK Higher Education system.

Most UK universities follow the same educational timetable as UK schools. The 'academic year' begins in late September or early October, and finishes in June or July the following year. Universities can either have three 'terms' beginning in September/October, January and May; or they may choose to adopt the American system of two 'semesters' a year, starting in September/October and January. It is also important to remember that although all universities are given rankings in national and global league tables, all UK universities, regardless of their rankings, will provide excellent teaching and learning opportunities.

Foundation modules

In addition to the main types of qualifications, some colleges and universities run special foundation or pre-sessional programmes for students who do not meet the normal entry requirements. These foundation programmes usually include more English language training for international students.

Bachelor's/undergraduate degrees

These are normally three-year degree programmes, although they might be longer if they involve work experience (internships or placements) or overseas exchanges, as part of the programme. These 'first' degrees are undergraduate degrees and are still called 'bachelor's' degrees because, originally, only males could study for degrees at university. These programmes lead to

5

awards such as Bachelor of Arts (BA) and Bachelor of Science (BSc). Both of these awards are at the same level, the only difference being that a BA is awarded in arts subjects, and a BSc normally only for 'science' subjects such as maths or engineering.

Many degree programmes now involve a year of 'placement' in industry, making the degree four years in total. This is sometimes called a 'sandwich' programme because, like the sandwich you can eat, it has something extra in the middle. Each year, undergraduate students take a number of 'modules' in their subjects, eventually getting enough 'credits' to be awarded the degree on completion of the three or four years. The degree can be awarded with 'honours' for those students achieving a higher number of credits

Master's/postgraduate degrees

Once students have obtained their undergraduate degree, they can apply for postgraduate degree study. Master's degrees are usually one-year programmes undertaken after completing an undergraduate degree. They often involve some extended research to produce a research report called a 'dissertation'. They are classed as taught postgraduate degrees and can be classified according to the subject area, for example, Master of Science (MSc) or Master of Arts (MA). You can also study for a Master of Philosophy (MPhil) which is a shorter research degree, completed to the same academic quality as a PhD, but suiting students who are not able to commit to a lengthy period of study.

All British master's degrees are 'research' degrees, although they include different taught modules. However, master's students are expected to develop independent learning skills. A master's degree is also a basic training in academic research, and requires intensive study and usually the production of a 'dissertation' which is a long research report on a topic that the student chooses, but is guided by a 'supervisor' in the choice. Research and critical-thinking skills are very important for this type of degree. Apart from studying other subject modules, students spend a significant amount of the time researching their specialist subject area by themselves.

Doctorates

A doctorate (PhD) is the next (and highest) qualification you can obtain in the UK. It normally takes three to four years to complete with full-time study. You normally need a good first degree, and a good master's degree, before you are accepted by a university for a PhD. Master's students can progress to a PhD if they have good academic results, and want to follow an academic career.

THINK 1.2

You can achieve excellent results wherever you study in the UK. How will a good qualification from the UK help you in your future life? Write some notes in the reflection box at the end of this chapter.

Adaptation issues

UK culture

Because the UK is a multicultural country, there is really no such thing as 'UK culture' – there are people of many different cultures living and working together in the UK. There are, however, general traditions and special ways of doing things, which you might see as very different from the way that people do things in China. One good way to learn about these differences is to make sure that you get out as much as you can, and travel on weekends and holidays to different places in the UK. Talking to 'home' students from the UK  will also be another good way to learn about cultural differences, as will watching British films, British TV programmes and watching and listening to British Broadcasting Corporation (BBC) news and current affairs programmes. This will also improve your ability to speak and understand English.

UK climate

An easy way to start a conversation with anyone in the UK is to mention the weather, e.g. 'It's a lovely day, isn't it?' Because the UK is a group of islands, the weather is particularly changeable, and is often very wet and cold in the winter. In winter – from November to February – the nights become dark quite early, around four to five o'clock in the evening. Some people get quite depressed at this time of year and 'seasonal affective disorder' (SAD) – sadness and depression – is said to often result. Many Chinese students, like UK citizens, find that the British climate affects them a lot. You may be used to a much warmer climate in Southern China, for example, or you may just find the rain and grey skies of an English winter a bit depressing. However, the weather tends to improve from spring (April) onwards.

Food and sleep

One important way to keep yourself happy is to eat well. Food is important to everyone, and is a especially important part of Chinese culture. Chinese students are especially interested in trying new types of dishes, as well as good Chinese food. Food in the UK is no longer just 'fish and chips' as many newly arrived Chinese students seem to think it is. There are many other local 'British' speciality foods and traditional dishes which you should definitely try, and the UK has many international restaurants and supermarkets from most countries in the world. There are also many specialist Chinese supermarkets in most towns and cities. Many supermarkets have their own economy brands which are very reasonably priced for students who need to be careful with their money. There are also many different types of 'fast food', outlets in the UK, many of which will be familiar to you from China. Italian food is very popular with Chinese students, possibly because the Chinese are said to have invented pasta noodles, and there are many Italian restaurants in the UK.

If you like Szechuan food, then you might like Indian and Thai food, which is also very spicy, and very popular in the UK, so there are many Indian and Thai restaurants in the UK. The Chinese restaurants in the UK make dishes according to British tastes, and the food may be different from similar dishes in China. Most Chinese students tend to cook their own food together, using fresh ingredients from Chinese supermarkets. Remember, this is also a good time to invite English speakers to your cooking evening; you can also practise English, as well as get information about other types of cooking from different countries.

It is also very important to make sure that you get plenty of sleep. As a student in a new environment, you might feel that it is very exciting to sit up all night with other students, but if you do this every night, you will quickly find that your studies will suffer and you will not be able to get up in time for your lectures. Try to make sure that you keep the weekend for socialising and the week for studying. A good 'work–life balance' is essential to be successful.

Communication issues

Adapting well to the new UK culture will be important to ensure study success. Communication issues and general homesickness can make you feel sad if you have not been to the UK before. This can be made worse if you feel that you had been a very good student in China, but because of communication issues, you are not able to show your ability to your tutors or other students in the UK. You might start to feel you are not doing very well, and you might feel it is impossible for you to succeed.

These are quite natural feelings, but most Chinese students manage very well once they have settled into their study routine, and made some friends. However, if you do experience personal problems, and you start to feel depressed, you must talk to your tutor or your international student adviser. In the UK, you are encouraged to discuss personal problems because we know that happy students will generally be more successful students.

Concerns about success

Although you will have an exciting time studying in the UK, we know that you will also be worried about keeping up with your studies and being successful. You might feel worried about your English, or saying and doing the 'right' thing in situations which are strange to you.

These feelings are common to many students. However, the reasons for feeling uncomfortable will vary. When you are listening to academic English, you may find it hard to admit to the tutor that you do not understand what was said. This might be because you don't want your tutor to think you are not a good student, or it might also mean that you are nervous about starting any conversation, because you feel you might not be able to think of the 'right' words to say in reply. Here is what a Chinese student, Xiao Zhou (Ava), has to say:

When I first came to the UK to study, I was too shy to talk to my tutor when I got the chance to. I was thinking about questions like: How do I organise my English to talk to him? How do I make him understand? If I ask a question in this way, would he think I should know the answer myself before talking to him? Therefore, I always lost my chance to communicate with him. But I realised that if I don't break my own barriers and be brave enough to ask, I will never learn and improve myself. I was also aware that although he was my tutor, I still needed to communicate with him as well as I did with the other students. I went to him and expressed these thoughts to him. My communication wasn't very organised, but he understood me quite well and we felt very relaxed, and it was easier to communicate with him after that. I also felt very pleased with myself for taking this opportunity.

ACTIVITY 1.1

What kind of student are you? A personal SWOT assessment is a general assessment which looks at your strengths and weaknesses, the opportunities you have, and any threats that you can see to your success. Complete a SWOT assessment using the headings below, and the space provided in the Appendix. You can repeat the SWOT assessment when you have finished the first part of your study in the UK to see if you have increased your strengths!

My current strengths as a student

My current weaknesses as a student

Current opportunities for my study success

Current threats to my study success

Induction

You will be given an induction (sometimes called 'orientation') period after you arrive at your institution. This is designed to give you all the basic information you will need, and often includes important things like meeting your tutors and choosing your modules. You will probably not get your timetable at this stage – you will be given this just before teaching starts – but induction is a very important process and you should not miss it. If you arrive late because of transport or visa problems, make sure that you contact the student advisers to receive this induction information. This induction period is also a very good time to start making friends.

Communicating with your tutors

In the UK, the relationship between students and tutors can sometimes appear to be very different from the traditional 'Confucian' view that you will have experienced in China. This can lead to misunderstandings when Chinese students come to study here. Chinese students often feel that their UK tutors are not as available as their teachers in China, but this is largely because of communication issues.

From our own experience of teaching in China, we know that Chinese students may be used to a closer relationship with their tutors – almost like a 'parental' relationship on the part of the tutors. Tutors in China tend to be more available largely because many tutors actually live on the campus with their students. As a result, there is often more socialising between tutors and students in China. In the UK, this will normally only happen during formal induction programmes, or perhaps as a special event during a module, but all your UK tutors will want to encourage you to communicate with them, and they want you to succeed. Your tutors have office hours during term time when you can 'drop in' and discuss any issues of your concern, or just for a casual chat about your studies and to say hello.

In some cases, Chinese students can feel that their UK tutors do not know them very well. This would be a wrong impression – all tutors are professionals, and always value their students highly, but they are very busy people, with many students to manage, and research projects to complete. Your tutors will want you to feel positive about your learning experience, but they will expect you to develop independent study skills, as outlined in Chapter 3.

Depending on the university or college student support system, you may be assigned a personal tutor, or you may have a student support unit which you can go to if you have any problems. All tutors are required to display their office hours and you do not normally need to book an appointment with them during these times, but just 'drop in'. You must do this if you feel you need to discuss any academic or personal issues with them that might affect your work and study.

Virtual learning environments

A vital source of communication with your tutors and other students when you are studying in the UK will be your VLE or 'virtual learning environment'. Universities and colleges put their learning and teaching materials on this special intranet learning platform. It's very important that you get to know this system quickly – ideally in the first week that you arrive, because it is your main study and information platform. It is very important that you check your module or module guides and news every day. Daily contact with your modules, tutors and other students through the VLE is a vital part of your education in the UK, and the only way that your language and study skills will quickly improve.

Your module guide, module syllabus, reading lists, timetables and module and university information will usually all be put on the VLE. Tutors put module materials on the VLE and use this portal to display lecture slides, class readings, further-reading lists, essay questions and video links. The VLE contains vital details regarding class times, locations and room changes, as well as being the place where you electronically submit your assessed work. The VLE is therefore a central part of your study experience in the UK and you should make the most of its capabilities. Many VLEs contain a place for interaction with other students, and interaction with tutors. This will give you a very good basis to develop your interaction and communication with your fellow students and your tutors.

Making friends

Friendship networks with other students will play an important role in helping you to adjust to the new environment. There are usually active Chinese student associations which can help you initially in this process, and then it will be a very good idea to join more general student societies and student union clubs and activities that will help you make friends with students from other countries. You need to 'work outside your comfort zone' and force yourself to be 'brave' like Ava, and try to form friendships with students from other countries in order to help improve your English. Most Chinese students have good intentions to 'mix' with students from other countries in order to improve their English, but often it seems easier to just socialise with other Chinese students. Try not to just take the easy way – it might actually be the longest road to study success. If you only mix with other Chinese students and watch Chinese movies all the time etc., then you will not be making the most of the great opportunity you have of living and studying in the UK.

THINK 1.3

What kind of person are you? Are you shy? Are you sociable? Do you make friends easily in China? How will you try to make friends with students from other countries when you are in the UK? Write some notes in the reflection box at the end of this chapter.

What is your name?

For people in the UK, Chinese names can sometimes be difficult to understand. For example, one of our students is called Yau Wai Ping in China. Her family call her 'Wai Ping', and her 'family' name is Yau. She decided to call herself 'Wendy' in the UK – partly because it also began with a 'W' sound – but also because she just liked the name, and she knew that it would be easier for her tutors in the UK to remember it. However, if you prefer to just use your Chinese name, that's fine – but make sure that your tutor pronounces it correctly, and in a way that you are comfortable with!

We've already introduced you to Xiao Zhou, and she actually prefers an English name. She decided to call herself 'Ava', but still uses her Chinese name sometimes.

THINK 1.4

If you gave yourself an 'English' name, which one would you choose and why? Do some internet research on possible English names and their meanings, and choose one that you think would be the most suitable for you (you don't have to have an English name – this is just an exercise to teach you more about English names). In the reflection box at the end of the chapter, write down an English name that you like and your reasons for choosing it.

Administrative issues

You will find that before you can begin your studies, you will have a lot of administrative issues to attend to. These will of course vary from institution to institution but, briefly, will generally include the following:

Registering with the university and paying fees

These regulations will vary but you should be proactive in this area yourself, although you can get help from your international student adviser. It's your responsibility to make sure that you are correctly registered on the right programme and that you have paid all the required fees before your module starts, otherwise this might adversely affect your degree programme.

Registering with the local police

This is a normal requirement for all international students and can be helpful if problems arise during your stay. The police can be very helpful to registered students, particularly with landlord problems, or problems with people who might try to cheat you or insult you. Although the UK is generally a very safe place for students, you will need to be careful about walking on your own late at night, and be aware that there are many pickpockets and thieves in the larger cities, as indeed there are in all cities in the world. It's a good idea to have the number of the local community support police on your phone. For emergencies, you only need to dial 999 from any phone.

Registering with medical services

Chinese and UK medical traditions are very different. Your university or college will have a health centre or nurse on duty, and you should make an appointment to register with the health centre as soon as you can. Alternative Chinese medicine is also widely available from practitioners in most large towns and cities.

Visa regulations and attendance

Your international student adviser will be able to update you on current visa regulations and the current rules regarding any paid part-time work which you might want to undertake while you are in the UK. Not all students will receive adequate financial support from their family for their studies. Therefore you might want to get a part-time job while you are here. This will also be a very good way of improving your English as well as giving you an income, but you must comply with current visa requirements about the number of hours you are legally entitled to work. As a student, you will be restricted in the number of hours you can legally work, and remember that your studies will take up most of your time.

Also remember to inform your module tutors if you have to go back to China for a long period during your study, because there may be a university and module requirement for you to remain in the UK while you are registered at the institution. All universities and colleges are required to strictly monitor attendance, and require that you register for each teaching week, so that they know you are attending your programme.

Opening a bank account

Opening a UK bank current account will still be essential for you in order to manage your financial affairs while you are in the UK. There are many banks to choose from, most with good connections to China. Some of them will charge you a monthly fee to have an account. You should check carefully. Many of the banks offer special deals for students, which often give special advantages. One special advantage that is very useful is insurance for your phone and personal possessions. Check if the bank account you are offered also gives you this insurance free of charge. Most banking is done on the internet or by phone, so you must make sure you have good virus protection software installed on your computer, particularly if you do lots of financial transactions online.

Chapter 1: Key words and concepts – English and Chinese

academic – 学术

adaptation – 适应

characteristic – 特征

comfort zone – 舒适区

Confucian – 孔子

critical thinking – 评判性思考

deals – 交易

democratic – 民主的

depression – 抑郁

dialogue – 对话

distance modules – 远程课程

drop in – 拜访

European Union – 欧洲联盟

exchanges – 交易

foreigner – 外国人

foundation – 基础

honours – 荣誉

impression – 印象

induction – 归纳

interaction – 相互交流

internships – 实习

judged – 评判的

kingdom – 王国

league tables – 排名榜

lifelong – 终身

module – 课程

monolingual – 单一语言

multicultural – 多种语言

online – 线上 / 网上

opportunities – 机会

orientation – 准备

parliamentary – 议会

placement – 职业

positive – 积极的

rankings – 排名

referencing – 引用

reflect – 反思 （动词）

reflection – 反思 （名词）

registering – 注册 （动名词）

research – 研究

resource – 资源

skills – 技能

state – 国 （名词）

strengths – 优势

supervisor – 论文导师

the right thing – 正确的事

threats – 威胁

tutor – 老师

update – 更新

weaknesses – 劣势

work–life balance – 工作生活平衡

CHAPTER 1: TEST YOURSELF

Put an ✘ for an incorrect statement and a ✔ for a correct statement.
Check your answers in the Appendix.

1   'Reflection' means to think about what you have done, and to think about how you can do it better, and how what you are doing now will help you in the future. .... ☐

2   The UK is one country called the United Kingdom. .... ☐

3   'British' is a word we use to describe anything that relates to the UK. .... ☐

4   The UK and the Republic of Ireland are also members of the European Union. .... ☐

5   Undergraduate degrees are called 'bachelor's degrees' because only unmarried men can study for them. .... ☐

6   A four-year degree is called a 'sandwich' degree. .... ☐

7   A high university ranking means excellent teaching. .... ☐

8   The VLE is a very good place for communication between students and tutors. .... ☐

9   You do not need to go to induction activities after you arrive in the UK. .... ☐

10   You will need to choose an English name when you study in the UK. .... ☐

Chapter 1: Reflection box

Write your THINK reflections here:

Think 1.1

What differences do you think you will find between your education experience in China and your new study home in the UK? Write some notes.

Think 1.2

You can achieve excellent results wherever you study in the UK. How will a good qualification from the UK help you in your future life? Write some notes below.

Think 1.3

What kind of person are you? Are you shy? Are you sociable? Do you make friends easily in China? How will you try to make friends with students from other countries when you are in the UK? Think about yourself and write some notes below.

Think 1.4

If you gave yourself an 'English' name, which one would you choose and why? Do some internet research on possible English names and their meanings, and choose one that you think would be the most suitable for you. Write down the name here, and the meaning, and your reasons for choosing it. Remember, the question says 'if' – there is no reason why you have to choose an English name!

2

Developing your academic English skills

Introduction

We know, from our experience of teaching many Chinese students for many years, that your biggest study challenge in the UK will be the English language, particularly more advanced 'academic' English, which is more complicated than general English.

The main problems with English will be:

  writing 'academic' English;

  listening to and understanding academic English;

  talking with your tutors and other students;

  understanding different English accents.

For all of us, our language and our culture affect the way that we think to some extent, so that people from different cultures often think differently about many aspects of the world. Most tutors and international students in the UK do not speak any Chinese, and may not have visited China and experienced its culture. You will have to use English most of the time. Unless you also complete a pre-sessional or foundation English module, you may not be able to take extra English classes – they may not be available, and you will be very busy with your subject studies. However, you will still be in one of the best English 'classrooms'

in the world – the UK – so you will be improving your English naturally while you are here. There are also many other methods you can use to help improve your English. This chapter outlines some of these methods.

Here are some comments from Xiangping:

In the UK, English is usually the medium of instruction. It is important for you to realise that English is the only language used in classrooms when you are studying in the UK. Therefore, ideally, you need to have a good foundation of English before you decide to come to study in the UK. There are very limited opportunities for you to take more English classes while you are studying in the UK. This is why the UK sets minimum English language requirements for learners of English to come to the UK to study.

You may also have tutors from many different parts of the world while you study in the UK. Some of these tutors may have different accents when they are speaking English, and you might find them difficult to understand. Therefore, a good ability with English is essential for your success. English is not only the medium of instruction in teaching and learning in the UK, but also the vital key to your successful experience in UK culture.

When you come from China to study in the UK, you can speak and write English, but you may find more advanced academic English difficult. One reason is because of the specialised vocabulary particular to each subject. Another reason is that most teaching is done through lectures. This requires that you can listen, write notes, and understand what the teacher is saying, all at the same time. This is very difficult for all students to do well.

So you may find some difficulties because English is not your native language and English is a very different type of language to Chinese. You will have to spend more time studying than an English-speaking student. You will also probably need to record the lecture so you can review it after the class.

Written English has a very different structure from written Chinese. There are also some basic differences between Chinese and UK thinking which influence the writing style. For example, UK education uses an 'evidence-based' approach. Chinese teaching often stresses the importance of the opinions of authority and well-known scholars who are experts in their subjects. Many

Chinese students refer to these authorities as 'famous scholars'. In the UK, you will be required to use a wide range of reliable 'evidence' to support your discussion, and not just rely on information because it comes from 'famous scholars'.

Chinese writing often repeats the same points because repetition seems to make the argument stronger. In the UK, you will be required not to repeat yourself, but to use an 'evidence-based' approach and many different sources of information and arguments. This means that you may find assignments in the UK difficult because of these cultural differences, and because of your lack of ability in more advanced English. Unfortunately, it is not enough to be good at English: you will also have to learn to think critically as well. But don't worry – most students, regardless of nationality, need to practise evidence-based writing and thinking. Chapter 3 will help you to develop these skills.

 **Chapter 2: Xiangping's study tips**

Here are Xiangping's tips about how to quickly improve your English while you are in the UK:

- 在英国学习，英语是永恒的课题。如果没有过硬的英语语言基础，在纯英语教学的国度，想在学术上成功或者有所建树是很困难的。这不仅包括英语口语，同时也包括英语写作。

英语口语：

- 你一开口，别人就知道你的英语水平，如果你连说英语都不准确流利，你的英语写作怎么会好呢？这也正是为什么很多国内的求职节目一听说求职者是海外留学归来的就让他们来一段英文的自我介绍，或者英文的对话。这无疑都说明了英语口语的重要。所以，提高英语口语是至关重要的。
- 提高口语的最重要的一点就是练习：多听、多说、多问！在学习的过程中不怕犯错误、丢面子，掌握了真本事才是真理。提高口语离不开听力，如果答非所问也是徒劳的。听和说是紧密相关、密不可分的。至于怎样练习听说，和谁练习的问题就是我们前几章里面提到的：

TABLE 2.1

☒ 不要	☑ 鼓励
✗ 千万不要一直和中国人扎堆	✓ 要和来自不同文化和国度的同学们交流
✗ 不要胆怯、羞涩、内敛	✓ 要大胆、勇敢、自信，鼓励放开自己
✗ 不要把自己从其他文化中孤立，不要有文化歧视	✓ 要加入校内外的社团组织，积极参加校内外的活动
✗ 不要怕自己说英文的时候犯错误，不明白的时候不要怕让对话者重复	✓ 要多听、多问、多说、利用这个机会，练习自己的英语，了解异国的文化和风俗

English language support

Most universities and colleges in the UK provide some English language support classes for international students. You should make sure that you attend these classes regularly, even though they might not seem to be directly related to your subject. It will be good practice, and the English language tutors will be able to suggest further ways in which you can improve your English while you are here.

'Language exchange' is also a good way to help yourself develop your English. You might find that the Student Union organises language exchanges. You can find someone who wants to learn Chinese and, in 'exchange', they can help you improve your English. Sometimes you can make lifelong friends this way!

Watching British television and news programmes, and watching English-language films are also good ways to improve, as well as taking any opportunities you can to speak in English. Don't feel embarrassed if you can't think of the right word or you are worried about understanding what is said to you in reply – if you don't try to speak, you will never improve!

Listening

You will need to develop good listening techniques while you study in the UK. One reason why you will not want to say very much in English is because you will be worried that you will not fully understand the answers you receive from people. So you will probably just pretend to understand, and then you will have to go and ask other Chinese students what to do. You must try not to do this, but to listen more effectively and use 'check questions' such as:

Excuse me, but would you mind just saying that again…

Sorry – did you mean…?

Can I check that I understand what you just said…

Oh, so you mean that…

Sorry, I didn't catch what you meant…

Pardon?

Remember

- Listening effectively should feel like hard work – don't think that this means that your English is not very good. The speaker's accent might be strange to you, or they may be speaking very quickly. You will need to concentrate hard on what is being said. Always try to link what you hear to other parts of your module or programme. While you are listening you should also be thinking about how this information fits in with other things that you know.
- Be well prepared. Ask the tutor if you can see the lecture slides before the lecture – many tutors will be very happy to do this because they know it will help you. If you have done some preparatory reading, you will listen more effectively and understand more of what is being said. You will start to make the essential connections between topics that will really help you understand your studies.
- This type of listening is called 'active listening'.

Listening is a very important skill, particularly for Chinese students who may not be confident with their understanding of English.

Make sure you are concentrating on what is being said. It's a great temptation to check your phone and emails during a lecture or tutorial, but not only is this regarded as bad behaviour, but also it will mean that you will miss a lot of what is being said.

Reading

Many Chinese students find the amount of reading required during their UK studies very challenging and they have difficulty in finishing all the required reading. It is certainly true that you will have a lot of reading to do, so you will need to develop the ability to read effectively in English. Reading is the key to successful study and to developing your thinking and writing.

However, if you just go through the reading process without understanding what you read, you will be wasting valuable time.

In the UK, you may often be expected to spend at least four hours' reading for every hour in class, so you can see the importance of quickly developing this skill. What should you read? Given that you might find reading to be a slow process initially, you should certainly be strategic, and read the most important things first.

Good personal management of your study time is a very important key to success. We call this 'smart study' – using your time well, and using effective study strategies. If you take a lot of time to read and understand every word of your module books, you will not be 'studying smart' – you will probably start to feel that you are falling behind in your studies. In China, you were probably taught to read and understand every written word – you might have been told to memorise everything that you read. In the UK, you will not be able to use this strategy because there will be too much that you have to read. However, your ability to memorise what you read will be helpful sometimes, particularly for exams. Here are some simple strategies to help you understand what you read in English:

Reading for 'gist'

The best way to understand compli-cated writing is to try to understand the general ideas first. We call this 'the big picture' or 'the gist'. The 'gist' is the general topic of the text. You will often hear tutors using this word. We also call any piece of writing a 'text'.

Many Chinese students think that they must read and understand every word of a text. If they do not, they will feel uncomfortable. However, this will mean you will get behind in your studies. Do not feel uncomfortable if you cannot understand every piece of text that you read. Ignore the words and phrases that you cannot understand and try to generally understand what the text means (the 'gist'). Even if you can only understand half of the text, this will be a good start. You can ask other students to help you understand the rest of the text. You can also go to general information sources to help you to understand the general topic of the text. For example, if you are reading some detailed information about different research studies, firstly try to understand the 'big picture' about what the subject of the research was. Once you have understood what the text is basically about, you need to read it critically.

What to read

The most important thing to read first is the 'module guide' for the module you are taking. You will have a number of modules to complete each semester, and it is very important that you understand what subject content and subject-related skills you will be learning on the module, and what your assessments will be. Each module will have a book list, but you may not need to go and buy each of the books on the list, and you may not need to read each book completely. Often, core textbooks are kept in the library or learning centre, in both hardback and electronic form (ebooks). You should try to borrow these books first and complete the required reading outlined in the module guide.

These books will be very popular and therefore difficult to borrow from the library, so you may have to buy them, but check online first because there are often cheaper versions available. Unlike in China, there is usually not a single set book to learn for each subject module, so it is important that you develop your ability for independent study. This will mean that you will often have to make your own decisions about which books and articles you should read in order to adequately prepare for your lectures and tutorials.

All modules have recommended reading lists and textbooks, but there generally will not be just one textbook that you are expected to 'learn' as you might

have experienced in China. In order to get the best grades possible, you usually need to demonstrate that you have read widely. This means reading more than your tutors' recommended reading lists in the module handbooks. Your reading also needs to reflect the learning outcomes for each module (found at the front of your module handbooks). You need time to read widely around your subjects to really understand them. It is certainly not enough to only read the lecture slides, handouts and some of the reading materials recommended in the reading list of your module handbook.

You also need to read background reading texts. This wider reading enables you to form your own opinion and contribute positively to tutorials and seminars. Include in your reading a range of academic sources that are recent and relevant for your task. Select material from a range of print and electronic sources, both practitioner (what companies do, for example) and academic sources (academic research journals for example). Consider what is being said in a text and compare and evaluate it to what other authors have written about the topic/subject. If you read broadly you can identify who agrees and also who disagrees with particular views on your reading topic.

It is important to have your dictionary at hand to look up words you are not sure about. As you research and read, collect the full reference details and the page numbers of all the sources you have consulted, in the correct reference style for your institution. This saves you a lot of time later when you draft your assignments, and also prevents you from losing valuable sources because you can't remember where you read something that you now want to include in your writing.

Manage your time well to work efficiently and effectively. When researching for an assignment, start your research early. Do not delay, as many students need to access the same textbooks. If all the hard copies of a text have been borrowed, you may be able to find an electronic copy. Remember that lots of texts are available in electronic form which you can download to your computer.

There is more advice on how to improve your reading skills and become a more effective reader in Chapter 3.

Using dictionaries

It is important for you to buy a good dictionary which gives you the different meanings of words in context. It is not sufficient to just assume that each word only has one meaning. In English, every word has a different meaning depending on the 'context'. The context is the sentence and paragraph that the word is part of, and what the sentence and paragraph are about.

ACTIVITY 2.1

Look up the meaning of each of these words in a good dictionary which gives you examples of how each word is used in a sentence. It's very important to make sure you are using the correct form of the word. For example, you will use the word 'analysis' quite a lot. Here are some of the forms it can take:

(Continued)

(Continued)

Analysis (a noun – a detailed examination of the parts or structure of something)

Analyse (a verb – the process of producing an analysis)

Analytical (an adjective – using, or skilled in using, analysis, e.g. an analytical approach, an analytical mind)

Only one of these examples below is correct. Why?

The student analysis the situation for the assignment. ✗

The student analysed the situation for the assignment. ✓

The student analyse the situation for the assignment. ✗

Here are some of the common forms for another word you might use a lot:

Economic

Economics

Economical

Economy

Use a dictionary to find out the differences between the meanings.

Taking notes from what you read

Making notes when you read can help you remember the main points from the text. But do not try to write down everything you read. If you try to do this, you will be wasting your time. You should try to make notes only about the most important things in the text – but you must decide what these things are, in terms of which information is the most relevant to the assignment you are working on. You can do this in many different ways. You can write down key words and ideas. You can use a highlighter pen or make small pictures showing the way that you think the ideas and points in the reading connect together. This is called a 'mindmap'. There are different ways to make mindmaps. Below is the beginning of a student's mind map on the topic of 'studying in the UK':

EXAMPLE

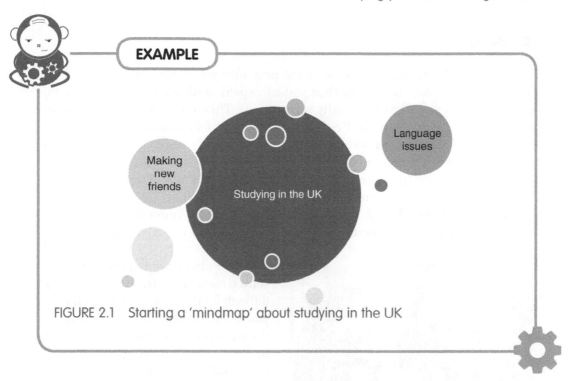

FIGURE 2.1   Starting a 'mindmap' about studying in the UK

When you are reading and making notes, make sure that you don't just copy exactly what you are reading. You must write down what you think is important, in your own words. This is called 'paraphrasing' and is an important skill for all your academic writing (see the section on 'paraphrase' later in this chapter).

Taking notes from what you hear

You might want to take some notes during lectures or tutorials. However, it is often best just to listen to what the tutor is saying. If you ask first, it is normally OK to record the lecture on your phone or other recording device. Most lecture slides and information are also put on the module site in the virtual learning environment (VLE) – often before the lecture – so you can look at the lecture slides and information before the lecture, to help you understand.

Speaking

Spoken English might give you the most problems when you study in the UK. You may not be very confident that you can speak without making mistakes, or that you can say what you really want to say. This may make you feel nervous about saying anything in English, so you might feel more comfortable saying nothing. This is understandable, but you definitely need to keep trying to communicate even if you feel that you might be making mistakes. You will only improve if you keep trying, and your tutors and fellow students will appreciate that you are trying to communicate well with them. When they reply to you, do not worry if you do not understand what they say immediately, but tell them that you do not understand. In this way, you will quickly improve.

You will also have to ask questions sometimes, and this can be very difficult for Chinese students. Firstly, you need to wait for a good opportunity, and then you must try not to be nervous, and speak clearly and loudly enough for everyone to hear. In the West, tutors like you to ask questions because it shows that you are listening and that you are interested, and that you are following the discussion. Everyone is entitled to ask questions but not everyone does so. This might be because of a lack of self-confidence, or because the discussion has moved on before the opportunity to ask a question arises.

Make use of any opportunity you have for asking a question and speaking to your tutors and fellow students. There may be opportunities to do this at the end of a lecture, or certainly during a tutorial or seminar. You could also prepare a question in advance. This will mean that the answer you receive will address the problem more precisely. Think about what it is that you would like to know; do you want your tutor to repeat what was said, or give an example? If you are asking a question, try to speak clearly and with enough volume so that everyone can hear. If you are too nervous to ask questions in front of other people, you could email your question to your tutor in advance.

Here is another comment from Ava, a Chinese business student. Her experience is very common, and you should also try to be 'brave', as she recommends:

It was my first experience as a student in the West. I had many things to learn. It was always easy for me to just say nothing, because this was less stressful. Even if I went to the fast food place, I was nervous. I did not know if I would understand the assistant and I did not want the other people in the shop to know I did not understand English very well. So I asked my friend to go and buy the food for me. But my friend told me that this was not the way to learn. He told me I had to be brave and take risks in order to learn. Of course, he was right, but I still found it hard to make myself talk in English. However, slowly, I got more confidence and now I don't mind if I can't understand what people say. I just tell people I don't understand, and ask them to explain to me again.

It may be possible for you to take an extra English module while you are in the UK. You might complete a module of English before you start your main programme (pre-sessional). You might be lucky to be able to take support English classes if your institution offers them. They are normally only a few hours a week, but if you have this opportunity, you should take it. Your success will depend on good English writing, speaking, listening and understanding.

The following simple strategies will slowly improve your English speaking:

- Taking extra English classes.
- Making English friends.
- Joining the English Society – most institutions have them, either run by students or staff, or both.
- Mixing with students from all nationalities – English will be the main language of communication.
- Taking every opportunity to speak to other students, staff, and people outside your education institution.
- Listening carefully to people speaking in different accents and in different dialects (e.g., Scottish, Welsh, Irish, Caribbean, etc.).
- Listening to English-language radio, TV and films.

Here is some more advice from Ava again:

I often had to communicate in English with my tutors and other students who were not Chinese. I knew that if I did not speak accurately, it would cause many misunderstandings and further problems. Therefore, I had to find a solution to this problem. What I did to overcome this problem at the beginning was to write myself a note before I talked to other people, no matter what the

content of the issue was. I wrote down bullet points and thought about how I was going to express myself before I went to them. I translated from Chinese to English in my head. It took me some time to do this but it gave me confidence and helped me to save time during our discussions. I also took my notebook with me all the time and quickly wrote down notes when people pointed out particular information, or when I heard about new words or new ways of expressing things. People were very helpful and my communication skills improved a lot with their help. I also lived with a host family – you can see them in the photo – and this really helped me improve my English very quickly because my host family were very kind, but they did not speak any Chinese!

More comments from Xiangping about how she improved her spoken English:

Students often ask me how to improve their English. My answer is quite simple: 'Practice makes perfect'. But determination is also very important. I remember when I first came to the UK. From the moment I landed

at the airport, I started to speak English at passport control, and I told myself that I would improve my English and make good use of the time in the UK to make the English language an advantage for me.

When I arrived at the university, apart from going to the programme talks, I joined in a wide range of social activities organised by the International Office. I went to the Quiz Night, although I did not know much about how that worked, but I did have a laugh! I went on trips to London, Cambridge, and Windsor Castle, and saw the different sights that I had only seen on TV and in pictures. I was very motivated and very determined to learn English well.

Secondly, confidence is vital. I was confident enough to step out and say 'hello' to others from different cultural backgrounds, and then start a conversation with them in English. At times, I had to keep saying 'Pardon?' (it means 'Could you say that again?') but I was not defeated by that. I found that people were not actually offended either. The more I talked to others, the more I learnt and the better my English became.

Some people say it is difficult to be confident if you know your English is not good enough. Well, I would say that your English will never be good enough if you are not confident enough to use it or practise it with others! So be confident and do not be afraid of 'losing face'!

I remember that for the first semester of my studies, I did not have a laptop, so I had to go to the library to complete my assignments. That also provided me with opportunities to meet other students who I could exchange ideas with in English. I always went out to join in various social activities during evenings and weekends. Also, I joined a number of clubs and societies which kept me busy and involved in organising and participating in different events in the university. That brought me not only the opportunity to speak English, but also worldwide friendships and broader horizons.

In particular, I would like to recommend staying with a 'host' family. Your university can arrange this for you, and it is a great way to practise English every day, and learn much more about English culture and all the strange expressions that you hear on the street! I had a fantastic time with my host family and would like more students to benefit from the experience.

THINK 2.1

What are your main concerns about using English in the UK? Write some notes in the reflection box at the end of this chapter.

Academic writing

Your ability to write clearly and in correct English will be very important for you at university. The English used in academic writing is referred to as 'academic' English, which needs to be formal and objective. The term 'formal' refers to academic style and the term 'objective' refers to 'evidence-based' writing which must look at issues objectively – from all opinions, not just your own.

You will also need to learn how to write in the appropriate 'academic' style. This can vary depending on where you are studying, but generally it refers to a type of writing that is based on evidence which you show by means of 'referencing' (see Chapter 3). The following sections briefly describe the main formal features of academic writing, which you will need to become familiar with.

English vocabulary

One big advantage of studying in the UK is that you will always have good opportunities to continually improve your written and spoken English and your listening ability. This section will give you advice about how to improve your accuracy with your communication in English, and extend the range of your English vocabulary.

Key academic vocabulary

One essential thing you must do is to record new vocabulary when you see it or hear it, especially those subject words which are 'technical terms'. These words are sometimes called 'jargon' words or 'terminology'. You can build up a good knowledge of the relevant jargon for your subject using the following techniques:

- Buy a small notebook and carry it with you always, writing down any new vocabulary. Or use your phone or computer to translate their meanings, as soon as you come across them. Take time to check you have entered the word or phrase correctly – check with the speaker if you can, or in a dictionary if it is a written source. This will slowly but very effectively build up your vocabulary.
- Use a thesaurus (a dictionary which gives you a choice of different words with similar meanings), either from your computer or in book form, to vary and develop your range of vocabulary. However, be careful when using a thesaurus to find alternative words, because they are given without any context, and small but important differences between similar words are not given. Make sure, therefore, that you have a suitable example of the use of a word before you actually use it.
- Do not read just for information about your topic but also for information about how professional writers write English – the expressions and words that they use, etc. Notice how academic articles are written, and how your textbooks are written. Try to write in the same way, using them as a model and guide.

Accurate use of words

It is important for you to use words accurately. This means choosing the right word for the situation, and this can be very difficult when you are still learning English. Use your dictionary to provide examples of the word in context. A good English dictionary will give you a full range of the meanings of the word, in example sentences.

> ### EXAMPLE
>
> Here are examples of words in academic English which are often misused:
>
> Informations ✗ (Information never has an 's' on the end – it is regarded as one thing).
>
> Information ✓
>
> Researches ✗ (Research is regarded as either one thing – in which case it is a 'research study' or if you are referring to more than one research study, you only need to say:
>
> > Research shows that... ✓
> >
> > A research study has shown that... ✓
>
> Check words you are not sure of in a good dictionary which shows the use of the word in a sentence (in context).

General English

Chinese students sometimes find it difficult to recognise the difference between 'general' English and academic English. General English is not just one type of English – in the UK, you will hear many different regional types of English, influenced by the varied cultures in a multicultural society. You will hear many new words spoken in many different accents which will often be very difficult for you to understand. However, academic English is much more standardised – there is really only one type of academic English, so if you get worried because you cannot understand general English, do not worry – many people in the UK have problems understanding different regional varieties of English, but all 'academics' use the same 'academic' language. Academic English is also more formal than general English.

> ### EXAMPLE
>
> **Formal, academic English style:** It has been suggested that Chinese Students should ensure that they have a small notebook in order to record new English words and phrases they encounter.
>
> **Informal, general English style:** Keep a small notebook with you so you can jot down new words.

Be careful with phrasal verbs

Phrasal verbs are made up from two parts – a verb plus an adverb or preposition – and are sometimes called 'two-word' verbs. They are generally associated with informal, general English, although they are very common in some subjects such as Business or Media Studies. Many of the things you will read in English newspapers and magazines – particularly about Business – will contain 'phrasal verbs'.

> ### EXAMPLE
>
> The company **ruled out** the option. (The company rejected the option.)

In the example above, 'rule' is the verb and 'out' is the preposition. This combination means that the original verb now has a new meaning depending on the context and has to be learnt.

For example, one general meaning of the verb *to rule* is *to dominate*, or *to exercise power*. If you add the small preposition 'out', as in the example above, the meaning changes completely. The phrasal verb *to rule out* means *to reject*.

The CEO ruled out the idea. (He/she rejected it.)

As phrasal verbs often have several different meanings, depending on the context, you need to make a special note of them. Your dictionary will give you examples of their use in context, and you can also buy specialist dictionaries of phrasal verbs. English-speakers use phrasal verbs a lot in informal communication.

ACTIVITY 2.2

Using your dictionary, find out what each of the following phrasal verbs means. Check your answers with ours in the Appendix.

Account for

Back up

Bail out

Catch up

Deal with

Drop in

Fill in

Get behind

Hang out

Head up

Roll out

Avoid 'short' forms and slang

In your academic writing, avoid shortened forms of words such as: *it's, they've, we're, don't*. Always use the full forms: *it is, they have, we are, do not*.

Avoid all **slang** words, as they are not appropriate in academic writing.

She got really stressed out. (✗)
She has suffered from stress-related illness. (✓)

Be precise

In academic writing, you need to be very precise with facts and figures wherever possible.

The term *a lot of people* is very general and vague. What does it mean?

- A lot of people = 100?
- A lot of people = 1 thousand?
- A lot of people = 1 million?

EXAMPLE

Other phrases you should not use in academic writing:

- It is generally known that... (How do you know?)
- Many people know this... (Who are they?)
- This proves that... (One example does not prove anything)
- Many scholars have shown this to be true. (Who are these scholars?)
- It is obvious that... (Who said so?)

Avoid first/second person

In the academic world, writers generally use what we call 'third person' (he, she or it) rather than first person (I, me, mine, etc.) because it makes the writing sound more objective, and we are always trying to be 'objective' (look at things without bias) in the academic world. A simplified explanation of the three 'persons' is given below:

First person: I, we, me, us
Second person: You (one person), you (more than one person)
Third person: He, she, it, one

EXAMPLE

Poor academic style: In this essay, I will talk about...
    As we can see from Figure 1...
Good academic style: This essay is going to discuss...
    As shown in Figure 1...

It is worth noting that, in some colleges and universities, you are allowed to use 'first person' in your writing (e.g., it's OK to say: 'I interviewed the manager'). However, in most institutions, you will probably have to use the more formal 'third person' in your writing (e.g., 'The manager was interviewed').

Avoid emotive language

Language that shows lots of emotion can be very subjective and can make your writing too personal. This is fine for when you are writing to friends or family, but it's too subjective for academic writing. Don't use words such as: *unfortunately, surprisingly, luckily, interestingly, thankfully*. These terms are too personal and emotional, but they can be used in reflective writing (see Chapter 3).

Avoid clichés

A cliché (pronounced 'kleeshay') is an expression which has been used too much by writers and the media so that it becomes too general and does not express things accurately. It is good practice to avoid these clichés in academic writing, as they are often viewed as overused, informal and vague. Examples of clichés in business English follow.

EXAMPLE

Thinking outside the box
Time is money
Blue-sky thinking
At the end of the day
The bottom line is…
The company was passionate about…
It was a win–win situation

Use inclusive language

Because the UK is a multicultural society, and also a society where men and women are treated as equal, you must also avoid non-inclusive 'sexist' or 'racist' language:

EXAMPLE

A manager must always do what he thinks is right. (✗)

A manager must always do what he or she thinks is right. (✓)

Managers must always do what they think is right. (✓)

The chairman ended the meeting on time. (✗)

The chairperson ended the meeting on time. (✓)

Use the passive voice

There are two special forms for verbs, called **voice**:

1. Active voice
2. Passive voice

The **active voice** is the 'normal' voice. This is the voice that we use every day. In the active voice, the **object** receives the action of the verb:

TABLE 2.2   The active voice

	subject	verb	object
active			>
	Students	read	books.

The **passive voice** is less usual. In the passive voice, the **subject** receives the action of the verb:

TABLE 2.3   The passive voice

	subject	verb	object
passive			<
	Books	are read	by students.

38

In the academic world, we often use the passive voice to make the writing look more 'objective' because we are more interested in what happened, rather than who did it (the agent).

Sentences

Make sure that all your sentences make sense, with a subject (topic), verb (action) and an object (the focus of the action). Sentences should be clear and concise. They should not be too long because this makes them difficult to read and understand. We call sentences which are too long 'run-on' sentences. They should be broken up into smaller sentences. Here is an example of a 'run-on' sentence, using this paragraph:

EXAMPLE

Make sure that all your sentences make sense, with a subject (topic), verb (action) and an object (the focus of the action) and sentences should be clear and concise and they should not be too long because this makes them difficult to read and understand and we call sentences which are too long, 'run on' sentences which should be broken up into smaller sentences.

KISS

Sentences should generally also be short and simple. You can remember this with the word 'KISS' ('keep it short and simple'). Avoid long sentences or 'embedded' sentences (sentences inside sentences, with too many clauses introduced by words like 'what', 'where', 'when' and 'who').

Paragraphs

It is important that all your essay and report assignments are written in paragraphs. A paragraph in English is a piece of writing which is basically about one topic, and separated from the next paragraph with a space. The topic should be developed with the following parts.

PEEL

A simplified way to remember how to construct good paragraphs is to remember the word 'PEEL' – like the skin of an orange, with an extra 'E'!

P = Main point of the paragraph, given in the first sentence or sentences

E = Example

E = Evidence

E = Explanation and evaluation

L = Link to the next paragraph, and your own opinion

In the example below, we have numbered them so that you can see the parts clearly.

Each paragraph below also uses references (Surname, year) in the text. We explain this important feature in more detail in Chapter 3.

1. **A first 'topic' sentence, introducing the main point of the paragraph (P):**

   As Surname (year) suggests, a very big problem for Chinese students is the difference between 'general' English and academic English. For example, general English is not formal, whereas academic English is formal. Further, general English is not just one type of English. As Surname (year) shows in a wide-ranging survey, in the UK there are many different regional types of English, influenced by an increasingly multicultural society. Chinese students may have problems with colloquial words and regional accents. However, as Surname (year) states, academic English does have an advantage in that it is much more standardised into one form of English. This implies that although you might worry about your colloquial understanding of English, your understanding of academic English may actually be better. In order to improve this understanding, it is necessary to look now at reading strategies.

2. **An example, or examples, to strengthen your argument (E):**

   As Surname (year) suggests, a very big problem for Chinese students is the difference between 'general' English and academic English. **For example, general English is not formal, whereas academic English is formal. Further, general English is not just one type of English.** As Surname (year) shows in a wide-ranging survey, in the UK there are many different regional types of English, influenced by an increasingly multicultural society. Chinese students may have problems with colloquial words and regional accents. However, as Surname (year) states, academic English does have an advantage in that it is much more standardised into one form of English. This implies that although you might worry about your colloquial understanding of English, your understanding of academic English may actually be better. In order to improve this understanding, it is necessary to look now at reading strategies.

3. Evidence to support your main point or points (E):

As Surname (year) suggests, a very big problem for Chinese students is the difference between 'general' English and academic English. For example, general English is not formal, whereas academic English is formal. Further, general English is not just one type of English. **As Surname (year) shows** in a wide-ranging survey, in the UK there are many different regional types of English, influenced by an increasingly multicultural society. Chinese students may have problems with colloquial words and regional accents. **However, as Surname (year) states**, academic English does have an advantage in that it is much more standardised into one form of English. This implies that although you might worry about your colloquial understanding of English, your understanding of academic English may actually be better. In order to improve this understanding, it is necessary to look now at reading strategies.

4. Explanation of the issue (E):

As Surname (year) suggests, a very big problem for Chinese students is the difference between 'general' English and academic English. For example, general English is not formal, whereas academic English is formal. Further, general English is not just one type of English. As Surname (year) shows in a wide-ranging survey, **in the UK there are many different regional types of English, influenced by an increasingly multicultural society. Chinese students may have problems with colloquial words and regional accents**. However, as Surname (year) states, **academic English does have an advantage in that it is much more standardised into one form of English.** This implies that although you might worry about your colloquial understanding of English, your understanding of academic English may actually be better. In order to improve this understanding, it is necessary to look now at reading strategies.

5. Evaluation of the issue – showing different points of view (E):

As Surname (year) suggests, a very big problem for Chinese students is the difference between 'general' English and academic English. For example, general English is not formal, whereas academic English is formal. Further, general English is not just one type of English. **As Surname (year)** shows in a wide-ranging survey, in the UK there are many different regional types of English, influenced by an increasingly multicultural society. Chinese students may have problems with colloquial words and regional accents. **However, as Surname (year) states**, academic English does have an advantage in that it is much more standardised into one form of English. This implies that although you might worry about your colloquial understanding of English, your understanding of academic English may actually be better. In order to improve this understanding, it is necessary to look now at reading strategies.

6. Your own 'informed' opinion on the basis of your evidence (E):

As Surname (year) suggests, a very big problem for Chinese students is the difference between 'general' English and academic English. For example, general English is not formal, whereas academic English is formal. Further, general English is not just one type of English. As Surname (year) shows in a wide-ranging survey, in the UK there are many different regional types of English, influenced by an increasingly multicultural society. Chinese students may have problems with colloquial words and regional accents. However, as Surname (year) states, academic English does have an advantage in that it is much more standardised into one form of English. **This implies that although you might worry about your colloquial understanding of English, your understanding of academic English may actually be better.** In order to improve this understanding, it is necessary to look now at reading strategies.

7. **Links to the next paragraph (L):**

As Surname (year) suggests, a very big problem for Chinese students is the difference between 'general' English and academic English. For example, general English is not formal, whereas academic English is formal. Further, general English is not just one type of English. As Surname (year) shows in a wide-ranging survey, in the UK there are many different regional types of English, influenced by an increasingly multicultural society. Chinese students may have problems with colloquial words and regional accents. However, as Surname (year) states, academic English does have an advantage in that it is much more standardised into one form of English. This implies that although you might worry about your colloquial understanding of English, your understanding of academic English may actually be better. **In order to improve this understanding, it is necessary to look now at reading strategies.**

A common mistake is to make paragraphs too short. Paragraphs should normally have the parts outlined above. In academic essays, it is not correct to make paragraphs that are too short, like the ones in the example below, and it is also not correct that there are no spaces between the paragraphs:

EXAMPLE

As Surname (year) suggests, a very big problem for Chinese students is the difference between 'general' English and academic English. For example, general English is not formal, whereas academic English is formal.

Further, general English is not just one type of English. As Surname (year) shows in a wide-ranging survey, in the UK there are many different regional types of English, influenced by an increasingly multicultural society.

Chinese students may have problems with colloquial words and regional accents. However, as Surname (year) states, academic English does have an advantage in that it is much more standardised into one form of English.

This implies that although you might worry about your colloquial understanding of English, your understanding of academic English may actually be better.

"In order…"

(These paragraphs are too short and there is no space between each paragraph.)

Quotation

A quotation is when you write exactly what someone said, enclosing it in speech marks like this:

> The manager said: 'The company must be more productive.'

This is another way you can use a source of information. However, you should generally try not to quote too much in an assignment and certainly keep the length down to about one or two sentences at most. It is considered bad academic practice to include lengthy quotations. This is because if you only copy down what someone says, it does not show that you understand – just that you can copy. It is generally always better to paraphrase. You should never have a quote as a separate paragraph without commenting on it. Showing your understanding of the material is more valuable than using too many quotations. Quotes have to be included in the total word count.

> Quotes must be in quotation marks, preceded by a colon (:) and have a reference at the beginning or the end, which must also include the page number.

EXAMPLE

Correct use of a quotation:

In a detailed discussion of outsourcing methods, Surname (year) notes the increasing popularity of different types since 1990, indicating that: 'a related trend has been offshoring, where core work is transferred to another country, typically overseas. Outsourcing has become a popular 'buzzword' in business and management since the 1990s. (Surname, year: page)

(A 'buzzword' is slang for a word that has become very fashionable.)

The problem with quotations

Using lots of quotations, or long quotations, is poor academic practice because it indicates that you might not have understood the text, and you are just trying to fill up your essay with things that you think might be relevant information.

Paraphrasing

It is usually best to paraphrase from your information sources. This means putting other people's ideas into your own words and not just copying them. You can also summarise the ideas that you take from these books and websites. Paraphrases are used to re-express a specific idea or piece of information from a text. In order to avoid being accused of plagiarism, you need to change the original words and sentences, and also add a reference to the source (where you got the data from). In other words, a paraphrase is what it says – a series of 'parallel' (but not the same) phrases or sentences that have the same meaning as the original source. Remember that a paraphrase also requires an in-text reference.

There are different techniques for paraphrasing:

1. You can use synonyms (words with similar meanings).
2. You can change the word and/or sentence order.
3. You can change between passive and active modes.

It is important to note that paraphrases need to be of similar length to the original text and with no change of the original meaning. Additionally, it is important that you should use a combination of the above-suggested skills.

Two important things to remember when you paraphrase a source are:

a. You should use at least 90 per cent of your own words and sentence structure – changing only 70 per cent is not acceptable, as this would still be part copying.
b. Even though you have used your own words, you must still acknowledge the source by giving a reference, because the information belongs to the original author. In academic writing, anything that does not have a reference is assumed to be the student's own idea or comment.

The processes of paraphrasing and summarising are quite similar, except that a summary will always have fewer words than the original, and a paraphrase might have the same number or more. Note that a paraphrase might also have fewer words than the original text because you are expressing the ideas more simply and perhaps more clearly than the original.

Summarising

The second way to use the source is to summarise the main points from the paragraph, although a summary will inevitably not include all the information contained in the original text. Summarising is just what you might expect – you make a summary of the main points from the original which is shorter than the original text. Remember, the summary must be mostly in your own words, and also have a reference to the source of the information.

It is also important to remember that a summary or paraphrase should *not* include your own ideas, comments or opinions. A summary or paraphrase should contain only the information that is given in the original source. Your own comments should come *before* or *after* the paraphrase or summary. Below is an example of two different paraphrases from an original source. One is a good paraphrase, the other is a poor paraphrase.

EXAMPLE

Original source text

Employers are increasingly requiring that graduate candidates have undertaken some kind of employment experience during their degree studies. This may be in the form of an internship as part of a 'sandwich' degree, or a work placement. Our research has shown that this is indeed the case, with one large UK employment agency reporting that it could only find permanent positions for graduates if they had gained placement or internship experience as part of their degree. This was equally as important as a good degree result. (Surname & Surname, year) (*90 words*)

Good paraphrase

As Surname and Surname (year) have stated, it appears to be the case that employers now require graduates to have evidence of employment experience as part of their degree module – usually in the form of an internship or placement as part of a 'sandwich' degree. Research by Surname and Surname (year) found that, generally, graduates could only expect to find permanent career positions if they had gained this experience, and that for employers, this experience was just as important as a good degree result.
(*85 words*, with most of the original words changed, and references given in the text, at the beginning of the paraphrase.)

Poor paraphrase

Employers are increasingly asking that graduate candidates have some kind of employment experience during their degree studies. This may be in the form of an internship as part of a 'sandwich' degree, or a work placement. Their research showed that this was certainly the case, with one large UK employment agency reporting that it could only find permanent positions for graduates if they had got placement or internship experience during their degree. This was just as important as a good degree result (Surname & Surname, year).
(*82 words*, with very few of the original words changed, and a general reference at the end, rather than at the beginning of the paraphrase.)

Checking your own work

You will have to develop the skill of checking your own work before you submit it, because this is your responsibility and not the responsibility of your tutor. This next section gives you some basic revision information about English grammar and punctuation for academic writing. You may not be confident about your English, and you will want an English speaker to check your work for you. In the UK, your tutor will not generally have time to closely check your work for you. You will naturally want someone to check your work, but unless you are lucky to make a good English-speaking friend who is happy to do this for you, you will need to develop your own skills in checking your own work.

Getting someone to help you check your work is not cheating or plagiarism – it is just a sensible procedure that all writers should adopt. Try to find an English speaker to do this, or failing that, get a fellow student from the same module to read it through for you – and you can do the same for them. With their 'fresh' eyes, they will see mistakes that you cannot. Use the basic editing section below to help you identify common mistakes in your writing.

Once you have edited your final draft and are happy with it, you should do some final checking (proofreading).

Proofreading tips

- Read your work to yourself. This can help you decide if your work makes sense, and you will 'hear' how your work flows and if there are grammatical errors. Some software is also available which enables your computer to 'read' your essay to you so that you can hear any problems.
- Check for spelling mistakes, such as typing or spelling errors. Look up doubtful spellings or ask someone. Use spell checkers (but be careful with grammar checkers, unless you already have a good knowledge of grammar). Read your work in sections, working back from the end of your assignment, when checking for spelling.
- Check for mistakes that you often tend to make, which your tutor has indicated in previous feedback to you.
- Check that you have answered the question or all the parts of the task. Check that you have the correct word length.

Peer checking

A final thing you can do is to swap assignments with other students to check. This is not collusion, but peer checking. It is what all writers have to do when they submit their work – they must get other people to check and comment on their work. In your case, these should be other student friends who know about the assignment. (Collusion is where two or more students write one assignment and then try to submit it as two separate assignments.) It is surprising how many problems a fresh pair of eyes can find. However, do not send electronic copies of your work to other people – they might be tempted to 'cut and paste' some of your material!

English grammar

Good English grammar is vital for academic success in both writing and speaking. There are many grammar books you can use to help you. However, you need to be careful if you use a grammar check program on your computer. Grammar check programs can be helpful because they will show you possible problems. However, you need a very good understanding of English grammar in order to make the right choice to correct the problems. It is better for you if a friend reads and checks your work and looks for common errors.

It is extremely important that your final draft is totally correct in terms of accuracy of grammar, spelling and punctuation. Remember that all your assignments are professional academic documents and must be presented to a high standard. If these issues are not addressed, you can lose marks. In this section, we have given some basic advice about areas of grammar and punctuation which we have found are a particular problem for our Chinese students. We discuss some general points to consider in the following sections.

Verb tenses

Verb tenses can be a particular problem for Chinese students since time (tense) is shown in a very different way in Chinese. Your English academic assignment writing will require many different verb tenses, depending on the subject. For example, a report is generally written in the past tense but references are generally written in the present tense. For example, we say 'Surname (year) states that...' even if the original research was many years ago. This is because we are referring to Surname's ideas at this current moment in time.

A common cause of errors when using verbs in English is in relation to what is called 'subject–verb' agreement – a plural subject needs a plural verb form. For example:

They takes (✗)	They take (✓)
Employees was (✗)	Employees were (✓)
The companies is (✗)	The companies are (✓)

Unlike Chinese, there are many verb tenses in English, so it is important to check your use of verb tenses very carefully.

Remember too that, in English, verbs are also *regular* (have the same verb forms) or *irregular* (have different verb forms). The irregular verbs have different forms which you need to check in a dictionary. For example, regular verbs make the past tense by adding 'ed' to the end.

Here are examples of how a particular regular verb – 'to talk' – and an irregular verb – 'to do' – could be used in different ways, depending on the context.

The regular verb 'to talk'

Present tense: I talk

Past tense: I talked

The irregular verb 'to do'

Present tense: I do

Past tense: I did

Here are some examples of the main tenses you will need to use in your academic English – past, present and future. Each one has a 'simple' form, as well as a 'continuous' and 'perfect' form. The perfect form is used to show that the action is perfectly (completely) finished, although the results of the action still have a current effect. The conditional form is used to express hypothetical actions ('If I work hard, I will succeed'). It also shows how certain you are of something, depending on the 'modals' you use ('I will/might/would see my tutor').

EXAMPLE

Past simple – I talked to my tutor yesterday about my essay.

Past perfect – I had talked to my tutor last week about my essay.

Past continuous – I was talking to my tutor about my essay when my phone rang.

Past perfect continuous – I had been talking to my tutor about my essay when he mentioned that I could use this book, *Study Skills for Chinese Students* to help me.

Present simple – I talk to my tutor every week during his office hours.

Present perfect – I have just talked to my tutor about my essay.

Present continuous – I am talking to my tutor now about my essay.

Present perfect continuous – I have been talking to my tutor about my essay, and now I understand what I have to do.

Future simple – I will talk to my tutor about my essay next week.

Going-to future – I'm going to talk to my tutor about my essay next week.

Future perfect – I will have talked to my tutor about my essay by next week, and hopefully, I will have a better idea what to do.

Conditional

These constructions can be used for speculating about future possibility so they are very useful for the recommendation and reflection section of assignments.

I'm certain: I will talk to my tutor about my essay (I'm sure)

I'm not certain: I might talk to my tutor about my essay (I'm not sure)

It's impossible: I would talk to my tutor about my essay (but he is abroad, so I can't)

Capitalisation

Knowing when to use capital letters (also called 'upper case') and when not to, is often difficult for students who may be used to different systems in their own language. Here are some basic rules:

- Use capitals after a full stop and at the start of a new sentence.
- For names and titles: Dr Xiangping Du.
- For all proper nouns: The People's Republic of China.
- For module titles: Contemporary Issues in Business.

Do not overcapitalise just because you think something sounds important. For example, the general words 'manager', 'company', 'government', 'education', etc. do not generally require capitals.

In titles and subtitles, normally only particular content words (not words such as 'and', 'the', 'of', 'in', etc.) are capitalised. For example:

Management Styles In UK Banks ✗
Management styles in UK banks ✓

Acronyms

You may find you need to use a lot of acronyms. These are words made from the first letter of each word in a title, for example 'UK' (United Kingdom).The general rule is that you must write the phrase in full first, followed by the acronym in brackets. From then on, you can use just the acronym.

EXAMPLE

The United Kingdom (UK) is a multicultural society. The UK has many citizens from many countries of the world.

English and American spelling

You can use either spelling system, but it is more usual in the UK to use the English spelling system. Make sure your computer spellchecking program is set to 'English spelling'.

EXAMPLE

Many **organizations** have training **programs** for staff. (American spelling)
Many **organisations** have training **programmes** for staff. (English spelling)
*when referring to computer programs in English spelling, 'programs' should be used

Appropriate linking and signposting phrases

When you introduce or change topic in an assignment, you can use 'sign-posting' words to guide the reader through your work by using effective linking words and phrases to link your sections and paragraphs. We give more guidance about how to use signposting in academic writing in Chapter 4. Here are some examples of signposting phrases.

EXAMPLE

Introduction

This assignment will firstly… then… next… finally…

Main body

However, (introducing a counter argument or point)
On the other hand, (introducing a counter argument or point)
Further/Furthermore, (expanding the point)
For example, (introducing an example)
With regard to… (changing the topic)
This leads on to… (linking the topic)

Conclusion

In conclusion,
Finally, to summarise the main issues…

Overgeneralisations

You should check carefully for any statements which are too general and not supported by appropriate referenced evidence. For example:

Most people shop online these days. (✗)

Other examples of phrases to avoid because they assume evidence that does not exist and/or make incorrect assumptions or overgeneralisations are:

> **It is true that** online shopping can bring many benefits. (✗)
> **It is obvious that** online shopping has many advantages. (✗)
> **Of course** online shopping has many advantages. (✗)
> Online shopping **must** have many advantages. (✗)

You could write 'Online shopping has many potential advantages', but this is still an unsupported statement that needs evidence and an in-text reference:

> According to Surname (year), online shopping has many potential advantages. (✓)

You must always present a balanced case and use a reference, even though this could mean showing the limitations of the evidence or argument. Be very specific about your claims on the basis of your data. For example, you could write:

> **A recent study (Surname, year)** suggests that online shopping **may** present specific advantages to consumers such as… (✓)

Avoid the kind of generalisations that are apparent in the example below:

> **As we all know**, online shopping is more convenient. (✗)

There are two generalisations here – one that 'we all' know something, and secondly, that online shopping is more convenient. How? Convenient for whom? Other common examples of overgeneralisations which you should avoid are:

> Research shows that… (✗)
> Research (e.g., Surname, year; Surname, year) shows that… (✓)
> Many authors agree that… (✗)
> Many authors (e.g., Surname, year; Surname, year; Surname, year) agree that… (✓)

Accurate use of vocabulary and jargon

Do not use elaborate and 'flowery' language in your writing, such as the 'famous' company, the 'noble' company, the 'honourable' managers, the 'famous' scholars, etc. You might be tempted to do this because in Chinese culture such terms are used as a mark of respect to people or institutions which are given high status in society.

In the UK, such terms are not used, and it is regarded as inappropriate to give such 'praise' in academic work. This is because it is too biased and subjective – you always need to be objective about the information you present in your assignments and avoid putting strong feelings into your writing. How do you know if the managers are actually honourable?

There are many 'technical' and 'jargon' terms you will need to use in your work. Record them, with their meanings, as soon as you come across them. You will soon build up good knowledge of the relevant vocabulary for your subjects.

Two other kinds of word are important in academic writing. One of these are 'signposting' words like 'next', 'however' and 'furthermore', which help your reader to understand your essay. The other type are cautious words which you should use when you want to show that something is not definitely a fact – you need to 'hedge' what you say. These are words like 'perhaps', 'maybe' and might'. We will tell you more about the importance of good signposting, later, in Chapter 4.

Fonts, headings, sub-headings and line spacing

If you are writing a report, you will need to use headings and sub-headings. Use appropriate academic type 'fonts' such as Times New Roman, Arial, or Calibri. You can also use headings and sub-headings in your work, especially for reports. This may vary depending on your assignment instructions and your tutor's preference, so it's always best to check. General assignment conventions are Times New Roman or Arial, font size 12, for the main text (often 1.5 spacing – check with your lecturer), and the following sizes for headings and sub-headings:

TABLE 2.4   General text-design conventions for assignments

Chapter title	20pt bold Times New Roman
Main headings	14pt bold Times New Roman
Sub-headings	12pt bold Times New Roman
Lower levels	12pt non-bold Times New Roman
Bullet points	10pt non-bold Times New Roman

Correct use of punctuation

All students need to be careful to use correct punctuation in their writing, and this can be a problem for Chinese students since the punctuation system in Chinese is very different. In Table 2.5, we have given examples of the most common punctuation errors we have found in our students' written work:

TABLE 2.5   Punctuation rules and examples of common errors

Full stops [.]

Every sentence must have a full stop at the end, and a space after the full stop, before the next sentence.

Example

Market research is essential before product development. It can take many forms, for example...

Question marks [?]

Question marks go at the end of sentences that are questions. However, in general, don't ask questions in your academic writing, because it is not good academic style.

Example

What is the population of China?

Exclamation marks [!]

Exclamation marks act as full stops. They are used in general English to show surprise, pleasure or emotion. For that reason, do not use them in academic writing, because they are emotive and 'informal'.

Example

It was a fantastic opportunity! That was a great essay!

Commas [,]

Commas can be used to put brief 'pauses' in longer sentences, breaking up the information so that it is easier for the reader to understand the sentence. In some cases, commas are vital to make the sentence understandable. In example (a) below, the sentence does not make sense without commas between the chunks of information.

Examples

a) My boss who was the team leader told me to finish the task however this was challenging. ✗
b) My boss, who was the team leader, told me to finish the task; however, this was challenging. ✓

Commas can also separate items in long lists. Note that the last item is always preceded by 'and' – not just a comma.

Example

There are a number of suitable cost-saving strategies, such as outsourcing, negotiating with suppliers, rationalising transport and cutting staff.

Colons [:]

Colons are used before a list or an explanation, as in the example below. They are often confused with semicolons (see below).

Examples

a) A SWOT analysis consists of the following components: strengths, weaknesses, opportunities and threats.

b) The company decided to adopt two main solutions: outsourcing and downsizing.

Semicolons [;]

Semicolons are normally used to separate two short sentences that are linked, and would otherwise be joined with a word, such as 'and', 'because', 'since', etc., to make a longer sentence.

Example

The company's first-quarter results were good; the strategy had clearly worked.

Semicolons can also be used for lists which contain many different phrases, rather than individual words. In most word lists, a comma is enough to separate the items. However, in a more complicated list, such as the one below, it is better to use a semicolon to make the list more readable:

Example

Good team work requires many things: a common team vision; clear leadership; clear definition of team roles; a mutual understanding of these team roles; positive commitment by team members; and clear deadlines for deliverables.

Speech marks [' ']

Speech marks are used for direct quotations. Only the words that were actually said are enclosed by speech marks. The first letter inside the speech marks must be capitalised. They can be single or double, but single is often used only for 'special' words.

Example

'We are pleased with these results,' said the CEO.

Another general rule is to use a colon after the introduction to quoted speech or writing.

Example

The CEO said: 'We are pleased with these results.'

(Continued)

TABLE 2.5   *(Continued)*

Apostrophes [']

Apostrophes next to the letter ('s) or (s') indicate possession or belonging. No space is needed before or after the apostrophe.

Examples

The employee's wages (the wages of one employee)
The employees' wages (the wages of many employees)
The bank's address (the address of one bank)
The CEO's statement (the statement of one CEO)

They are also used to show missing letters in shortened words, for example:
Isn't (Is not)
It's (It is)
(However, remember that short forms of words should not be used in your academic writing.)

ACTIVITY 2.3

Using the information we have given you in the section on checking your own work, see how many problems you can find with this paragraph of student writing. Our feedback is in the Appendix.

As we all know, online shopping is very popular and has many advantages Research shows that the number of consumers shop online has increased lately. This is because it is easier to shop online. You don't need to go to the shop only have to wait for the delivery. why would you want to go to the shop when you can have this service? It's a very convenient way to buy things! Many people are using this service nowadays. I always use this service.

THINK 2.2

Reflect on your own personal problems with academic English. Make a list of the main problems you have now. Then think about how you can improve during your stay in the UK.

Make a list of all the things you plan to do to improve your academic English, using the ideas in this chapter and any others you can think of yourself. Write your ideas down in the reflection box at the end of this chapter using these two headings:

Current problems with my academic English

What I plan to do to improve my academic English while I am in the UK

Common Latin words in academic writing

Latin is an old language which many years ago was very important for scholarly academic work. We still use some Latin words today in academic writing. Here are some of the more common Latin phrases and abbreviations which you will find in your academic textbooks.

e.g. (exempli gratia) = for example, such as, for instance

Only use 'e.g.' in brackets, like this: (e.g., China and India).

etc. (et cetera) = and so on, and others

Try not to use this common Latin abbreviation in academic writing, because it lacks the detail that academic writing needs. It is mainly used informally like this:

You can take your luggage, computer etc. on the aeroplane, but it must be the correct size.

i.e. (id est) = namely, that is to say

If you use 'i.e.' in academic writing, you must list all the things you are referring to, not just one or two examples:

Students have to write different types of assignments, i.e., assignments, reports and case studies.

et al. (et alii) = and other authors (usually three or more)

Use 'et al.' in your academic writing and referencing to refer to three or more authors:

Surname et al. (year) stress the importance of good study skills for success at university.

N.B. (nota bene) = take note

Only used in notes and footnotes – do not use in the main body of your academic writing:

N.B. it is important to check and proofread all your assignments before you submit them.

Ibid. (ibidem) = the same work as the previous one mentioned

This is a useful referencing convention for some reference systems such as APA, but cannot be used with all of them (it is not used with the Harvard system, for example). It is mainly used for footnotes:

Surname, year, pages 40 to 45.
Ibid., pages 101–105.

cf. (confer) = compare with

Used in footnotes or in brackets in the main text to draw the reader's attention to another author who has written something different:

Surname (year); cf. Surname (1960)

viz. (videlicet) = namely, that is to say

'viz.' has a similar meaning and use to 'i.e.' but 'i.e.' is generally preferred. As with 'i.e.', you must list all the things you are referring to – you cannot use it as a general term to cover everything:

Students have to write different types of assignments, viz., essays, reports and case studies.

Sic (sic) = signifies an error which has been made in the original text

'sic' is used if you want to use a direct quotation but there is an error in the original, and you do not want to change it yourself because it might be important. In the example below, the word 'plagiarism' has been spelt incorrectly by the original author:

Surname (year) stresses: 'The importance of written accuracy in academic work, and the importance of avoiding playgarism [sic]'.

Things to remember about using Latin abbreviations and phrases

- Latin phrases are not capitalised, except for the abbreviation 'N.B'.
- The abbreviation 'etc.' You should not use this for academic writing because it lacks the required detail.
- The abbreviations 'e.g.' and 'i.e.' are too informal to use in your assignments unless you use them within round brackets (called parentheses).
- The abbreviation 'N.B.' is too informal and general to use in assignments.
- Don't confuse 'e.g.' and 'i.e.' – they have different meanings.
- If you do use an abbreviation, make sure you use full stops and spacing correctly.
- For common Latin abbreviations, do not use italics (except for *sic*) because they are now part of the English language.
- Latin abbreviations are not capitalised except for the abbreviation 'N.B'.

Chapter 2: Key words and concepts – English and Chinese

accurate – 准确的

acronym – 缩写

brave – 勇敢的

cautious – 谨慎的

colloquial – 非正式的

critically – 评判地

evaluation – 评估

exchange – 交换

font – 字体

gist – 概要

heading – 标题

hedging – 躲闪 (不确定)

inclusive – 包含的

induction – 归纳

Latin – 拉丁

objective – 目标

orientation – 预备

overgeneralisation – 过度泛化

paraphrase – 改述

proofreading – 校对

quotation – 直接引用

signposting – 标识

slang – (当地) 俚语

smart – 聪明的

source – 来源

stress – 压力

subjective – 主观的

surname – 姓

tentative –试探性的

vague – 含糊不清

verb tenses – 动词时态

CHAPTER 2: TEST YOURSELF

Put an ✗ for an incorrect statement and a ✓ for a correct statement.
Check your answers in the Appendix.

1 Language exchange is a good way to develop your academic English............. ☐

2 Academic English is informal.. ☐

3 Academic English uses mainly second person. .... ☐

4 Academic English is generally tentative.. ☐

5 This is correct: 'A manager must do what he thinks is right.' .... ☐

6 You should generally use quotations and not paraphrase. .... ☐

7 A perfect verb tense is used to show that the action has completely
   finished.. ☐

8 A colon is used before a list or an explanation....................................... ☐

9 Semicolons can be used to separate two short sentences that
   are linked. .... ☐

10 You should use 'etc.' in academic writing to show that other things
   are also possible.. ☐

Chapter 2: Reflection box

THINK 2.1

Write your THINK reflections here:

THINK 2.2

Current problems with my academic English

What I plan to do to improve my academic English while I am in the UK

3

Developing your academic study skills

Introduction

This chapter will help you develop the main study skills you need in order to study successfully in the UK. Study skills are often taught separately in UK Higher Education colleges and universities, but frequently you are expected to develop these skills yourself. This is also why we have written this book.

Study skills include a wide range of capabilities – for example, knowing how to get the best results from your lectures, seminars and tutorials, and knowing how to work in groups and give presentations. All of these skills also depend on the basic skill of using English effectively, as we explained in the last chapter.

You will notice that this chapter contains a lot of advice about 'becoming' – becoming an independent learner; becoming an effective learner, etc. This is what we mean by 'developing' your study skills. Be patient – things will not change in one day, but over the course of your studies, if you follow this advice, you and your tutors will be very happy to notice a positive difference in your academic ability and your self-confidence!

Chapter 3: Xiangping's study tips

- 要在英国的大学中成功，首先要了解中英大学不同的的学习环境和氛围：

TABLE 3.1

中国	英国
一般每周5天都有课	每周可能只有2天有课
每门课程都有教科书，老师的教程一般是按照某本固定的教科书进行，基本不特别要求你课后阅读其他资料，因为你只需要把教科书研究好了就能在期中和期末考试中得高分了	不会有固定的教科书，不过老师会推荐给你很多的阅读书籍和资料，需要你自主地课后自己阅读，课堂上，老师会利用这些材料做案例分析；研讨课上也可能会探讨这些资料；所以，很多时候都靠你自己课后自学，因为以后的作业、考试中你需要提及和引用这些资料。
喂养式：注重基本的理论知识的传授和灌输	散养式：注重对学生综合分析、批判以及应用能力的培养
学生很少质问老师讲的任何事情，因为"老师就是真理"	老师鼓励和欢迎学生提出任何问题和质疑，没有完全的对和错，只要有足够的证据
学习期间很少有作业评估，一般只有期中和期末考试。所以，学生平时的学习可以比较轻松，在学期末"临时抱佛脚"也可能会高分。	除了期中和期末考试外，学习期间会有很多课堂和课后测试，作为最终成绩的一部分。所以，学生平时需要认真对待每部分的作业，因为他们都影响总分的。
老师会像"妈妈"一样"无微不至"，叮嘱和提醒你重要的事件和截至日期，如早操，活动和作业	老师不是你的"秘书"时刻提醒你要做什么：什么时间上课，交作业等。

- 其次，要了解学习中老师对你的学术期待。你所学习的学历越高，老师对你的学术期待就越高：从'基本的记忆 - 对知识的'理解和阐述'- 理论联系实际 - 深入地分析总结 - 综合推断模式或者趋势 - 批判性地评论并发自己的见解。

所以，中英教学和学习中有很多的不同，其中很重要的一点就是批判性思维。

TABLE 3.2

在中国的学术氛围里，学生很少质问老师讲的任何事情，因为"**老师**就是真理"；**也很少**对自己阅读的信息提出质疑，因为1）**可能是出于尊重**2）**只要**发表的资料都会被视为权威。	**在英国的学**习中，无论对阅读还是写作，都需要有批判性思维；老师鼓励和欢迎学生提出任何问题和质疑，因为没有完全的对和错，只要有足够的证据。

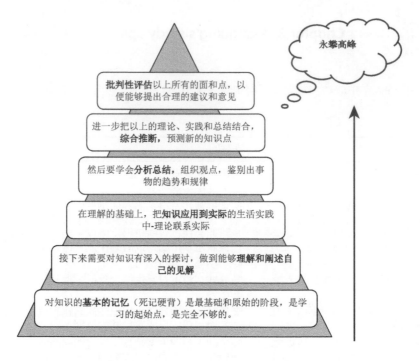

FIGURE 3.1

无论是阅读还是写作的时候，需要具有批判性。比如阅读时候要批判性地接受你的阅读资料。

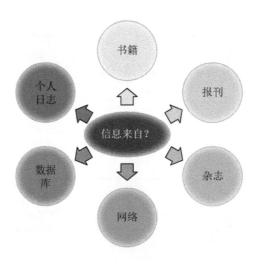

FIGURE 3.2

另外，在阅读和利用这些信息的时候，还需要考虑以下一些方面：

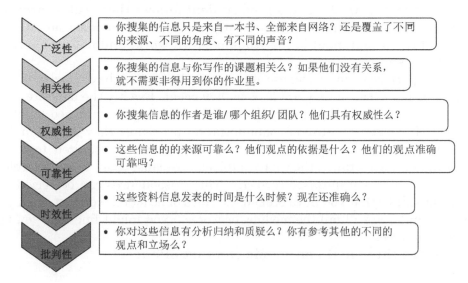

FIGURE 3.3

Becoming a responsible learner

Everything that you are taught in the UK will be 'evidence based' and you will be expected to acknowledge the source of the evidence and be able to 'evaluate' this evidence as part of your university training. By 'evidence', we mean the supporting information (the 'data') you need in order to complete your assignments. This 'evidence' can come from books, journals, news, websites, and other independent sources of information.

The first important step is to understand how to correctly use this evidence in a Higher Education context. It is very important that you understand some of the dangers of not using evidence sources correctly in your studies. You should understand the rules of what is called 'academic conduct' in the UK. This is a very important feature of UK university life. Here are the general rules you should know, although each institution will have its own policies which you will be made aware of.

Academic misconduct: Cheating, collusion and plagiarism

Academic conduct is the system of rules about how to study and learn correctly and ethically. It refers to the 'rules' you need to follow when you are using other people's ideas and work for the information you need for your assignments. In the UK, a good student follows these rules carefully and writes assignments which are 'original' – this means that all the content of the assignment is the student's own work, and not copied from anywhere else.

In our experience, many Chinese students find that they have academic conduct issues not because they are lazy or they cheat. Exactly the opposite – we find that our Chinese students try very hard and are very concerned to follow the rules. However, because of communication problems, they do not understand what they are required to do, and how they are required to do it. Unfortunately, sometimes they have problems because they have not referenced correctly or paraphrased correctly. The consequences can be serious. If your tutor thinks that you have broken the rules of academic conduct, then you may find that you will fail the module, or worse – you might find that you fail the whole degree!

There are three main academic conduct offences:

- Cheating
- Collusion
- Plagiarism

TABLE 3.3   Defining cheating, collusion and plagiarism

Cheating This is any attempt to gain an unfair or dishonest advantage in the assessment process	1) Impersonation – this is where a student allows another person to take an assessment on their behalf or to present themselves as being that student, or where a current student takes an assessment on behalf of another student.
	2) Obtaining or attempting to obtain unauthorised access to examination papers.
	3) Copying, or attempting to copy, the work of another candidate in an examination, or another student in a class assessment. This can be by looking at what he or she has written, or by asking him or her for information about the answers.
	4) The introduction into an examination room (or any other room in which a formal assessment is taking place) of devices which can contain information to help answer the questions. This can take the form of paper notes, writing on hands, arms, etc., or use of smartphones, computer tablets, books, or other devices of any kind other than those permitted. This includes, for example, unauthorised information stored in the memory of a pocket calculator, personal organiser or any other device.
	5) Requesting a temporary absence from an examination room (or any other room in which a formal assessment is taking place) with the intention of gaining, or attempting to gain, access to information that may be relevant to a formal assessment.

6) The falsification of research data for assignments, projects and dissertations.

7) False statements made in order to receive special consideration by tutors and examiners, or to obtain extensions to deadlines or exemption from work.

Collusion

This is when you pretend that your assignment was written only by you but it was really written by you and someone else

Submitting an assignment which you claim to have been written only by you, but which was actually written partly, or wholly, by another person.

Plagiarism

This is when you use other people's work and ideas, but you don't admit this, and you pretend that the work and ideas are yours

The representation, whether intentionally or otherwise, of another person's work as your own, or the use of another person's work without acknowledgement. This includes:

a) The use of another person's exact words, without using quotation marks and identifying the source.

b) Making a copy of all or part of another person's work and presenting it as your own work.

c) Making extensive use of another person's work, either by summarising or paraphrasing the work inappropriately, or by changing the sequence of the material without other changes (you might include a reference, but you still have used far too much of the original).

d) Using the ideas of another person without any acknowledgement of the source or the work which is mostly that of another person.

e) Filling your writing with other people's views which are properly referenced, but there is no original work of your own (the purpose of using others' views is to show how they are connected with the topic you are working on and to comment on them, and to show your opinion – otherwise, there is no point in just listing what others have said).

Unfortunately, there might be differences between what many Chinese students think about using other people's ideas, and what your tutors might think about it. For example, for cultural reasons, some Chinese students think that by using large parts of an author's work without adequate referencing, they are actually complimenting the author and acknowledging the author's status.

It is therefore important to fully understand the issue of plagiarism. If you don't understand how to reference correctly, whatever the reference system your university or college uses, then you might be accused of plagiarism. Good referencing is one of the best ways to avoid the charge of plagiarism.

TABLE 3.4   How to avoid academic conduct offences

Cheating: Don't be tempted – you will be found out.

Collusion: It's OK to get advice from a friend with your assignments, but don't let anyone else contribute to the writing without acknowledging them. Make sure that if you send an electronic version of your assignment to a friend in order to start a discussion about the assignment, that you are sure your 'friend' will not misuse it, and try to 'cut and paste' parts of your work. It's probably best never to let anyone but your tutor have electronic copies of your work.

Plagiarism: Learn how to reference well and use your referencing system correctly. Always put sections from books into your own words (paraphrase) but always with a correct reference to your source of information. Don't use your old assignments – all your work should be original. You can use old assignments for revision and perhaps use some of your old references, but that's all.

Referencing and citing academic information

You will need to include other people's evidence in order to support your own argument in your assignments. In order to avoid being accused of plagiarism, you will need to reference every source you use and to develop your ability to summarise and paraphrase and also quote properly. If you don't do this, you could be accused of plagiarism accidently – you didn't intend to cheat, but your tutor is not sure that the essay is entirely yours.

'Citing' in an academic document means giving a reference to the source of the information. When you cite a data source, you say where the data comes from. It should not be confused with 'quoting', which is writing down exactly what someone said or wrote.

You will need to constantly support your points in your academic writing by referring to experts – this is what is meant by a 'reference'. When you refer to these experts, you should use an appropriate reporting verb ('states', 'suggests', 'concludes' etc.) that accurately reflects what the author does in their writing and shows your tutor that you understand this, e.g.:

Surname (year) suggests that…	Surname (year) indicates that…
Surname (year) claims that…	Surname (year) maintains that…
Surname (year) argues that…	Surname (year) defines X as…
Surname (year) believes that…	Surname (year) states that…
Surname (year) explains that…	Surname (year) concludes that…

Each of these reporting verbs means something slightly different. Make sure you choose carefully, so that if you use the verb 'believe', this is what you mean. If you are unsure how to link the idea with the researcher, then use one of the more general verbs such as 'states' or 'suggests'.

Generally, it's safe to use the present tense – even if the date of the research was in the past, for example 2000 or earlier. This is because you are referring to the research result as something which is still currently available.

There are many different referencing formats, such as Harvard, Oxford, APA and MLA. These are all 'in-text' systems, meaning that the author of the information, and the date of publication, are placed in the text and not at the end of the article, as in the footnote system explained below.

There are two main types of referencing system in use in Higher Education in the UK. The first is called an 'in-text' system because you acknowledge the source of your information in the actual text of your essay or report. The second system is called the numeric, or footnote, system. This is because you put your references at the bottom of the page, or at the end of the text, and you refer to each reference in the text with a small number (see below).

However, both these systems require that your references need to be used at two places in your assignment – in the text, and in a final list at the bottom of the page or the end of the text.

In-text citation system

In-text citations are the references used in the body of your work, which only need the author's surname and the publication date for Harvard style. You do not use the author's first name. For example, in the Harvard system, if the author of the book you want to reference is John Wong, then you only use his family name (called a surname) and the year (year) when the book was published. This is what it would look like in your assignment:

> Wong (year) states that good referencing is essential in order to avoid being accused of plagiarism.

It is usually best to put the reference at the beginning of the sentence. However, sometimes you might also want to put both the surname and the year in the bracket at the end of the sentence, like this:

> Good referencing is essential in order to avoid being accused of plagiarism (Wong, year).

It is worth noting that the full stop needs to be after the reference and not before the reference.

Final reference list

All your work should have references in the text and also in a final reference list (if you are using an 'in-text' system). This is called 'References' or sometimes it is called a 'Bibliography' if the list also contains other books and websites that you read, but you didn't actually use in the final assignment.

EXAMPLE

References

Courtney, M., and Du, X. (2015) *Study Skills for Chinese Students*. London: SAGE.

Depending on the reference style you are using, there are different styles for different types of information. For example, information from the internet usually has the following features:

Surname, first letter of first name. (year of publication) Title. Available at: *web address.* Retrieved [or accessed]: *date of retrieval/access.*

Remember also that:

- The references should cover a wide range of sources instead of being limited only to books.
- The references must be organised alphabetically according to the author's surname – if there is more than one author, the surname should be the first author's.
- For the specific format of different types of references, you need to refer to your institution's style guide.

If you are using an older style of referencing system such as the numeric or footnote system, then your references might look like this:

EXAMPLE

Numeric/footnote system

For example, if the sentence below was the fifth reference in your text:

> Courtney and Du (year)[5] state that good referencing is essential in order to avoid being accused of plagiarism.

And in your final reference list, at the foot of the page (footnote) or at the end of your essay (endnote):

> (5) Courtney M., and Du, X. (2015) *Study Skills for Chinese Students*. London: SAGE.

The importance of referencing can be seen from Xiangping's experience:

In China, we never have to include references in our writing to acknowledge where we got the information from, because we consider that the information or knowledge is published for others to use, so there is no need to reference it. However, in the UK, if students do not write down the references, it will be considered plagiarism, which as we have seen is a very serious academic misconduct issue. Students will not only be marked down, but may also be called into meetings with academic conduct officers, which can be quite scary!

When I was doing my first assignment in the UK, I didn't know that I had to write down references for the information collected from various sources, and I got many comments from my tutor: 'How do you know?', 'Where did you get the graph from?', 'You need to acknowledge the source', 'Go and find some support with your referencing.' For referencing, I learnt that references need to be used in two places in the text: 1) in the body of the work, which is called an in-text citation, and 2) in a final list of references. For in-text citations, usually only the author's surname and year are needed, but for the final list of references, full details of the source are required.

Additionally, there are different referencing formats, e.g. Harvard, Oxford, American Sociological Association (ASA), and American Psychological Association (APA). Each department in a university usually follows one particular format. Therefore, it is important for students to quickly learn the correct referencing system and follow the correct style guide.

Becoming an independent learner

You will often hear tutors talk about the importance of becoming an independent learner. This does not mean always working on your own and never asking your tutors about anything. It means that you need to develop confidence and ability in making good decisions about your own learning and development, using the advice and support of your tutors and your institution.

In China, teachers often tell students what to do, how to do it, and when to do it. However, in the UK, you might not feel that you are being guided in this way. This is because in the UK, students are expected to be 'independent' learners. This means you will have to make a lot of these study decisions yourself. Tutors are there to deliver lectures and tutorials, or facilitate seminars, and support you when you need some help. However, they are not there to 'spoon-feed' you – to tell you which book to read and when to read it. They will treat you as an adult and expect you to take responsibility for your own study organisation and learning. In order to be a successful student in the UK, you have to be an active and independent learner. What does it mean to be an independent learner?

Here are some characteristics of independent learners:

1. **They are proactive:** they do not wait to be told what to do, but start to read and research for their modules even if the tutor has not specifically told them to. This might be a problem for Chinese learners because you may feel uncomfortable about doing anything that you

have not specifically been told to do. In China, your tutor usually gave you very precise instructions about what to read and write, and when to do it.

2. **They are self-motivated and well organised:** in our experience, Chinese students can be very well organised, so this is not a problem. However, with regard to being self-motivated, Chinese students are often worried about doing the 'wrong' thing, so will be uncomfortable with being told to be proactive and self-motivated. This is also a problem for many students, and it isn't necessarily a bad thing, since it does mean that you will be very careful about checking details – and this is also an important study and life skill. However, it is still the case that Chinese students often think that only tutors can 'teach' them anything, and this is a very narrow view of learning in Higher Education.

3. **They are detail-minded:** independent students don't just rely on their friends either. If you always ask your friends what you need to do, then this is not developing your own independence. You must get into the habit of finding the information that you need yourself, from reliable sources such as module guides and tutors. You must develop the habit of checking details yourself, and not just rely on your friends.

This is Xiangping's experience when she first came to the UK to study:

Unlike in China, I wasn't given any textbooks for the subjects I studied, so I mistakenly thought that this would make my study life much easier because I could just go to classes without reading any books. However, I soon realised that I was wrong because the tutors recommended to us a long reading list of books and journals which we were expected to read before the lectures! All of this information was in the module guide, but at first I didn't read this guide, so I didn't know about the reading list.

Additionally, I found that only sitting in classes was never enough for me to understand, so I had to read (as recommended) after class in order to have a better understanding of what was taught in class.

It was surprising that the tutors never checked on whether we had read as required, because they said they treated us as adults. Neither would they check whether we had done our homework or assignment. There was a kind of freedom to some extent. However, the most important thing I learnt was how to become a more independent learner.

I learned this from a hard lesson when I missed the deadline of my first ever assignment in the UK, because I thought the tutors would tell me or remind me when the deadline was approaching. However, the tutor did not because it was all set and written clearly in the module handbook.

That's when I got to know that students on each module will have a module handbook with information related to the whole module. The module handbook contains the tutors' contact details, teaching schedules, module work syllabus, assessment tasks and assessment criteria, and other important information.

Data handling skills

A key part of successful independent learning is being able to work confidently with academic data (information). It is essential that you can identify appropriate information sources, and search and retrieve appropriate information. Then you will need to evaluate the quality of the information, and use it to create new information for your assignments and research.

Becoming a proactive researcher

It is also worth noting that although you are enrolled onto a taught programme, you are expected to conduct a great amount of research for your assignments, and study independently. If you only rely on the time in class, or just reading the tutor's notes, this will not be enough.

Using the library

As well as the VLE, the library is a very important place for your study, and you should learn to use it well. Many books are now available electronically as 'e-books', and you will find that this is a useful way to access the books that you need for your modules. Because there will only be a limited number of core course textbooks available in the library, and many students will want to access them, using e-books or buying your own copies will be the best options.

Buying textbooks

Module textbooks can be expensive, so it is worth checking to see if there is a second-hand facility run by the institution or the department, to recycle module book copies used by previous students. However, it is important to check the edition number to make sure that these copies are up to date for your current module.

Decide if a source is relevant for your exact task

Avoid wasting time looking through sources that are not related and that will not increase your understanding. To quickly identify whether a book or other data source is relevant for your purpose, you need to check the following things:

- key words in the title of the book;
- the back cover summary, which will indicate whether there are useful chapters/sections;
- the table of contents for key words in chapters;
- the index (at the back of the book) for key words;
- the chapters for sub-headings.

To quickly check whether a journal article is relevant to you, check:

- key words in the title;
- the abstract (the small summary of the article at the beginning);
- the sub-headings;
- the conclusion.

THINK 3.1

What kind of reader are you now? Complete this reflection activity. If you answer yes to a lot of these questions, then you probably need to improve your reading ability, using the tips underneath this THINK exercise.

TABLE 3.5   What kind of reader are you now?

When I read an article, ...	YES	NO
I need to read every word to understand the article.		
I feel scared that I will not understand some parts of the article if I don't understand every word.		
I always think that everything I read is correct.		
I only read things that I am interested in.		
I try to remember everything I have read – to learn it by heart.		
I never make notes when I read.		
I only read what my tutor tells me to read.		
I only read what I need to read for assignments, tests and exams.		
I never use a dictionary when I read because it slows me down.		
I don't enjoy reading – it's too difficult for me.		

How to improve your reading

As we indicated in Chapter 2, it is not usually advisable to read word by word as it takes too long and many parts could be irrelevant. If you often need to read and re-read sections or you avoid complicated texts, you may need strategies to help you get the most from your reading.

Processing and understanding text

Remember, you do not need to read and understand and remember every word you read for your academic studies. To try to do this all the time would mean that you will always get behind with your reading and start to feel very unhappy. In the same way, you do not need to make lots of notes from things that you read. Tutors do not just want descriptions copied from books and lecture slides and lots of quotations. You are expected to understand what the text was 'about', both in terms of the 'gist' and the detail, and what the article implies in relation to the topic in general. To do this you need to examine ideas, to question, to engage with the text, and to reflect on what you have read in order to make connections with others' ideas, to use and apply in your assessments.

Reading academic articles

You need to recognise the style of the academic text you are reading (book, case study, report, journal, etc.). When you are familiar with the different types, it is easier to find what you need.

Being an active reader helps you interact with the text to improve your concentration and keep you focused as you read. You do this by asking questions, taking notes and highlighting key points. You could colour-code the different points you note, e.g. main points in yellow and examples in blue. Try to do these things when you read:

1. **SCAN** the text quickly to get a quick general overview of a topic, to separate important relevant information from irrelevant information. If relevant, plan to read further, and if irrelevant, ignore.
2. **SKIM** to gather as much information as possible from a section/article /chapter in the shortest possible time. This reading style provides you with the gist of the text by using visual clues in the text. For example, you can look for key words, nouns, verbs and link words in order to get an overview of the text. You probably already skim the internet for relevant sites/ information you want to read more about, so you are probably quite naturally good at this.
3. **QUESTION** the text. How do you do that? Keep the exact assignment focus in your mind, or make sure you have it written down, and question: What is written? Who said/did what? Why? When? Where? How? When you actively search for answers to questions, it helps you analyse the text as your mind is engaged in the learning process. This helps you remember and understand more information and use the material more effectively.
4. **READ** useful sections and divide them into smaller ones to read the details of the text carefully, making notes of possible answers to your questions (see above) and referencing important points. This takes time but it is worth it because it helps your understanding.
5. **REVIEW** – read the text again, rewrite, refine the structure of your notes, or repeat, in order to fix it in your mind, as repetition of material will enhance your recall and memory. If you read the assigned reading before your lecture, then the lecture will act as a useful review of the information you read.

Reading journal articles

As we show you later in this chapter (critical evaluation of data), academic journal articles are among the best sources of data because their research is thoroughly checked by other experts in that subject before the article can be published. So reading and using academic journal articles for your assignments will potentially get you much better marks.

The best place to start when you are trying to read an academic journal article is the small summary of the article at the beginning, called the 'abstract'. Skim the abstract the article summary and conclusions to get an overview of the journal article. Check the abstract and discussion sections to decide if the article is useful for your particular assignment and which information is relevant. Read the article carefully, asking yourself questions and searching for the answers to focus your reading. Read critically, analyse and evaluate the findings.

EXAMPLE

The table below shows you the typical structure of an academic journal article.

TABLE 3.6   The structure of an academic journal article

Journal article section	Author's purpose
Abstract	Gives the reason for the research, the main results and a statement about the interpretation of the results.
Introduction/ background	This section will put the context of the article – the researcher's position; the hypothesis or main argument, if the article is exploring a new or specific point of view; introduction of the theoretical context so the reader can relate the author's findings/ideas to earlier research.
Methods (may/may not be included, depending on the type of article)	Indicates different methods used, i.e. a case study or a survey. This is useful information when comparing two articles to interpret reliability of the research. This section may not be included if the article is a discussion of a theory/premise.
Results/findings	This section presents data, either in statistical form or qualitative findings, and is often descriptive.
Discussion	Presents the researcher's interpretation of the results; the author may try to persuade the reader to a way of thinking. This section will be critical of how the research was conducted so the reader must be aware of flaws.
Conclusions/summary	Provides a summary of the research and the implications of the research for the subject, topic, organisation, issue, etc.

Using internet sources

Students increasingly use the internet for sources of information. With all data sources, you need to be careful about the information and the claims made, and this is especially the case with internet data. You can access many good data sources and relevant academic sources using databases set up on your institution's VLE or by using commercial web browsers. You can also use internet encyclopaedias to get initial information about a topic, and perhaps a list of better references which you can follow up. However, your tutors will not want you to use internet sources entirely. With all internet sites, you need to know who the author is and what their credentials are. Ask yourself: Is this source reliable? Relevant? Current? Objective? Ask the advice of your tutors when accessing internet sources.

What to look for in an academic article

Use the questions below to 'question' a text when you read it:

TABLE 3.7   What to look for in an academic article

Question	What to look for
Is the article based on balanced research evidence or is it just the author's point of view?	Does the author reference other academics to support his or her points?
Are there links to other texts/research?	Look for words such as: • *According to...* • *A research study by...* • *Evidence supplied by...* • *(cited in Surname and Surname, year)*
Is the argument sound/ strong?	• Is there good evidence or is the author generalising? Look for examples of other research/information which backs up the line of argument – you may have to check other sources to find out. • Look at other sources for disagreement. This will help you decide which has the most convincing argument that is backed up by evidence.
Is the evidence reliable?	• Is the author an expert? • What does your tutor say about the author? • Research the author: has she or he been involved in other research? What other articles has he or she written?
Is the author's research reliable?	• What do other experts say? • What methods were used to gather evidence?
Does the conclusion reflect the evidence/ information in the text?	• Check back from the conclusion to the discussion and findings. Can the author really make these claims?

Improve your reading by increasing your reading speed

Your reading speed will vary depending on the complexity of the text and how you engage with it. When reading complicated sentences and technical terms, your speed will slow down to cope better. To help you improve your speed while still understanding the material, try the tips shown in Table 3.8.

TABLE 3.8   Tips for improving your reading speed

Read faster	Tell yourself that you don't need to understand each word. The more you practise reading quickly, the more you will learn even though you may not understand all you read.
Increase the number of words that you read at one time	Practise reading a phrase at a time rather than individual words. This will gradually increase the length of the phrases you read and gradually increase your reading speed.
Read more quickly to improve comprehension	Quickly repeat-read difficult sections of the text.
Improve the flow of your reading	Resist the temptation to stop and go back – keep reading forwards.
Recognise the style of the subject and the subject jargon. Spend some time after you have read the whole text to focus on key words and meanings	Practise reading key subject words out loud, making sure you pronounce them correctly – there are many internet sites which will pronounce the word correctly for you, and give you the meaning in Chinese.

(See also 'Becoming a critical reader' later in this chapter.)

Becoming an effective learner

Lectures

In most colleges and universities in the UK, lectures are the main way that modules are taught. A lecture is a talk by a module tutor on a set topic in the module syllabus. The lecturer talks, usually with the help of audio-visual aids, and students listen and take notes. There is an opportunity for questions, but most students will want to leave these for the smaller group seminars and tutorials, so there is not much interaction. There may be hundreds of students at one lecture.

Normally, lecturers also expect students to prepare for the lecture in the following ways:

1. Complete the relevant reading for the lecture, as shown in the module guide.
2. Read and view any lecture material published before the lecture.

During the lecture, most students want to take notes. This can be a good idea, but a better idea is to prepare for the lecture beforehand by doing (1) and (2) above, and then recording the lecture on a small recording device so that you can listen again after the lecture. If you try to take notes as well as listen during the lecture, you might miss a lot of the information, so it's best just to listen. Most lecturers do not mind if you record the lecture – they will often record it for all the students themselves, as they lecture. In any event, it is polite to ask the lecturer first if you can record the lecture. They will normally be very happy for you to do this.

Seminars, tutorials and workshops

Seminars, tutorials and workshops are all very similar types of teaching method. They are basically small group meetings of students with a tutor – usually around four to twenty students.

A **seminar** is a group discussion on a specific topic related to a lecture. The discussion is held between students on the module and a seminar tutor who might or might not have been the person who gave the lecture on the subject. Typically, a seminar might consist of twenty students. Personal opinions and questions are encouraged and expected.

A **tutorial** is individual or small group tuition which allows a focus on individual student needs and understanding of the topic. Typically, a tutorial might consist of one to four students. Personal opinions and questions are encouraged and expected.

A **workshop** is an opportunity to learn a more practical application of a theory or a skill. Typically, a workshop consists of a facilitator and ten to twenty students.

Questions and participation are expected. Workshops may be extra to the module syllabus – a workshop on academic writing, for example.

You may not be familiar with the seminar and tutorial teaching format. These methods offer advantages over the lecture method since the group sizes are smaller and interaction with the tutors is encouraged. It is your chance to get to know your tutor and some of the other students in the group. In these smaller classes, students and a tutor discuss a specific topic from the module. Topics are given in advance, and preparation and presentation by the student is often required. This normally makes Chinese students feel quite stressed because you will have to speak and give your opinion. However, remember it is also stressful for most students, particularly in their first year of study, so don't feel worried by this. The more that you speak out, the easier it will become for you, and it will also increase your confidence with spoken English. The key to successful seminar participation is to prepare adequately before the seminar. Tutors do not like it when students say nothing because they have not done the required reading.

Experiential learning: Work placement and overseas exchanges

A popular Chinese government slogan in the 1980s was 'Practice is the only way to test the truth', and in the UK, practical experience is also highly valued. Increasingly, on many UK Higher Education modules, there is a practical element. This often means that the student will work for one year of the degree programme in a placement or internship in order to gain work experience. This is called 'experiential' learning – or learning from practical experience. On some modules such as tourism, there will be field trips away from the institution. How this 'experiential learning' is integrated into the learning outcomes and assessment pattern may also be unfamiliar to Chinese students.

It is also possible to study at another partner university during your degree programme, as an exchange student. This also gives you very valuable experience of living and studying in another culture.

Here is Ava's experience again:

> From my placement year, I found that I have become more organised and my self-confidence and self-management skills have greatly improved. I can now manage my time well and use my time effectively. I also improved my writing and speaking skills, and I believe that all of these improvements will help me in my final-year studies, as well as my future career. I further believe that the industry practice I had during placement year will enhance my understanding of my final-year modules because I have gained the experience of putting theories into actual practice so that I now know the theories very well.

Becoming an effective organiser

As an international student studying in the UK, you will be responsible for yourself. There will be a lot of research to do and independent study to complete. You also have to do cooking, housekeeping and shopping, as well as making time for socialising with friends, travelling around the country and participating in some events. Therefore, managing your time well, organising yourself and prioritising your tasks are vital for a successful stay in the UK.

Below are some tips about organising your studies effectively:

1. Make sure you keep an updated timetable of your lectures, seminars and tutorials in your diary. Make a note of your tutors' office hours and room numbers on this timetable.
2. Before the study week starts, prioritise your weekly study tasks, reading, preparation for seminars and assignments, etc.
3. Make sure you attend all your lectures, seminars and tutorials, and use all the recommended study resources.
4. If they are available, download and print a copy of lecture slides before the lecture. Read them, and use the module or module guide to help you find pre-lecture reading which might be necessary.
5. Prepare well for seminars and tutorials – this will make them more enjoyable because you will have something to contribute. Complete any tasks necessary and make a list of questions you want to ask.

6. Make an email or social network 'study group' with other students on the module; exchange ideas and information, and discuss any problems. Keep group members' contact details.
7. Record lectures (if they're not already recorded for you by the tutor) so that you can listen again and take notes, or check the notes you took during the lecture.
8. Keep a small notebook in your bag to record new vocabulary and important module information.
9. Make a personal weekly planner or study timetable to help you organise your time effectively.
10. Learn how to use the library and VLE study resources – attend modules which will help you do this.
11. Start your list of references as you plan and read for a piece of coursework – don't tell yourself you will do it later. You can always delete references you don't need when you have finished.
12. Start revising at least four weeks before exams, using a revision plan.

Groupwork: Becoming a team-player

Besides independent study, you will often have to complete assignments in groups. Group work is a very popular method of teaching and assessment in the UK. This might be difficult for you at first because you might not have much experience of this type of task and assessment. You may get an individual mark for your work, but often group members are awarded the same mark, which means that you need to be able to work very effectively as a group.

Group assignments normally involve a group presentation and a group report, and maybe a reflective piece of writing where you write about your experience in the group. Groups are usually from two to six students, and it is very important that your group works well together to achieve success. It will be quite obvious to your tutor whether you have worked well as a team or not, because normally you also have to provide a group 'log' where each group member records exactly what they did in the group.

Group work is designed to encourage team-working skills, and generally we have found that Chinese students work very well in this type of assessment.

However, group members may find they have different views and expectations about how work will be shared and how decisions will be made. Don't see this as a problem. It is normal in multicultural groups for students to have very different viewpoints. You should see this as a great opportunity to improve your communication skills in English, and to learn more about other cultures.

Xiangping considers that:

Working in groups can be a good or bad experience depending on who the group members are, and how well you work together as a team. In a diverse learning environment in the UK, it is likely that you will be working in a diverse group where your group members are from different cultural backgrounds and have different ways of looking at issues.

I generally had very positive experiences of working in groups, where everybody agreed on a schedule, attended meetings, worked on the part as allocated and completed it on time. However, it was inevitable that there were times of disagreement, but as long as we discussed any problems, there was always a good solution.

Occasionally, there were unpleasant times, especially when I was ignored because others thought they had better English than me. They expressed their own ideas without allowing me to contribute mine. I found that the way to deal with this situation was to confront it and speak out. I needed to make myself and my ideas heard. Their attitude changed towards me and they listened to my ideas, and valued them more.

So we can truthfully say in a good TEAM, 'Together Everybody Achieves More'!

Getting the group started

It is usually your responsibility to contact other members of the group to arrange the first meeting and exchange telephone numbers and email addresses. Each group member should have read the assignment task in order to discuss it at the first meeting.

The first meeting

At the first meeting, the group needs to agree on some rules and who will do each part of the assignment. You could divide tasks up according to the experience, expertise or strength of each member. You could also do it on the basis of building on a student's inexperience and areas of weakness.

Establish a regular programme of meetings to review the group's progress. The group should keep in regular contact, so you need to arrange a regular meeting place. This could be at the university, group members' homes, or via a social networking site.

Agree to keep good records of meetings, with details about what was said and agreed and who agreed to do each task. You can also keep a personal journal and record your own progress, issues and successes, plus any problems so that you can avoid them next time. You will probably also need this information to complete a reflective report after the assignment. In this report, you write about what went well, and what went badly during the group assignment process.

Establishing group roles

In order for the group to function successfully, achieve goals and maximise time in meetings, separate roles have to be taken on by each group member. Some people are better at creating good ideas, and others might be better at motivating and organising the group, or writing reports, etc. All these functions keep the group working well towards the group goal.

Working with people of other cultures and ethnic backgrounds is a great opportunity to learn about others and yourself. Make the understanding of group members' backgrounds and points of view an explicit group objective. Try to be aware of how factors such as the age, social status, occupation and/or educational background of group members is affecting the way you interact with the group. Do you need to improve your attitude to the group, and if so, why?

Addressing conflict

You will often find that some group members will be difficult to work with, and will not come to meetings or produce work on time. The rest of the group should discuss any issues like this, and agree a united approach to the problem, perhaps arranging to talk to the difficult group member. This can be quite difficult if you generally prefer to avoid situations of potential conflict. If this is the case, you might have to see your tutor confidentially, and ask for your tutor's advice.

Any conflict needs to be resolved without creating bad feeling amongst group members, and successful resolution can usually be achieved by discussing the issues with the whole group. Remember that you do not have to like people to work with them, but you do have to learn to work with them in the group. This will help you to develop good interpersonal skills. It is important that the group tries to address any conflict themselves before involving a third party; and most importantly, do not ignore problems – the success of the group will depend on achieving group harmony. Below are some steps you can take to achieve this.

Steps for preventing or resolving conflict within the group

- At your first meeting, agree on how any future disagreement will be resolved. If conflict does occur, establish the nature of the disagreement.

   o Do members perceive things differently?
   o Do they disagree about ways of working?
   o Are members operating with different values?

By exploring the cause of the disagreement, the group may be able to come to a better understanding of the task and its context. Solutions can then be suggested by the group.

- Encourage an atmosphere of openness and honesty – say if you are unhappy, or post a note on the group social networking site.
- Be polite and honest. Don't personalise the issue by blaming other group members – be positive and let other group members know that you are only motivated by getting the best marks for the group.
- Agree that all members should: participate fully, always put their views forward and consider other members' feelings. You should decide to put the needs of the group before your personal needs.

See Chapter 4 for information about writing group reports, and reflections on group work.

Becoming an effective communicator

Communication in English can be the biggest problem for Chinese students. However, effective communication with your tutors does greatly improve your chances of success with your studies in the UK. In this section, we give you some advice about using other very popular methods of communication with your tutors – email and telephone.

Emails

It is important that when you write emails to your tutor, you write them clearly and appropriately. Keep your emails short, and try to say exactly what you want to say, politely and clearly. If you need to discuss things more fully, then only use the email to arrange a face-to-face meeting with your tutor, during office hours.

EXAMPLE

Here is an email from Ava, requesting help with an assignment question she does not understand. It is written in an appropriately polite style for communication with her tutor:

Dear Dr Surname,

I am writing with regard to the new assignment, 'Critically evaluate the importance of corporate social responsibility'.

Although I have done some research for the assignment, I still do not fully understand the assignment question you gave us last week. I have asked my friends, but I am not sure that they are giving me the correct information. Would it be possible to come to your office at some time which is convenient for you so we can discuss the question? I really want to make sure that I answer it correctly. I will be very grateful if you can help me.

Regards,

Xiao Zhou

ID number 123456

Telephone communication

As well as face-to-face conversations with tutors, telephone conversations can be a major source of stress for Asian students in general. Some students are very scared about talking to tutors by telephone since they are worried that they will not understand what the tutor is saying and will not know what to say in reply. If you avoid the problem entirely, you will not learn anything.

You can use some simple clarification requests if you don't understand what someone has said, and your tutor will not be offended. You can use phrases such as:

> I'm sorry – could you repeat that? I don't understand.
> Could I just check with you that I have understood what you have just said?
> I'm sorry, but I didn't quite get that.
> Excuse me – so what you are saying is…
> I'm sorry, I really didn't understand that last point.
> I'm sorry – could you say that again, more slowly – thanks.
> So, what you are saying is…

REMEMBER – you must turn off your phone in lectures, seminars and tutorials, and never send or receive calls during these times, or check your emails, etc. It is considered very bad behaviour to take phone calls during teaching sessions.

Different ways of thinking

This next section looks at some important ways in which students in the UK need to think about the subjects that they are learning. The most important of these is called 'critical thinking'.

Becoming a critical thinker

A very common criticism of most students – including Chinese students – from tutors in the UK is that students do not critically evaluate what they read and write.

This is an issue for most students, regardless of nationality, and we also know from our experience of teaching in China that Chinese students may have particular difficulties in this area because of cultural differences. So,

one of the most difficult things for Chinese students in the UK is to read, write and think critically – to critically evaluate.

The word 'evaluate' is important. It means to make judgements and decisions about something. When you read information for your modules and your assignments, you need to make judgements about what the information means, how reliable it is, and what other experts say about the same issues. This is critical evaluation. The UK education system teaches students to critically evaluate information because of the important idea that all 'truth' is actually 'constructed', and it is therefore the tutors' and the students' responsibility to 'deconstruct' (analyse – break into important parts) this information, not to just describe it and accept it without question.

These abilities are highly valued in the UK education system, and a good critical ability will get you the most marks in your assignments. This next section will show you how to develop this skill, but let's firstly look at why it is such an important learning skill.

孔子

In China, the education system has always been highly influenced by the principles set out by Confucius, the sixth-century-BCE Chinese philosopher and teacher. He emphasised the importance of respect, ritual and harmony, and maintaining the proper order of social relationships, especially within the family. He thought that education was the best means to create this order, and the best way to achieve social status and material success. These beliefs are still strongly held in China today.

Since you will have come from this mainly literal and 'fact-based' educational culture, you might feel that what the 'experts' in your textbooks write is the factual 'truth' – to be learnt by heart and not to be questioned. Consequently, many Chinese students generally think that 'research' is finding out as much as possible about a subject and then presenting this in an unquestioning description.

As a result, Chinese students often write about 'famous' academics, theories, brands and companies, etc., and praise them just because they are well known or well established. In the UK, we do not use the word 'famous' like this in academic essays, because famous people can always be wrong, just like anyone else. You must always allow for new research to present new evidence which might question current opinion. In UK education, we require a more critical and evaluative approach to 'knowledge'.

In China, you probably were taught all the 'facts' about your subjects – including the opinions of the expert scholars – and you did not question them. So, 'knowledge' was a much more certain commodity in China, and that is why you were often required to memorise these so-called 'facts', rather than question them.

Therefore you might only feel comfortable if you are told 'the facts' about your subject. You can memorise 'facts' and copy things from 'expert' sources, rather than evaluate them and give your own opinion. This is how you studied and wrote your essays in China.

Unfortunately, this method means not only that you do not learn to develop your thinking, but also that you might be accused of cheating or plagiarism. Your job as a critically thinking student is firstly to try to analyse this information and then, secondly, to critically evaluate it. In China, this kind of analysis is not encouraged, so it will be a new experience for you. You may think that just describing situations is enough, but you need to always go further and try to find evidence that explains the situation: Why do people do what they do? Why does a company behave in a particular way?

The status of education remains high in Chinese culture. This is reflected in the high degree of parental interest in education, and you may feel a lot of pressure from your family and friends in China to succeed in your studies here. You may also be aware of the financial sacrifices that your parents and relatives may have made to send you here to study, and this is all extra pressure for you. As Xiangping explains:

> In China, we consider tutors to be the fount of all knowledge, and we expect them to know everything. In return, we give them great respect. We feel that whatever is said by our tutors is correct, so we actually believe in our tutors more than our parents. Thus, learning is more of a passive exercise and we believe everything we are taught, read and see, and would never question 'authoritative' tutors.

> However, it is quite different in the UK because tutors encourage us to discuss and critically evaluate topics that they teach. This requires us to be

critical thinkers. Instead of simply accepting everything, we need to think about questions such as: What does this really mean? Why are they saying this? When was this theory established? Where can I find other views about this? etc. During this process of questioning, you must also be aware of the different interests of each person in the discussion – they will have their own bias, just as you do. Especially with further research, different opinions from different sources can emerge, and what theorists claim can be different from what professionals actually do in their work. Interestingly, I realised that the more research I did, the more critical I became.

Additionally, the critical thinking required in my studies has trained me to be a critical thinker in life, and critical thinking has become one of my characteristics, which I find very useful to help me evaluate different situations in my personal life.

Postmodernism

One of the biggest problems for Chinese students is that UK Higher Education generally uses what is called a 'postmodern' approach to the issue of knowledge and how we can know things. This is very different to the Chinese approach to 'knowledge'. 'Postmodern' refers to Western intellectual developments which came after the 'modern' period of development in the twentieth century. Postmodern thinking questions the accepted principles and practices of previous generations.

The next part of this chapter will show you how to change the way you think about 'facts' so that your assignments will be evaluative and successful.

What is fact and what is opinion?

It is important to realise that most information that we deal with in this new 'information age' is actually opinion, but often stated in ways that make it look factual and 'true'.

EXAMPLE

Your friend thinks that it is a 'fact' that British food is not very good. She has only eaten fish and chips and pizzas in the university restaurant in the UK. This is not a 'fact' – it is just her opinion, which she has 'constructed' from her experience of only eating fish and chips and pizza.

If you take your friend to London and show her all the many different kinds of food available, your friend will construct another opinion – that English food can be very interesting and tasty. She has increased her 'evidence' base, and revised her opinion.

ACTIVITY 3.1

Which of the following statements is a 'fact'?

1. Hong Kong was given back to China by the British in 1997.
2. 100 divided by 4 is 25.
3. The best way to improve your English is to practise as much as possible.

(See answers in the Appendix.)

ACTIVITY 3.2

Think of a discussion you had recently. Perhaps your parents told you that they wanted you to study in the UK because they wanted you to have an educational advantage. Their perception is that a UK degree is 'worth more' than a degree from China. Is this 'true'? Is this a fact?

(See the discussion in the Appendix.)

What is knowledge and what is academic truth?

In the modern world, 'knowledge' appears to be available easily – on our smartphones, for example. We can easily find out where the nearest restaurant is, or how many yuan there are to the sterling pound. Nowadays, it is very easy to get information about any subject you want just by using the internet connection on your phone. This information is knowledge – but the problem is that knowledge is not a certain and quantifiable thing. These are 'general' facts which we call 'correspondence' truths (they are called 'correspondence truths' because x yuan corresponds to y sterling pounds). These are also sometimes called 'empirical' or 'real-world' facts. There are many 'general' 'facts' that we could not live without, so we don't question them. However, not all knowledge is 'truth'. If we ask you to tell the truth about a situation, you will still only tell us what you choose to tell us, based on your memory of the events and your opinion about what happened.

So how do you know whether or not the 'knowledge' that you have gained through your reading, for example, is 'true'?

EXAMPLE

Facts, opinions and truth

Beijing is the capital city of China

You might think that this is a 'fact' – it is now, but it was not always a fact. This is 'correct' and 'true' today, but of course, this depends on the historical date. For example, Anyang was the capital during the Yin period of the Shang Dynasty (estimated between 1600 BCE and 1046 BCE): called Yin (殷). This is an example of a type of knowledge that we can call a 'correspondence truth' or 'general fact'. The problem is that apart from these 'general facts' – like the address of your house, or the number of your student ID – there are not many 'facts' in the world. Most knowledge is actually opinion, even though it might be 'expert' opinion that is often presented as 'fact'. People often say 'The facts of the situation are…' when what they should say is 'Personally, my opinion is…'.

In the academic world then, nothing is permanently 'true' because a new researcher may present new research which changes the way we think about things. Many years ago, people thought it was 'true' that the earth was flat, and not so long ago, that the atom was the smallest particle in the universe. Now we know that both statements are not 'true' anymore. Most statements and assertions by people, whether written or spoken, are actually opinions.

So when you write your essays and reports, try not to use the phrase 'it is true that' or 'this proves that' because in the academic world of research, it may not be true and you can never 'prove' anything. Of course, you can use these phrases in your everyday life – we all do – but as a student researcher, you need to be very careful with these words!

Theory of knowledge

There are many theories about what 'knowledge' is. We have seen that most knowledge is actually opinion, and therefore, open to discussion and more research. Every Higher Education student in the UK should understand the theory of knowledge – it is essential for every subject. However, it is not always taught, and you may only have to think about the important issues of academic knowledge and academic truth when you read the feedback from your tutor, who questions your statements in your essay.

The problem can be particularly difficult for Chinese students. The way students in China are taught to think about knowledge is often quite different from the way students in the West are encouraged to be critical about what they are told. As we have discussed, this is often because of different cultural traditions and the different interpretation of what 'knowledge' is in the Chinese educational system.

What does 'being critical' mean in academic study?

It is important to remember that the word 'critical', as used in academic study, does not have the same meaning as the way we use the word 'critical' in everyday life.

EXAMPLE

- 'My friend was very critical of me – she said I was lazy!'

This use of *critical* is a negative *accusation* – the friend accused you of not working hard. We use the word like this in everyday life when we want to accuse someone of something.

- 'The experiment was at a critical phase.'

This use of critical here means 'to reach a very important or vital point'.

- 'Give a critical account of global climate change.'

This essay title asks you to be critical in the academic sense of 'critical evaluation'. Being critical in this context does not mean being negative about global climate change. Being critical in this academic sense means to research expert opinion about global climate change and to write about the different expert opinions from many sides of the discussion.

Evaluation

'Evaluation' in everyday life means making a judgement about how good or bad something is, or how useful or not useful something is. We do it every day:

My tutor is great! He really helps me with my studies. (Positive evaluation)

My tutor is not good! He doesn't explain things clearly to us. (Negative evaluation)

In the academic world, evaluation is not concerned with good or bad, but relevance and irrelevance, strengths and weaknesses, and effectiveness and ineffectiveness. To critically evaluate means to use your analysis, evidence and reasoning to form a view on the accuracy and/or value of something, rather than just using your own personal experience or opinion. You need to assess the 'pros' and 'cons' (strengths and weaknesses) of a situation, issue or idea in order to make a judgement on it, draw conclusions, state key points, and propose implications and solutions. Critical evaluation is an important life skill and an ongoing process in your personal and academic development.

Critical evaluation normally requires that you analyse a situation or issue first, and then write about the advantages and disadvantages of the strategy or theory, or the strengths and weaknesses in an argument. You are not normally required to do this from your own experience or personal knowledge. You do it by comparing and contrasting the 'expert' views. One important reason to come to university is to develop an 'informed' opinion by learning from 'experts', so you will not be expected to personally criticise the experts.

You might be asked to critically evaluate many different things – for example: a research article, your own learning on a module, a topical issue connected with your module, or a theory.

EXAMPLE

- **Critical evaluation of an article** (for a review or critique of the article)

Example: Surname's article (year) gives a useful overview of the issues; however, as Surname (year) indicates, Surname apparently does not include the perspective of the individual employee – only that of the company. This may be neglecting a very important aspect of the issue. On the other hand, Surname (year) does give a comprehensive account of the company macro-environment.

- **Personal critical evaluation of a module** (for a reflective essay on what you have learnt from a module)

Example: I learnt a lot from this module which will be very useful in any future business-related career. I particularly enjoyed the inclusion of business practitioners in the teaching schedule. This made the end-of-course conference particularly useful, since it gave us the opportunity to learn from their real-world experience of business, rather than just from the textbooks.

- **Critical evaluation of research**

Example: There have been many research studies on this issue (e.g. Surname, year; Surname, year; Surname, year). However, these studies have all focused largely on the company perspective and not that of the individual employee. As Surname (year) suggests, it may be that more research on the individual employee perspective will be important to get a better understanding of the effects of the changes the company is currently undergoing.

- **Critical evaluation of an issue**

Example: According to Surname (year) this issue is an important one for the industry to resolve. However, as Surname suggests, unless all stakeholders are involved, then only token progress can be made to improve the situation. Further, as Surname (year) also points out, it could be the case that a final resolution is not possible, since the issue is changing all the time. What is required is a better understanding of the change process rather than how to solve a particular problem at a particular time.

- **Critical evaluation of theory**

Example: Surname's (year) theory of employee motivation provides a useful analytical framework of factors which might impact on workplace motivation in general. However, more recent research by Surname (year) has suggested that the criteria he uses are too limited in scope. For example, the theory only includes office workers. It might be that the motivation of workers in other workplaces is based on different criteria.

Becoming a critical reader

To read critically you must question, reflect and evaluate what you read, i.e. engage with the text in a number of ways, such as:

- understanding the context of a variety of texts;
- reflecting upon what various writers have written;

- evaluating what you have read from different sources;
- developing your own ideas;
- trying to work out why the writer has a particular viewpoint.

You can really only read critically if you read widely from a range of different sources to develop your knowledge and understanding of your subject/topic. Reading critically does not mean looking only for negative aspects, but evaluating the strengths and weaknesses of information or of an idea.

A critical reader does not look for information alone but for ways of *thinking* about a topic. A 'surface' reader only memorises information, whereas a 'deep' reader understands the information too, and can apply knowledge. (Remember that a key assessment learning outcome is: 'To be able to show a knowledge and understanding of...'.)

A deep approach to reading requires:

- trying to understand what the author is really saying;
- interacting with the text by constantly asking questions;
- relating new ideas to previous knowledge;
- relating concepts to everyday experience;
- relating evidence to conclusions;
- examining the logic of the argument.

So deep reading should result in you actively building up your knowledge and understanding of the topic/subject so that you can appropriately use the ideas and concepts, with correct definitions and terminology. Your tutors will be impressed if you assess the key writers in the topic area, and if you are able to evaluate, reflect upon and synthesise different people's ideas, concepts and opinions. As a critical and deep reader you will show that you can evaluate the credibility, limitations and relevance of other people's ideas, as well as developing your own.

THINK 3.2

Are you using critical reading skills when you read? Complete this self-assessment.

TABLE 3.9   Critical reading skills self-assessment

	Yes	No
1. Do you think about what you are reading and question what the author has written?		
2. Do you refuse to accept everything the article says as 'facts'?		
3. Do you question how much the author knows about the subject?		
4. Do you often disagree with the ideas as you are reading?		
5. Can you follow the arguments in what you read?		
6. Are you able to synthesise key information and make connections between what different authors are saying?		
7. Can you make judgements about the arguments in a text?		
8. Do you try to evaluate how reliable the information is?		
9. Can you see the underlying assumptions that the author makes (the subtext)?		

If you answered yes to __all__ these questions, then you are reading very critically – well done!

As you read to gather information and evidence for your assignments, you need to think critically about it and 'interact' with the text. Higher grades are usually given for work that demonstrates an approach to reading with a critical understanding, and the ability to analyse and synthesise. It is also important for you to read every day. Read quality weekly newspapers, your textbooks and recommended reading given by your lecturer – this will help to keep you up to date, extend your vocabulary, and increase your reading speed, as well as your understanding of your subjects. Create a notebook of technical terms from your specialist area to help you learn the terminology.

ACTIVITY 3.3

Choose a chapter or an article from one of your module textbooks and answer the questions in the space provided in the Appendix (refer back to the tips we gave you earlier about how to read an academic article).

Evaluation and knowledge

As we have said, in the West, teaching students how to evaluate has been a major goal of education. This is largely because of the influence of a particular

TABLE 3.10   Critical reading of an academic article

Question	What is your evidence from the text?
Who do you think the article was written for?	
Why do you think the article was written?	
What is the main argument in the article?	
Are there any other arguments in the article?	
What assumptions lie behind the evidence/ arguments?	
Is adequate proof provided and backed up with examples of evidence?	
What are the general weaknesses of the argument/evidence?	
What are the general strengths of the argument/evidence?	
Give examples of what other expert authors have to say on the same subject	

model of learning and knowledge which is used by many educational institutions. This model is called 'Bloom's taxonomy'.

A taxonomy is a theory about the relationship between different elements of a process. Bloom's taxonomy was originally a theory about the classification of learning objectives within education. It was first proposed in 1956 by a committee of educators chaired by an American educational psychologist called Benjamin Bloom. The model shows a theoretical relationship between the different learning objectives that educators regard as important skill development goals for students. Bloom's taxonomy divides educational objectives into three 'domains':

Cognitive (mental)

Affective (emotions and feelings)

Psychomotor (knowing how to do practical things)

According to Bloom's theory, learning at the higher levels is dependent on having attained a capability with lower-level learning skills. As you can see from the figure below, in the original theory, evaluation was given the highest level of importance. We still regard evaluation as the most important skill that a student can develop. The lowest level of knowledge is the memorisation of 'facts' – this is an essential skill but, without the higher level skills of analysis, synthesis and evaluation, it is not considered to be the best kind of learning. Chinese students are generally very good at memorising 'facts', but are not confident with evaluating opinions. This is why it is important to develop the skill of evaluation as you study and learn.

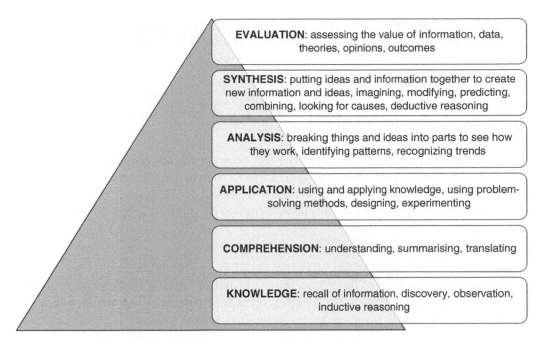

FIGURE 3.4   Bloom's taxonomy (1956) of knowledge development

Evaluating information

There are four main types of information you will need to critically evaluate when you read or write for your assignment:

1. The data or information you collect for your assignment.
2. 'Expert' academic research relevant to your assignment.
3. Theories and models relevant to your assignment.
4. 'Practitioner' data – information about what organisations, companies, people, nations, etc. actually do.

Critical evaluation of data

The first step in critical evaluation is to critically evaluate the sources of information you are going to use – your data. In very simple terms, we can grade data in terms of its academic status and reliability. This is only a very rough guide, but it shows you how to begin to evaluate information. Remember that all data can be evaluated – there is no such thing as information that is absolutely 'true' for all time: most data is only reliable until new research suggests something else. That is why it is very important to always try to read the latest research and expert comment about your subject. So what is the best kind of data to use in your studies? Let's call it 'five star' data!

Five star data

This is academic, credible and reliable data which can be used for your academic studies. 'Five star' data would include:

1. academic research journals – these contain articles or 'papers' which are checked (refereed) by other expert researchers in the subject, before they are published;
2. academic textbooks – written by experts in the subject and recommended by your tutors;
3. reliable and established industry publications and news media (practitioner sources).

Two star data

We can call this type of data 'two star' because it is data that is not reliable. We don't know if it comes from experts, from research or is just biased opinion. For example, this category includes data which is from:

1. internet sources not in the above five star categories;
2. other news and media sources;
3. trade magazines and popular newspapers.

One star data

We can call this type of data 'one star' data. It is really data that may be interesting to read or listen to for entertainment, but cannot be used for academic work. This is generally just unsupported and biased opinion from unknown sources such as:

1. blogs;
2. many internet sources;
3. gossip – what other people say.

Critical evaluation of research

This type of critical evaluation should compare and contrast the different views of academic authors on the reliability and validity of the relevant research (see also Chapter 5).

Reliability is the degree to which an assessment tool produces stable and consistent results.

Validity refers to how well a test measures what it is supposed to measure.

If you are familiar enough with the research, you might also indicate your own assessment of any shortcomings that you see in it. Express your assessment in the third person, e.g. 'It might be the case that the sampling technique used affected the validity of the results.'

EXAMPLE

An example of critical evaluation of research

The example below is taken from a student essay about shopping. We have put some tutor feedback and improvement tips in a separate column so you can see what a tutor might think about it.

TABLE 3.11   Analysing a student's critical evaluation

A student's critical evaluation of research about shopping	A tutor's comments
Recent research (Surname, 2009) has shown the growing popularity of internet shopping and a dramatic drop in town centre spending in the UK. A retail analyst, Company Name (year), has found that for the first time in 20 years, the amount of money spent by families in the high street has dramatically fallen.	*A mainly descriptive introduction – description is necessary in many parts of your assignment writing, but make sure you have some evaluation as well. Also make sure that when you say 'recent research', it is recent – the research cited here (2009) is no longer recent!*
Total spending on the high street dipped to £120 billion per annum, as online spending increased to £10 billion. Company Name (year) suggests that the present condition of the UK economy, unemployment issues and rising living costs are the main factors influencing cautious consumer spending on the high street.	
However, an internet research group, Company X (year) indicates that a major shift in consumer spending patterns has been underway for some time, and that transitional economic factors may not be as influential as the rather narrow research analysis suggests. Company X (year) points out that the Internet has already enjoyed a 400% increase in online shopping since 2005. In contrast, high street spending has been forecast to grow at just 0.1% over the next five years.	*The word 'however' signals some critical evaluation of the previous paragraph. Typically, it consists of another research study which points to other important factors to consider, and by implication, questions the 'narrow' conclusions of the previous research. This is good critical evaluation. The student adds supporting evidence from other research by Company X (year).*

(Continued)

TABLE 3.11   (*Continued*)

Company X (year) also points out that pricing was an early challenge. Initially, online retailers substantially undercut offline competitors, and although prices are now closer, many consumers still perceive the internet to be significantly cheaper than the high street. A further two factors in the shift to internet shopping have, firstly, been the increases in online payment security, so that consumers are now more comfortable buying products over the internet, and secondly, improvements to websites so that consumers are more confident navigating online stores (Company X, year).	*The student adds another point of supporting evidence from Company X – 'they also point out that. . .' – and then presents a more substantial case to question the conclusions of the Company X research. The evaluation finishes with another in-text reference to the Company X research to give the source of the evidence.*

Critical evaluation of theories and models

The word 'theory' has many meanings, depending on the context. In science, a theory is a testable model of the way in which a set of variables interact. A theory is useful if it provides explanations and predictions about the 'real world', verified by empirical (real-world) observation of what actually happens. A theory is never 'true' or 'false': it is just useful or not useful. You cannot 'prove' a theory to be true or false. You must supply evidence to show that it has useful explanatory and predictive power. The word 'theory' is also used to indicate an opinion, speculation or hypothesis. It is often used interchangeably with the word 'model'.

A hypothesis is a guess about what is going on in a situation, and can form the basis of a theory.

Two types of theory

In your studies, you will be using two main types of theory: analytical and descriptive theories; and explanatory theories.

Analytical and descriptive theories

These are theories which present a framework or list of criteria which you can use to break an issue into important parts which either might be influencing (impacting on) the issue, or causing the issue. They are sometimes called models. 'Models' are often smaller theories, related to a bigger theory. These are sometimes called 'taxonomies'. These are descriptive theories which describe how the parts of an issue can be classified. A common analytical theory in business studies is a PESTLE. This theory states that before creating business plans or making decisions, it is important to 'scan' the external business environment. You can do this effectively with a PESTLE analysis, i.e. an investigation of the **p**olitical, **e**conomic, **s**ocial, **t**echnological, **l**egal and **e**nvironmental influences on an organisation.

Explanatory theories

These are theories which claim that they can be used to help explain why things happen, and predict how and when they might happen. Examples of this type of theory include the theory of gravity, the theory of supply and demand, and Maslow's hierarchy of human needs.

Theories are initially formed from inductive guesses about how things might work. It's important to realise that theories are only somebody's guess about how the real world works, although the 'somebody' may well be an expert researcher with a lot of knowledge in that particular area. Academic theories are more complicated guesses, but they all start off with a simple 'hypothesis'. A hypothesis is an initial guess from initial observations, about what is going on in a situation. A hypothesis is also a prediction about what will happen in the future. For example, when you bought this book, you did so because you hoped that it would help you with your studies in the UK. So your initial hypothesis was this:

> If I read *Study Skills for Chinese Students* I will get better results from my UK studies.

Is this a 'true' theory? No – theories are not true or false – they are 'useful' or 'not useful' depending on how well they predict what will happen. We can only 'evaluate' them on the basis of how well they seem to predict what happens in the real world.

Of course, Xiangping and I hope that your hypothesis above was a 'good' one, and that when you successfully finish your studies in the UK, you will feel that this book helped you a lot!

Applying theory

Using theories is sometimes called 'applying' theories; it is a very important academic skill. One of the most difficult writing tasks for all students is to use theory correctly in assignments. Most students just tend to define and describe the theory without trying to apply it to real situations in their assignments. However, it is an essential skill to develop if you want to be working at the highest academic level. Tutors give high marks to students who can do this accurately and well.

Applying theory can involve four steps, which we explore in the following sections.

Step 1: Identifying relevant theory

When tutors ask you to include theory in your assignment, they expect you to identify the relevant theory or theories, and provide an appropriate reference. Sometimes this is done for you by the tutor, but if there is no guidance from them, then these are some basic principles you can use to select relevant theory:

i. Check the module guide, lecture slides and recommended reading list for theory relevant to the assignment.
ii. Try to make sure you use current theories. The only reason you would want to include an 'old' theory is if it is 'seminal' (this means that it is a very important and influential theory) and therefore recommended in the module guide or slides.

Remember that this is only the first step – identifying and just describing a theory is NOT applying it. You need to go on to step two.

Step 2: Applying the theory

You tutor wants you to use an appropriate theory, but they don't need a detailed description of the theory. They know the theory very well, and it is not useful for you to just copy out the theory again from lecture notes or a module book. What they want you to do is to show you understand the theory by 'applying' it to a real-world issue, or linking it relevantly to a real-world issue. This is the same with definitions. Definitions are only theories too – they are not 'right' or 'wrong' but are only opinions about what things are or how they work. Because they are also theories, definitions need to be evaluated too.

A very basic theory in business studies is a SWOT theory. This says that if you look at the **s**trengths, **w**eaknesses, **o**pportunities and **t**hreats in relation to a business, then you will get a basic picture of the current situation of the business. In order to 'apply' this theory, you need to research the business and then write about each of the four categories. From your research, you can describe the impacting factors and their possible influence.

EXAMPLE

Here is an example of applying the 'S' in the SWOT for a company called ABC. This means that you need to detail the apparent strengths of the company, from your research:

The ABC company already has a good market share in the luxury goods market, and they have increased the number of their luxury goods shops in the

UK. They will be opening two more shops in the Kensington and Knightsbridge areas of London. This will further strengthen their market presence and enable them to serve more Chinese visitors. Chinese visitors to London are the most important customers for ABC because they come to the UK to take advantage of lower luxury goods prices here, compared to luxury goods prices in China.

Step 3: Evaluating the theory

After you have applied a theory, or you have investigated how someone else has applied the theory, you are often asked to evaluate how well the theory worked. However, remember that theories can be used as evidence to support or argue a point, but they do not 'prove' things. In general life, we use the word 'prove' in a different way to the way we use it in the academic world. In the academic world, you cannot 'prove' that a theory or a belief is right or wrong – you can only provide evidence that supports or does not support the theory or belief. At university, the modern view of 'knowledge' is that it is 'constructed' by individuals and interest groups to suit their own purposes. Of course, there are 'general facts' such as Beijing being the capital of China, but most other 'knowledge' is actually theory – in the form of beliefs and opinions.

In the example above, where a simple 'SWOT' theory was applied to a company, a good evaluation of the theory might include comments from another 'expert' that a SWOT analysis was too simple, and not comprehensive enough to produce a good picture of both the company's external and internal strengths and weaknesses etc.

Generally, you can critically evaluate theories with the following method of comparing and contrasting different 'expert' opinions, not forgetting to add what you see as the implications of the difference in opinion.

EXAMPLE

Surname's theory of effective management (year) states that managers are only effective if they are also good communicators about company policy. However, Surname (year) suggests that the most important characteristic of a manager is that he or she cares about the employees, and the employees are aware of this. This might suggest that Surname's (year) theory of management is too narrow, and needs to also consider employee motivation.

Step 4: Testing the theory

Finally, one other thing you can do with a theory is to test it to see if it does what it says it does. This is not usually required in undergraduate work, but you may be required to do this at postgraduate level if you are doing scientific research which allows you to control the experiment. Testing a theory means setting up an experiment that allows you to see if the predictions of a theory are supported by the results of your experiment.

Normally, theory testing is only really possible with theories that generate quantitative data – numbers and statistics. However, it can be done with qualitative data as well.

For example, if you wanted to test a theory about how consumers make purchasing decisions, you would interview some consumers and see if they made their decisions to buy things in the same way that the theory predicted. The results from your 'test' might then either support or not support the theory, although the results would not be very 'reliable' if they were only from a small sample (see Chapter 5).

Critical evaluation of practice

Here 'practice' means what practitioners (companies, organisations, business people and professionals) actually do, and the regulations, strategies and methods with which they work.

EXAMPLE

An example of critical evaluation of practice

As Surname (year) shows, after the ABC company outsourced their production to China, they found that their production costs decreased because of the generally lower wages paid in China. However, according to Surname (year) they also found that because of their new extended supply lines, this advantage was soon cancelled because of the increased costs of shipping products from China back to the UK.

An advantage is stated because of a new company policy.

A corresponding disadvantage is stated to give a balanced view of the effect of the new policy on the company.

Remember: When you write a critical essay or report, it must focus on the issue, rather than your own feelings about the issue. Remember the difference between your own feelings and academic evidence. It does not matter what you believe about an issue, but rather how you can support your belief, drawing upon evidence found in the text itself, and other researchers.

Criticism does not mean you have to attack the work or the author. It means you are thinking critically about it, exploring it and discussing your findings in relation to how useful these findings are to your task.

All claims made about the work need to be supported and referenced in the correct referencing style. If you want to write: 'Internet shopping is the most important retail development', then you must find referenced evidence from a relevant research report to support this claim.

Use evidence from your data sources. If you want to argue that an author appears to have a narrow view of an issue, back it up with evidence from the article itself as well as from similar research articles on the same issue which have taken a wider perspective on the issue.

Review what critics write about the issue(s), then research other critics' similar views. To achieve a balanced argument, use expressions such as:

- **On the other hand**, it may also be the case that capital financing decisions are equally important (Surname, year).
- **However**, as Surname (year) indicates, capital financing decisions may be equally important.

Do more than simply provide a summary of what critics have written about the author or the article – evaluate. The assignment must use an appropriate academic style. Write in the passive mode wherever possible and avoid the first person, i.e. I think that...

Additionally, vary the types of sentences you use:

- **According to** Surname (year), capital budgeting is central to the corporate financial process.
- **It has been argued** (Surname, year) that capital budgeting is the central corporate financial process.
- **Research** (Surname, year) **indicates** the centrality of capital budgeting to the corporate financial process.

Critical evaluation: Comparing and contrasting

As we have seen, one way to evaluate is to compare and contrast – find out similarities and differences, and advantages and disadvantages. 'To compare' means to find out how things are similar. 'To contrast' means to find out how things are different.

This is actually what we do when we decide to buy something. For example, if you want to buy a new smartphone, you will first of all find out what new models are available (analysis). Then you will summarise the information that is relevant to your needs (synthesis) and finally make a considered judgement about which phone would be the best choice (evaluation). In order to make this evaluation, you will consider the advantages and disadvantages between the different models. This is the same process when you are evaluating theories. However, you must remember to avoid the mistake of comparing 'chalk and cheese' (two very different things). For example, you cannot compare the management structure in company A with the market position of company B.

Comparing means considering how things are **similar**.

Contrasting means considering how things are **different**.

A simple organisational structure for this information in your assignment would be:

DASEY:

1. **D**ESCRIBE the issue(s)
2. **A**NALYSE the issue(s)
3. **S**YNTHESISE the information
4. **E**VALUATE the information
5. **Y**OUR OPINION on the basis of your analysis and evaluation.

All critical evaluation essays and reports should have these five important parts.

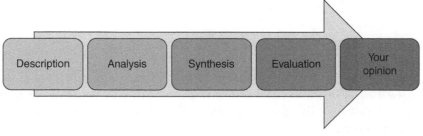

FIGURE 3.5   The DASEY structure for assignments

Cici Zhang

EXAMPLE

Here is a short example assignment written by a Chinese student, Cici Zhang. You can see her in the photo on the previous page and you will meet her again in Chapter 5. The essay is about a general subject, perhaps the kind of essay you might be asked to write for an English test, or a pre-sessional course. If you read the stages of her essay below, you will understand how to make your writing more 'academic', and it is easier to see this development with a simple, general topic.

For her essay, she used the three important processes of **analysis, evaluation and synthesis**. She was asked to discuss the statement:

'Studying abroad is a valuable educational experience for all students.'

She had to make a plan first, based on some initial brainstorming and research about the topic. Below are the notes from her research. She did primary research by asking her friends and thinking about her own situation. She also did secondary research by reading what other Chinese students had posted on their social networking sites, and by reading academic articles about how to learn.

Assignment task: 'Studying abroad is a valuable educational experience for all students' Discuss.

TABLE 3.12   Cici's initial plan for the assignment

Studying abroad: advantages	Studying abroad: disadvantages
Experience of another culture	Unfamiliar with the way things are done in the new culture
Extend my comfort zone to help me develop and mature	Makes me feel uncomfortable because I'm out of my comfort zone
Make many new friends	Leave good friends behind
Develop independence from family	Become homesick and miss my family
Improve job opportunities	Miss out on local job opportunities at home
Improve my communication skills	Experience many problems because of communication difficulties
Learn new ways of doing things	Forget about old ways of doing things

(Continued)

(Continued)

Studying abroad: advantages	Studying abroad: disadvantages
Foreign academic qualifications have high status and are necessary to compete in the job market when returning home	Many employers in China want local qualifications and experience and regard time away from the home country as only a holiday
Can take a part-time job	Very expensive to support myself as a student with cost of accommodation, flights, weekly living costs, etc.
Advantages for all stakeholders – me, my parents, future employers and my future family	Disadvantages for all stakeholders – expense, stress, communication problems, etc.

Here is Cici's assignment (without references). It is in three main parts, but the discussion part of her essay was further divided into the two main parts of advantages (the 'pros') and the disadvantages (the 'cons').

EXAMPLE

Introduction

What the essay is about and how she will address the essay task.

Discussion

Advantages of studying abroad
Disadvantages of studying abroad

Conclusion

A summary of the points she feels are important, to finally give her own opinion on the basis of her discussion.

Cici's first draft of her assignment

EXAMPLE

'Studying abroad is a valuable educational experience for all students.'

This assignment will discuss the advantages and disadvantages of studying abroad. It will finally draw a conclusion in relation to the stated argument that studying abroad is a valuable experience for all students.

There are many advantages to studying abroad. For example, experiencing another culture is important in terms of students developing their independence and knowledge of the world. Such an experience also presents opportunities to make new friends and improve communication skills in the new language. There may also be other advantages in the future in terms of improved career opportunities because UK university degrees are generally seen as high status.

However, there may also be disadvantages to studying abroad. For example, it can be very stressful because there is so much more to learn about the new culture other than just the academic subject you are studying. Language issues will mean that you will not be able to understand your tutors very well and you will have problems writing assignments in the foreign language to the high standard required. Furthermore, you may find that you become unhappy because you have to leave your family and friends behind. Finally, you may not give yourself the competitive edge in the career market that you had planned. Many local employers now value people who have remained in the local job market and gathered good consistent experience there.

In conclusion, as can be seen from the above discussion, there are many advantages and disadvantages to studying abroad. Some of these advantages are connected with personal development, and some are connected with career prospects after graduation. However, on balance, it does appear to be the case that the longer-term benefits of studying abroad in terms of personal development – maturity, independence and a broader world view – outweigh the temporary disadvantages and discomforts of studying in a foreign country.

If Cici rewrites the assignment to make it more 'academic' and to correctly 'cite' her sources of information (this means to tell us where she got the information from) with correct references to her sources, it will look something like the new version below. In this version, she has used an 'in-text' referencing system and has used a more formal and academic style of writing. For example, she has stopped using 'first-person' words such as 'I' and 'you', and is now using 'third-person' words such as 'students' and 'themselves'.

The assignment also has three clear parts (with references): an introduction which states how she is going to answer the question; a discussion which compares and contrasts the advantages and disadvantages as stated by academic 'experts'; and a conclusion which answers the initial question on the basis of her 'evidenced-based' discussion.

Cici's new, more 'academic' draft of her assignment

EXAMPLE

'Studying abroad is a valuable educational experience for all students.'

This assignment will discuss the advantages and disadvantages of studying abroad. It will finally draw a conclusion in relation to the stated argument that studying abroad is a valuable experience for all students.

According to Surname (year) there are many advantages to studying abroad. For example, experiencing another culture is important in terms of students developing their independence and knowledge of the world. Surname (year) shows too that such an experience also presents opportunities to make new friends and improve communication skills in the new language. Furthermore, there may also be other advantages in the future in terms of improved career opportunities because UK university degrees are generally seen as high status (Surname, year).

However, Surnames (year) suggest that there may also be disadvantages to studying abroad. For example, it can be very stressful because there is so much more to learn about the new culture other than just the academic subject of study. Language issues will often mean that students will not be able to understand tutors very well and they will have problems writing assignments in a foreign language (English) to the high academic standard required. Furthermore, as Surnames (year) point out, students may become unhappy because they have to leave family and friends behind. Finally, they may also not give themselves the competitive edge in the career market that they had planned. Many local employers now value people who have remained in the local job market and gathered good, consistent experience there (Surnames, year).

In conclusion, as can be seen from the above discussion, there are many advantages and disadvantages to studying abroad. Some of these advantages are connected with personal development, and some are connected with career prospects after graduation. However, on balance, it does appear to be the case that the longer-term benefits of studying abroad in terms of personal development – maturity, independence and a broader world view – outweigh the temporary disadvantages and discomforts of studying in a foreign country.

References

Surname, G. (year) *Going to University Abroad*. London: XYZ Publishers.
Surname, J. (year) *Studying Abroad: A Handbook for Students*. Hong Kong: ABC Publishers.
Surname, A., and Surname, T. (year) *International Education*. Shanghai: ZYX Press.

Analysis

As we saw from Bloom's taxonomy, an analysis is the first step in the process of critical thinking and writing. Before you can evaluate something (judge how useful or relevant something is), you first need to find out more about it – analyse it, or make an analysis.

Remember that 'analysis' is the noun, and 'to analyse' is the verb. We also 'make' an analysis – not 'do' an analysis.

To analyse means to break down and to identify the different factors or parts of something, with the aim of then examining and evaluating it. Analysis therefore requires taking apart an idea or statement. This is often referred to as 'deconstructing' or 'unpacking' the concept or the situation – in just the same way as you 'unpacked' your suitcase after you came to the UK. You took out all the things and then you organised them into clothes, books, etc.

When you analyse, you also examine the different parts to see how they might be interrelated. Analysis means considering the answers to questions that begin with 'What?', 'Who?', 'When?', 'Why?', 'Where?', 'Which?' and 'How?'

Your analysis forms the basis of your evaluation, so it is important to make a thorough analysis. There is no such thing as a complete analysis, because it is impossible to include all the aspects of a situation, but you do need to make sure that you have investigated all the important things relating to the task by addressing these questions:

What are the main issues?

What are the main problems?

What are the main successes?

What is being said?

Who is saying it?

Where are they saying it?

When are they saying it?

Why might they be saying it?

What are other people saying about the same issues?

Why are they saying this?

Remember that your analysis should be based on the best and most reliable information and it should be as 'objective' as you can make it (not biased).

You can evaluate the situation and make conclusions after you have completed your analysis.

EXAMPLE

If you have to write an essay about studying abroad, like Cici, you could use the following steps and plan to complete it:

Analyse and critically evaluate the statement: 'Studying abroad is a valuable educational experience for all students.'

Firstly, analyse the question or the task. In this example, it is a statement which asserts the theory that studying abroad is a beneficial activity for students.

Stage 1: Analysis – Brainstorming the topic (questions to ask yourself)

What does studying abroad mean? How long does the study have to be before it is beneficial? What does 'beneficial' mean? Who benefits and why? How is the experience valuable? Is it really valuable for all students or are there some students who would study better in their home country? What is my own personal bias? Do I think it is beneficial for all students?

Stage 2: Research the topic

Look in academic books and academic research journals about the best ways to learn and the benefits of travel. Look at actual written accounts such as blogs, by students who have studied abroad, to understand more about what their experience was.

Stage 3: Structure your own argument

You can organise what you have found out from your research into a list of themes, or a list of advantages and disadvantages (sometimes called 'pros' and 'cons') using the information you have obtained from your reading.

Synthesis

Let's look at the next step in Bloom's taxonomy, which is 'synthesis'. Think of synthesis as the opposite of analysis. If analysis is breaking something down into its constituent parts, then synthesis is putting things back together. 'Synthesising' means to pull together all the results of your critical analysis, to reach a conclusion for an essay question, or to suggest new ways to look at an issue in a report, or to suggest new and different connections between things in research.

> **EXAMPLE**
>
> Surname (year) and Surname (year) both share the view that governments should not attempt to control markets. In contrast, Surname (year) suggests that this is actually a key role of governments in certain cases.

You will need to synthesise when you review what researchers have written about particular topics, and when you summarise and bring together different viewpoints. Being able to see patterns in information and being able to group information into relevant types for the purpose of an assignment is an essential information management skill. Some people do this easily, but most of us have to learn how to do it through practice. A common place to report the results of your synthesis of information is in the conclusion to an essay or report. Here, you are entitled to give your own 'informed' opinion because you have done the research to inform yourself.

Developing your own 'voice' in your academic work

Your 'voice' means your opinion. Many students naturally want to know how they can show their own opinion in their work. Tutors want to encourage this too, provided it is 'informed' opinion, and is presented in a good academic style, on a good evidence base. Your tutors want you to express this 'informed' opinion, after you have done the necessary reading and research for the assignment. Remember that this opinion is 'evidence-based, informed opinion' and should be expressed cautiously and objectively, using the third person, as in the example below.

> **EXAMPLE**
>
> It appears to be the case that...
> From the evidence presented, it could be concluded that...

Your 'voice' is very important to your tutors and they want to see that you understand the 'expert' views and arguments that you are studying. The 'wrong' way to express your voice is directly and informally, like this:

> Personally, I think that this author's ideas are very good.

What you should say is:

> Surname appears to have contributed useful insights to the debate, and these are insights which are supported by other researchers, such as...

Always use cautious language for your opinion

Expressions like '*appears to be*' are called 'cautious', 'tentative' or 'hedging' language. Academic writing uses cautious language because you can never be certain of anything in the academic world. It's always possible for other researchers to find new information which questions the old information. Therefore, in order to allow for this, and to try to be objective, you should use cautious or 'tentative' language when you are showing your own opinion.

EXAMPLE

Tentative verbs:	It **appears**...; It **seems**...; It **may be**...
Tentative adjectives:	**Possible** consequences might be...
Tentative adverbs:	It might **possibly** be the case that...
Tentative nouns:	The results show a **possibility/probability** that...

After having critically evaluated other experts' views, you are also expected to present your own views on the basis of this expert evidence. This is very important because tutors want to see that you are learning and developing an 'informed' opinion about what they are trying to teach you.

Chinese students are often confused by the idea of showing their own opinion in assignments because this is something which is not generally done in China. This is not the same as arguing that you are right and everyone else is wrong. It means that after you have presented the arguments of the experts, you indicate to the reader in your conclusion, and at various stages in the main body of your assignment, what you think are the strongest and most convincing arguments and why. However, it is important to make sure that you give your own opinion in the correct 'academic' way. For example, you must not write too assertively like this:

Personally, I think that this definitely shows that… ✗

But write in the third person, and tentatively, like this:

From the evidence presented in this report, it appears to be the case that… ✓

It is very important to remember that arguments, like theories, are neither true nor false, so forget about 'proving' that your argument is right. You need to find valid evidence to support particular viewpoints. For a 'balanced' essay, you should also look for evidence that does not support these perceptions, and include it as well.

There are basically three ways to give 'your opinion':

1. In the main body of your writing, directly after you have introduced the expert views of the issue.
2. In the evidence that you choose to present, and the way that you choose to present it – for example, for some essays and reports, you are required to argue for a particular viewpoint. The section on arguments and narratives below explains this in more detail.
3. In the final conclusion of the essay or report.

EXAMPLE 1

Here is an example of a student's opinion in the main discussion part of an essay. We have underlined the opinion so that you can see it clearly:

Surname (year) states that managers have to be good leaders. However, Surname (year) disputes this view, suggesting that managers must firstly be good communicators. **From this debate, it might be concluded that good managers should be both good communicators and good leaders.**

The last sentence (underlined) is your own opinion on the expert views you have presented to us in your discussion. If you don't tell us what you think about the implications of the issues you present, then your tutor might say: 'So what? Why are you telling me about this particular issue? What are the implications (consequences)?'

However, be careful that you are not too personally opinionated in your essays – like this:

Surname (year) states that managers have to be good leaders. However, Surname (year) disputes this view, suggesting that managers must firstly be good communicators. **Personally, I feel that both these ideas are wrong. I think that good managers should just know how to do their jobs well.**

EXAMPLE 2

Your own opinion in the conclusion

Another place in your assignment where we expect to see your opinion is in your conclusion. In the conclusion, you summarise the evidence you have presented to us in your discussion, and finally answer the essay question, or finally indicate that you have completed the task. A typical conclusion has the following parts:

A signpost word to show us it is your conclusion (i.e. one of these):

> In conclusion…; To conclude…; In conclusion…; Finally…; Lastly…

A summary of the main evidence which is the most relevant evidence necessary to answer the question or finish the task:

> As can be seen from the evidence presented above…

Finally, your own personal opinion:

> From the evidence presented, it seems to be the case that…

EXAMPLE 3

In the following example, a business student has researched and written an essay on the subject of outsourcing – contracting out a business process to a third party. The question asks:

> Is outsourcing a company's production a good business strategy?

After presenting the researched evidence to give a balanced answer, stating some advantages and disadvantages, the student gives a final opinion (underlined in the example below) in an appropriate 'academic' style.

> In conclusion, as has been discussed, many companies have considered outsourcing their production in order to save costs. However, as the evidence shows, moving production to a new country such as China may also involve extra costs from a number of sources. These extra costs can come from increased supply chain costs, and increased costs of adapting to local government policies and the local culture and environment. For example, when companies move to a new overseas location, they may have to invest in training the local workforce and building suitable accommodation for factory workers. Further, local workers are increasingly comparing their wages with workers in other national locations, and are not prepared to work for a lower wage. **Therefore, from the above discussion, it can be seen that the policy of outsourcing production to a new location**

is one that has to be considered very carefully, since the theoretical advantages in terms of reducing production costs may be outweighed by the extra costs and necessary expenditure required for successful relocation.

VERY IMPORTANT: Make sure you always answer the assignment question in your conclusion. Your tutor will always check to see you have done this.

Arguments and narratives

A related area of difficulty for many students, particularly Chinese students, is the concept of 'arguments'. In everyday life, we know that people are always arguing – giving their own opinions, and trying to convince other people that their opinions are the 'right' ones.

Your tutors may tell you that they want to see your 'argument' in your essay, because this is the way that the academic world advances knowledge through argument about the meaning of research results. What do your tutors mean when they say that they want to see your argument in your essays?

Firstly, your essays and reports should contain lots of 'arguments' from other expert researchers, and you need to be able to understand what position(s) they are arguing for, and why they are arguing this. You then compare and contrast the different expert arguments, as we have shown, to finally enable you to make a conclusion about which argument(s) you personally find the most convincing. This whole process – combining expert arguments with your own informed opinion – is called 'argumentation'.

Secondly, the way that you present these different expert arguments also reveals your own argument, or what we sometimes call your own 'story' or narrative.

EXAMPLE 4

Let's look at an example question:

What do you think is the main cause of climate change in the world today?

The question asks you for your own opinion about climate change – the way in which the planet changes its weather, temperature, rainfall patterns, etc. It seems to be more variable now – is this kind of change mainly caused by the activities of humans on this planet, or is it a natural process which always happens to the earth over long periods of time?

Imagine that you do a lot of research for the essay, and you gradually form a personal opinion that the evidence clearly seems to you to suggest that it is human activity that appears to be the main cause of the current changes in world climate – more extreme weather, hotter summers, etc.

This then becomes your own personal viewpoint that you want to argue or 'put forward' in your essay, but firstly, you need to present the expert evidence for and against this position. This means presenting the expert 'arguments' from academic researchers.

However, the evidence you choose to present to us, and the selection you make of this evidence, is your own choice. As we have seen, in these types of discussion, there are no 'right' or 'wrong' answers (even though many people hold very strong views and might think that they are right!). You might be tempted to choose only evidence which supports your own opinion, but this would not be a 'balanced' essay. Even if you want to argue that it is human activity which is largely responsible for climate change, you should present 'both sides' of the argument (although, in reality, there are as many 'sides' to arguments as there are participants, or stake holders – people with an interest in the argument).

But there is nothing to stop you presenting more of the strongest arguments which appear to support your own position, and this would then form your own 'narrative' about the issue. Tutors might say that they want to see your own narrative in your essay; what they mean is that they want to see your own argument, supported by evidence from expert researchers.

There are different types of argument which you should be aware of:

1. **Experiential arguments** – based on what people do.

These arguments are of the type: 'Company XYZ uses this strategy, and they have been successful, so it must be a good strategy.'

These are not good arguments in themselves, since they generalise too much, and are reductive, in that they assume that there is only one reason for something, which is never the case. Using experience from the real world to support your arguments can be an effective part of most argumentation in assignments. It is good to give examples from real-world practitioners, but you will also need to supply research and theory to support your arguments.

2. **Theory-based arguments** – what theorists think.

These arguments are based on theories and models. Models are also theories, but usually a proposed way of understanding a complex issue, for example Maslow's hierarchy of needs. This is a well-known theory in psychology which theorises about the order in which human needs should be addressed – the most basic level of needs must be met before the individual will be strongly motivated to try to address higher-level needs.

It is important to remember that theories like Maslow's are neither true nor false but continue to be used only if they are useful in helping us explain and predict 'how the world works'.

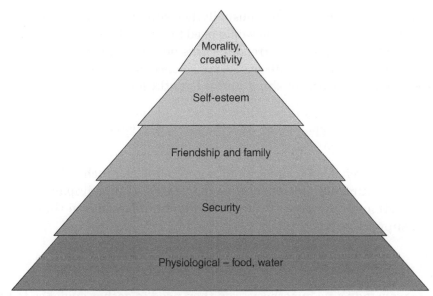

FIGURE 3.6   Maslow's (1943) theory of needs

For example, supply and demand theory in economics and business is still used today since it appears to explain a lot about consumer behaviour and enables us to make reasonably accurate predictions about that behaviour. So, a good theory or model is one that explains a cause–effect chain in a satisfactory way. But you can never 'prove' this kind of theory or model: you need to tell us why the theory is useful and why it supports your main argument in your assignment.

Inductive argument

Inductive argument is the starting point for all knowledge acquisition. It is how science progresses – by observation of what appears to happen in the real world. This is a reasoning process we use in general life, whereby we take evidence from initial observations of one or more specific cases (or what has happened so far) to generalise and draw a more general conclusion (also called an inference).

The problem is that if you rely on induction alone, you can come to some very wrong and dangerous conclusions. You cannot 'jump to conclusions' on the basis of one or two observations – although, unfortunately, we tend to do this in real life.

Importantly, the larger the evidence base used as a premise, the more confident we can be about the conclusion. If your evidence base is too small, your conclusion will be an over-generalisation. Unlike in deductive reasoning (see below) a conclusion arrived at through induction is not reliable. For example, just because you experience one unusually hot summer, it doesn't mean that climate change is responsible – you would need to collect data over a much longer period of time to see if there is a trend towards hotter summers each year.

Inductive arguments are the way that science progresses, and they are therefore essential for establishing initial hypotheses, e.g.:

> I observe that summers are getting hotter now, and winters are getting colder. Therefore I hypothesise that human activity on the earth may be affecting global climates.

You should research good sources of data to provide as much evidence as you can for your arguments. You should also gather evidence impartially (keep an open mind) and take note of counter-evidence, i.e. evidence that does not appear to support your argument.

Deductive argument

Following your inductive hypothesis, you then need to gather evidence to try to 'deduce' a better description of the issue, particularly in terms of causation – what is causing the issue. A deductive argument is based on a form of logic whereby you reach a conclusion through logical reasoning.

More precisely, in logic, *to deduce* is when you use general principles (premises) to arrive at a specific conclusion. In a formal deductive argument, the premises guarantee/entail the conclusion – if the premises are valid, the conclusion must also be valid. For example:

> Climate affects everyone on the earth. I am on the earth now, therefore I will be affected by any changes in the climate.

Another way to think about deduction is to think about what the police do when they come across a crime scene:

1. The detective firstly analysed the evidence from the crime scene.
2. The detective then made inductive guesses (hypotheses) about what might have happened, based on the evidence from their analysis.
3. The detective then tested each of these guesses (hypotheses) by deduction – collecting more evidence to support or reject each hypothesis, thereby deducing what the causes of the crime might have been – who did it and why?

Chapter 3: Key words and concepts – English and Chinese

abstract – 摘要

academic conduct – 学术行为规范

affective – 情感的

analysis – 分析

arguments – 论点

cheating – 欺骗

citing – 引用

cognitive – 认知的

collusion – 合伙共谋

domain – 领域

evaluation – 评估

evidence – 证据

experiential – 实验性的

generalising – 概括（动名词）

implications – 影响

independent – 独立的

interactive – 相互的

literal – 文字的 / 有文化的

narratives – 叙述的

offences – 冒犯

overseas – 海外的

plagiarism – 抄袭

presentation – 演讲

proactive – 积极主动的

quoting – 引用（动名词）

resolving – 解决（动名词）

role – 角色

scan – 浏览

scholar – 学者

spoon-feed – 填鸭式教育

self-motivated – 自我激励的

seminar – 讨论会

skim – 略读

synthesis – 综合

taxonomy – 分类

tutorial – 个别辅导

workshop – 研讨班

CHAPTER 3: TEST YOURSELF

Put an ✗ for an incorrect statement and a ✓ for a correct statement.
Check your answers in the Appendix.

1　The three main academic conduct offences are cheating, collusion and plagiarism. .... ☐

2　It's not plagiarism as long as you give a reference. .... ☐

3　It's always best to use quotation and not paraphrase. .... ☐

4　There are two main types of academic reference systems – in-text and numeric. .... ☐

5　When you read an article, you must make sure you understand every word.... ☐

6　You should make sure you focus on taking notes in a lecture. .... ☐

7　An independent learner does not need to ask the tutor about anything. .... ☐

8　It's a fact that London is the capital of England. .... ☐

9　Bloom's taxonomy shows the facts about learning. .... ☐

10　Theories are either right or wrong. .... ☐

Chapter 3: Reflection box

Think about your current ability with the study skills we have covered in this chapter. Assess your current ability with each of the skills below. Be honest with yourself. Give yourself a score on a scale of 1–10 for each skill (1 = poor, 10 = excellent). Then for any score lower than 8, write down in the final column one thing you can do to improve this study skill.

Academic study skill	Current score (1–10)	One thing I can do to improve this skill
Personal study organisation		
Responsibility – understanding plagiarism and how to avoid it		
Referencing – acknowledging sources of information in my work		
Module reading		
Theory of knowledge awareness: understanding the difference between opinion and fact		
Independent learner		
Team/group work		
Critical thinking		
Critical evaluation of information/data		
Critical evaluation of research		

4

Assignments, assessment and feedback

Introduction

In UK education systems, assessments of your progress are normally made with 'assignments', which are usually in the form of essays and reports, although you will also have many other types of assessment such as in-class tests, multiple-choice tests, presentations and debates. Furthermore, there are many different types of essays and reports.

This chapter shows you how to write standard essays and reports. Make sure you always check with your tutor's instructions for the exact requirements of your assignment. This chapter also covers other types of academic writing such as reflective writing, portfolios, team projects and persuasive writing for marketing modules etc. Your assignments are very important because they are the main way that you will be assessed for your qualification.

Chapter 4: Xiangping's study tips

英国的测试方式多样，除了学期末的考试外，很多时候学生的课堂表现也可能会被纳为评估的一部分，另外，英国平时的课外作业比较多，有学术论文、报告、演讲等不同的形式。

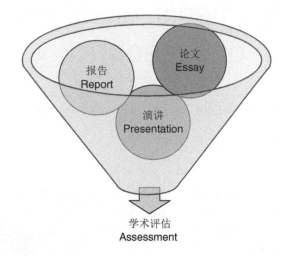

FIGURE 4.1

- 课堂表现：英国课堂除了大课 堂（Lectures）外，还有小组的研讨课（Seminars）、个别的指导课（Tutorials）、工作坊（Workshops）。为鼓励同学们积极发表阐述自己的意见、回答老师的问题、激励同学间的相互交流，英国大学老师有时会把每个同学的课堂表现作为最后评估的一部分。
- 学术论文：是英国常见的一种课后作业形式，字数1000–2500不定。一般老师给一个学术专业课题的命题，让学生根据自己的研究调查，阐述自己的论点，然后写成由不同的段落组成的一篇连贯的学术文章；格式上一般没有大小标题。
- 报告：一般报告是在商业工作中使用的，格式比较清晰有大小标题、可以有图片、表格、图表。英国大学让学生学习写报告是为学生在以后的工作中准备的。
- 演讲：除了书面的写作外，英国大学也考核学生的口头表述交流能力，所以演讲就成了测试的一种。有些演讲是个人的；有些演讲是集体的，每个人演讲一部分。
- 反思论文：反思论文也是其中的一种作业形式，一般在学期中或者学期末的时候老师置给学生的一个回顾以前学习、反思自己长短、以便在以后学习中取长补短的文章。
- 考试：考试分为：开卷考试和闭卷考试。开卷考试的时候，学生可以带着自己准备的资料（一般是一个文件夹）在规定的时间内完成答卷。有的开卷考试是在线上的，学生在规定时间内完成题目后在网上递交文章。闭卷考试一般是在老师的监考下进行的。
- 值得一提的是，这些课后作业，是除了上课外，占英国学习的很重要的一部分，而且这些作业都是学生在课后自己独立完成的。为完成这些作业，学生必须要阅读大量的资料（书籍、杂志、报刊文章、线上资料）。所以，在英国学习，大部分时间是自己的学习，学生一定合理利用时间，正确对待在英学习。

Module guides and learning outcomes

A very important document for you to read and keep with you to refer to is the written guide for each of your modules. This will be available from your VLE, or will be given to you as a booklet by your programme or module tutor. It will give you essential details about your lecture and tutorial timetable, your syllabus and assignments, together with reading lists, etc. Importantly, it should also tell you what the module is trying to teach you, so that you can show your tutors in your assignments that you are achieving the required module outcomes. Assignments are always designed to test module learning outcomes.

Three types of learning outcome

It is very important that you understand that all of the learning and assessment activities throughout your programme modules are designed to help you develop three types of learning outcome:

- **Learning outcome 1**

  These are the basic concepts and ideas of your subject. For example, if you are completing a marketing module, it would be things like basic marketing theory, consumer behaviour theory, etc.

  We can call this outcome 'What you should know about your subject at the end of the module'.

- **Learning outcome 2**

  These are the subject-related skills – how to organise a marketing campaign, how to write a marketing mix plan, etc.

  We can call this learning outcome 'What you should be able to do in your subject, at the end of the module'.

- **Learning outcome 3**

  These are key 'transferable' skills – this means they can be used in other areas of your life and career. These would be skills such as team-working ability, presentation and communication skills, etc.

  We can call this learning outcome 'What you should be able to do generally at the end of the module that will be useful to you in other areas of your life and career'.

All your assessments will be designed so that you can show your tutors that you have achieved all three of these learning outcomes.

EXAMPLE

Typical learning outcomes and marking descriptors

A typical set of learning outcomes and marking descriptors used in UK Higher Education might look like this (the example is based on a postgraduate module in marketing):

Learning outcomes being tested

1. To develop competency with the principles and practices that underpin marketing and marketing communications theory.
2. To understand the role and importance of marketing and marketing communications within organisations.
3. To understand key communicative and language strategies relevant to the business environment.
4. To develop competency with the analysis and evaluation of marketing outcomes in the light of environmental analysis.
5. To develop the ability to create written reports of a standard acceptable for a master's-level programme and in business use.
6. To develop the ability to critically evaluate personal and transferable learning.
7. To develop the ability to conduct communication exercises based on marketing content.

ACTIVITY 4.1

Read the learning outcomes above. Identify each of the outcomes. Are they type 1, 2 or 3? The answers are in the Appendix.

What is assessment like in the UK?

Read Xiangping's experiences about assessment in China and the UK:

In China, my assessments mainly consisted of course work and exams, which always took place at the end of a semester. The main emphasis was on the 'end-of-semester' exam, so students only needed to really work hard on revision before the end-of-semester assessment. This is why, in China, we regard university as 'heaven' compared to the more intensive and competitive high-school exam system.

In China, most of the time, students can pass with some revision beforehand. The pass rate is very high and students can usually get very high marks in China, because we can always find answers to the questions from our textbooks which are given at the beginning of a semester. Therefore, as long as we can memorise the information in the textbook, we would have the right answer and get a good mark.

However, in the UK, I realised that, apart from the end-of-semester assessment, there are also 'in-semester' individual assignments, group assignments, presentations and in-class tests. So, most of the time, Chinese students in the UK are very busy – going to classes, doing coursework, arranging group meetings and preparing for tests, apart from the many social activities that you need to get involved in.

One of the main things that makes UK study more challenging is that there is no textbook for each subject, but a long reading list with books, journals, magazines and websites related to the subject. Additionally, tutors always require students to use the VLE databases to find current research data. Also, in your assignment, you cannot just use information from only one textbook – you need to read widely and use a combination of information from different sources. A lot of the time, there is no right or wrong answer; all answers must be supported by sufficient evidence.

In summary, assessment in the UK consists of many different components, and Chinese students will have to work hard all semester – not just for the final exam – in order to gain good grades.

Assignment writing skills

Firstly, check with your tutor or the module handbook for precise instructions, i.e. the prescribed report/essay structure, word count and deadline. Most essays and reports will be module- and assignment-specific, so the structures given below are only very general structures. However, all assignments require good attention to small details. These are details such as accurate referencing, good clear English, professional presentation, clear structure, and no spelling, grammatical or punctuation errors.

Summary of things to check for in your assignment

- Use of 'academic' style
- Correct structure and argumentation
- Use of plain English
- Linking and signposting words and phrases
- Avoidance of plagiarism
- Avoidance of generalisations
- Avoidance of clichés and non-inclusive language
- No short forms or slang
- Accurate vocabulary and jargon
- Accurate grammar
- Accurate spelling
- Accurate punctuation
- Correct layout and use of headings (if appropriate)
- Check that you have included page numbers and a footer, containing your name, ID and module code, in your assignment. Do not forget to include a title page with your work.

Understanding the assignment

An assignment 'question' asks you to answer a question. An assignment 'task' requires that you do a number of different things – it may not require you to answer any questions.

Understanding your assignment title is therefore very important. Don't make the mistake of reading the title quickly, assuming that you know what it means, and then doing a lot of reading which is not going to help you answer the question well. You must break down the assignment title and analyse it in detail to make sure that you answer the title exactly.

For any assignment, break down the title using the three categories given below. (Note that a word or phrases in an assignment title will sometimes fall under more than one category.)

1. **The function words** – does the title ask you to describe, analyse, argue, or some of these things together?
2. **The concept words or phrases** – words related to the content of the topic. You will often need to say how you are defining a term; how you define something (e.g. whether you define *law firm* as only a firm of partners or any type of legal organisation) will partly determine the scope (how much you need to include) of your assignment or report.
3. **The scope of the title** – what you are asked to cover and not to cover. If the scope is not clearly stated in the title, you will need to decide on the scope yourself.

Use these three categories to break down and analyse your assignment title. It is also a good idea to discuss the assignment title with your tutor and other students if you are not completely sure what it means.

EXAMPLE

Let's analyse two assignment titles:

1. Assignment title from a business studies module called 'Work and Organisation'

TABLE 4.1   Assignment 1 analysis

Assignment title	Key words in the task assignment	
Describe the connection between wages and job satisfaction in organisations. How relevant is this connection today in motivating employees?	*Describe* – Just describe, do not analyse or evaluate. *How relevant?* – Are the changes not relevant, a bit relevant or very relevant? You will need to also give your reasons and evidence for your decision.	*Job satisfaction* – How are you going to define this? *Connection* – Is there just one thing connected, or several? *Today* – Make sure that you do not talk about how relevant the methods were in the past or might be in the future. *Motivating* – How will you define motivation?

2. Assignment title from a business studies module called 'Managing People'

TABLE 4.2   Assignment 2 analysis

Assignment title	Key words in the task assignment	
Discuss the benefits and challenges an organisation might face when trying to address the diversity agenda in the workplace.	*Discuss* – Means to state and describe, but also to evaluate different arguments. *Might* – This is a modal verb; it indicates a degree of uncertainty or possibility.	*Benefits and challenges* – Keep to just these two themes; do not talk about other areas.

(Continued)

133

(Continued)

Assignment title	Key words in the task assignment	
	Diversity agenda – the word 'agenda' implies a policy requirement that the organisation is implementing. 'Diversity' means employing people from all backgrounds, nationalities, age groups, etc.	*The workplace* – This is a general term, but you could illustrate your answer by referring to particular types of workplace.

Task-based assignments

Sometimes, your assignment will not be a question but a task which includes several things that you have to do. Here is an example of a typical task-based assignment from an economics module. This type of assignment often involves three things:

1. individual research;
2. group presentation;
3. group report.

The task is built around a 'scenario' which is a typical imagined situation, based on 'real-world' issues:

EXAMPLE

Assignment – Forecasting: Group Assessment

Assignment brief

You are required to:

- write a group management research report (MRR);
- present the findings of your report.

You must form groups of four.

Report

You are required to write a management research report on the scenario below. Your report will be approximately four pages in length (not including appendices) and marked as a group report.

Presentation

You will present your findings during the tutorials as per the module guide. The presentation will be given by the whole of your group but you will each be marked for your individual performance.

Your group must give a group presentation for 20 minutes, to the general manager and one other senior manager. You will be assessed individually so you should each speak for approximately the same amount of time. Guidance on dress code is in the marking guidance.

Scenario

The company was established in 2000

It has approximately 100 employees

All manufacturing and packaging is on one site

You work for a small company established in the year 2000 and you report directly to the general manager. The company manufactures and sells energy drinks. As they are a relatively new company, they have just four products:

TABLE 4.3   Example energy drink products

Product	Product description
A	Pre-exercise high-energy drink
B	Protein food replacement drink
C	Zero-calorie drink
D	High-protein milkshake

Your role is to analyse each of the four products in terms of their growth and apply two appropriate profit forecasting methods to each of your products. Choose the best profit forecasting method for each product (data set) and calculate forecasts for sales of each of the four products for this year.

Your presentation should include:

- introduction: a brief introduction on yourself, and an outline of the areas covered in the presentation;
- product growth since 2010;
- forecasts for this year;

(Continued)

(Continued)

- any diagram or chart which helps you present your findings;
- summary of what you have presented.

The management research report should include:

Title

Acknowledgements

Executive summary

Table of contents

Terms of reference

Introduction

Methodology

Findings, analysis and discussion

Conclusions

Bibliography

Appendices (including group report log)

ACTIVITY 4.2

Understanding the task

Read the task above carefully. Answer the following questions to check that you understand what you are required to do:

1. You need to make your own scenario for this task.   YES NO
2. You need to complete this task individually.   YES NO
3. You need to produce a management research report.   YES NO
4. You need to write the report individually.   YES NO
5. You need to speak for approximately five minutes in the presentation. YES NO

(The answers are in the Appendix.)

Assignment instructions

There are standard words that tutors use to tell you what they want you to do. For example, you are asked to 'describe' and 'discuss' in the assignment questions above. Following is a list of some of the most common instruction words you will find in your assignment questions:

TABLE 4.4   Common instruction words used in assignment questions

Term	Meaning
advise	Give suggestions based on your judgement/views about future actions, with explanations/evidence/reasons.
analyse	Break a topic, issues, concept etc. into the main parts as you see it. How do the parts interrelate? Who said what? Why did they say it? Who is interested in this topic or issue and why?
apply	Use a theory in part of your essay or report to help you analyse an issue and to show that you understand the theory.
appraise/assess	Judge the importance/value/quality/worth of something and give reasons.
argue	Show what 'experts' think about an issue and then give your own opinion based on these expert views.
calculate	Work out/find out using your judgement; determine; weigh reasons carefully.
classify	Arrange things into groups/divide according to class or type.
compare	Talk about the similarities in different things (sometimes tutors also want you to discuss the differences, although this is actually 'contrast').
conclude	Give an answer/summarise/reach a decision about something based on the evidence you have presented in your previous discussion.
contrast	Discuss the differences between things.
create	Generate/construct/design/invent some original thought/idea/thing/product.
critically.../ critique	Comment on the merit of data/theories/opinions/relevance; judge evidence; weigh up strengths/benefits and faults/weaknesses.
debate	Question/dispute/argue a view or case.
define	Explain precisely; state the meaning of; give details to show boundaries/distinguish from others.
demonstrate	Show clearly by giving evidence/examples. Develop the idea by reasoning and example.
derive	Obtain results/draw from/develop.
describe	State a detailed account; information showing what?/why?/when?/where?/how?/who?
design	Devise, plan, invent, draw up plans, propose, formulate.
determine	Find out something exactly; establish, decide.
differentiate	Explain; show how something is different from something else.

(Continued)

TABLE 4.4   *(Continued)*

Term	Meaning
discuss	Consider from several points of view and explore implications; put the case for and against a proposition, and end with some statement of your own position (often means 'critically evaluate').
distinguish	Identify the differences between; separate, discriminate.
estimate	Predict; form an opinion as to the degree/nature/value/size/amount.
evaluate	Make an appraisal as to the worth of something; judge effectiveness/value/quality/nature/use of/amount of; compare and contrast advantages and disadvantages, different viewpoints etc.
examine	Consider; look closely at a question to find out.
explain	Make clear and understandable; give reasons for; interpret and account for.
explore	Discover more about; look carefully for; investigate; seek; find out about something.
express	Clearly state, show an opinion/a fact/a feeling.
find	Discover something, e.g. information, reveal meaning, locate, obtain.
forecast	Predict; estimate or calculate possible results linked to criteria, complete or incomplete facts, or reasoning.
formulate	Express, compose; devise something by using a formula, model, or specific words or definitions.
highlight	Emphasise, stress, underline; make prominent; focus on; place attention on; give prominence to.
identify	Name, specify; point out; pick out key facts, features, criteria.
illustrate	Make clear by using examples; use figures or diagrams to explain; show the meaning of something by giving related examples.
implement	Make it happen; put into practice or action a plan; apply, employ, instigate.
indicate	Show; point out; draw attention to; give evidence of; make clear.
integrate	Incorporate; put things together; combine ideas, theories and/or practices.
interpret	Give an account of the meaning; use your judgement, indicating relationships to others or ways of looking at something.
judge	State opinion; view based on evidence/examples; ascertain to what distance/amount, to what extent, to what degree.
justify	Argue, defend, support an issue or case; provide explanations and reasons, facts, information, strong evidence and examples.
list	Catalogue; name items in a sequence; mention briefly.
organise	Put in some order; sort out people, plans, facts, issues; arrange, systemise.
plan	Arrange something or an event, with aims, times, stages, sequences, outcomes.
prepare	Get ready, set up, practise.

Term	Meaning
present	To introduce and deliver; depict, portray, display, demonstrate, show, put forward arguments for; argue a case; bring to notice.
produce	Make, create; construct something or make something.
propose	To offer, or put forward for consideration or acceptance, something to be undertaken.
prove	Give evidence to support an argument. (Note that, because you can never 'prove' anything completely since new evidence can always be produced, it's best not to use this word in academic writing.)
quantify	Express/measure the amount or quantity of something.
question	To critically evaluate by asking and answering questions about the topic.
recognise	Identify, recall, recollect, acknowledge, notice, endorse, accept as valid, appreciate.
recommend	Suggest possible actions/routes/outcomes, linked to and based on previously shown knowledge and understanding – may include your own views and advice.
reconcile	Bring together, settle/resolve issues, e.g. levels of acceptance of a statement/proposition.
record	Register data, make accurate note of facts, evidence.
reflect	Consider and assess strengths and weaknesses/usefulness/quality/performance and draw conclusions.
relate	Show/establish how things are linked to and impact upon each other.
report	Say what happened or what was done; give an account of; inform, recount, relate, record.
review	Make a survey of, examining the subject critically; consider and judge carefully.
schedule	Plan and identify the order of actions or events within a set timescale, agenda, calendar.
state	Express main points carefully, completely, briefly and clearly; specify.
structure	Organise and arrange ideas/things in a clearly formulated way; construct a plan.
summarise	Draw the main points together to produce an answer to the question.
synthesise	Put the information together in an organised way.
tabulate	Put things in a table or chart to show information or results.
test	Question and check material/views; experiment to find limitations.
to what extent	State the amount; estimate how much.
translate	Interpret, convert, decode and explain.
use	Employ, apply something; apply and draw on experience, knowledge.
validate	Confirm, authenticate, certify, endorse, support with evidence.
verify	Check to ensure that something is accurate/true.

Referring to the assignment instruction list above, what do you have to do to answer the following questions? The answers are in the Appendix.

1. To what extent is student life in China different from student life in the UK?
2. Discuss the problems that Chinese students might experience in the UK. Critically evaluate the advantages and disadvantages of studying in the UK.

Assignment structure

Once you have analysed your assignment title you should be much clearer about exactly what you need to read about, and what questions you want answered. You should also have a clearer idea about what *types* of sources you will need, such as:

- module textbooks;
- key, established (seminal) works on the topic;
- recent academic journal articles on new developments or ideas;
- non-academic (practitioner) views from independent websites or quality newspapers.

When you write an answer to the assignment question, try to make your answer very easy to read. Firstly, plan the basic structure:

Analyse the title and make sure you understand what you have to do – is it an essay or a report? Do you need to describe or to evaluate, or both?

Introduction

Discussion

Conclusion

References

Signposting

Successful assignments guide the reader with 'signposted' introductions. Signposts are words such as 'Firstly', 'Next', 'Furthermore' etc., which tell the reader what you are going to do next. Here is a useful list of typical signposting words which will help anyone who reads your work follow your narrative. This is particularly important in essays, where you don't normally use headings and sub-headings to help readers understand your structure:

TABLE 4.5   Useful signposting words for narratives

Showing the order of your answer	To begin with; Firstly; Secondly; Thirdly; Next; Turning now to; With regard to; In relation to; To conclude; Finally
Adding to a point made	Furthermore; In addition; In the same way; Similarly; Equally; Another related point is
Introducing examples	For example; For instance; such as; This is shown by
Stating the same point differently	In other words; Another way of looking at this is; Alternatively; In that case
Stating an alternative point	However; On the other hand; On the contrary; Conversely; In comparison; In contrast; Alternatively
Showing the results of something	Therefore; Consequently; As a result; This suggests that; It follows that; This implies that; The consequence of this is
Summing up or concluding	In conclusion; To conclude; To summarise; To sum up

Introductions and conclusions

A good introduction is essential because it provides the reader with the information required to understand what follows in your assignment.

Good introductions

A good introduction should have the following parts:

1. A short opening sentence about the topic to be discussed.
2. An identification of the main issue to be discussed and why it is important.
3. A reference to an important research study about the topic and why it is relevant to your assignment.

TABLE 4.6   Example introduction

Parts of the introduction	Purpose	Typical expression
1 A short opening sentence about the topic to be discussed	WHAT the assignment is about	*This assignment aims to discuss (link to the task)...*
2 Background information about the topic which would include a) brief explanation of key academic terms and b) the context (e.g. industry/company) in which the topic situates; this usually leads to an identification of the main issues to be discussed and why they are important	WHY this topic is worth addressing	*The issue is important because...*

(Continued)

141

TABLE 4.6   (Continued)

Parts of the introduction	Purpose	Typical expression
3 An explanation of how the assignment will proceed	HOW this assignment is structured (in the main body)	*This assignment will start with... then... thirdly... last but not least...*

4. An explanation of how the assignment will proceed.
5. A final sentence, linking with the next paragraph.

Good conclusions

A good conclusion should have the following parts:

1. A signpost word, indicating that you are concluding: 'In conclusion…'
2. A summary of the relevant points from your assignment discussion, in which you will need to finally answer the assignment question or complete the task.
3. Finally, your own answer to the assignment task – this is where you can write your own opinion on the issue, but it must be an 'informed' opinion which you have reached from your research of the opinions of the 'experts'.

TABLE 4.7   Example conclusion

Parts of conclusion	Purpose	Typical expression
1 A signpost word, indicating that you are concluding	Clear signpost of conclusion section	*In conclusion* *To conclude*
2 Refer to the task that has been addressed in the assignment	WHAT the assignment has done	*This assignment has discussed (link to the task)...*
3 A summary of the relevant points from your assignment discussion which you will need to finally answer the assignment question or complete the task	WHAT are the main findings from the discussion in the main text in relation to the original question or task?	*As discussed above, it can be seen that ...*
4 Finally, your own answer to the assignment task – this is where you can write your own opinion on the issue, but it must be an 'informed' opinion which you have reached from your research of the opinions of the 'experts'.	WHAT is your opinion on the topic? (You need to be cautious in your claims)	*This implies... It is likely to suggest...*

Drafting

Every time you write an assignment, you should produce at least two 'drafts' of your work. A draft is a rough version of the finished essay. You can change things and add to your draft until you are satisfied that the assignment answer is the best work that you can produce. Here are some tips about how to draft:

Draft 1: A quick draft to get ideas down

Use your assignment plan. At this stage do not worry too much about academic style or good English.

- Focus on the exact question: write out your interpretation of the title.
- What is your core idea? Write out your central idea or main line of reasoning.
- Develop a mindmap by writing headings and sub-headings from your plan, but leave these out of the final draft.
- Add in the details below each heading. Link headings and points into sentences.
- Use your plan: keep looking back to it after writing each paragraph.
- Make sure you put all your references into the draft, in full, even at this stage. You can always remove any references that you don't use when you write the final draft.

Draft 2: Fine-tune the structure

- Check that information is grouped and ordered into paragraphs. If not, cut up the text and rearrange it, or colour-code and number paragraphs in the order in which you will need to rewrite them. Make sure each paragraph is not too short and is about only one topic.
- Check that the discussion is linked from one paragraph to the next. Add sentences to link ideas if necessary. Make sure you keep to the task set. Check that you are addressing all the parts of the question or task.

Draft 3: Fine-tune the style and content

- Read to yourself what you have written. How does it sound? Can you improve the flow or style? Add sentences or details where needed. Now is the time to improve your academic writing style. Ask someone with better English than you to read through your work and point out any errors in your English.

Most students collect a lot of information when trying to complete a task, but not all of it is relevant and so it needs editing. You may give a lot of great information, but your tutor can't give good grades if what you write does not answer the question exactly. So make sure that you keep focused on the task, and that the relevance of each section of your work is clear. When quotations, facts and diagrams are included, check that they link to the point(s) you wish to make. You should make it very clear why you have included particular information. Use the information we gave you in Chapter 2 on 'Checking your own work'. Make sure you can answer these important questions about your work:

Content and argument

Does the text answer the question?

Have I given enough words to the main points?

Is all the information included relevant?

Have I included enough examples and evidence to support my points?

Have I used various quotes and references appropriately?

Structure and grouping

Have I linked my ideas?

Have I used well-structured paragraphs?

Is it clear how one paragraph links to another?

Style

Is the language appropriate for the module?

Does the text 'flow'?

Is the text written in 'academic' style?

Is the text free of slang?

Does the text repeat itself?

Does the text sound right when read aloud?

General

Have I written a clear introduction?

Have I written an effective conclusion and recommendations where necessary?

Have I referenced my work thoroughly?

Have I followed the assignment brief, in line with the subject's learning objectives?

Have I taken into account feedback from my past work?

Essays and reports

Essays and reports in the UK may be different from the assignments that Chinese students are used to writing in China, as Xiangping describes:

When I was studying in China, I never heard of the term 'essay' or 'report' because these things were both referred to as an 'assignment'. Therefore, I did not know that 'essays' and 'reports' referred to different formats of writing and that there were differences between them. The first essay I wrote in the UK was in the format of a report, which I received a very low mark for.

Gradually, I learnt that there are similarities between academic essays and reports, for example:

1 They are both evidence based and require references to support the points of the writer.

2 They both need to follow academic style and be formal and objective.

However, there are some important differences:

Essays are generally:

1 long 'flowing' documents using paragraphs to separate topics, without any headings/sub-headings, bullet points, numbers, graphs or tables in the body;

2 used by tutors to assess student understanding of course content, application of the knowledge in defined contexts, and student ability to analyse information, synthesise and critically evaluate;

3 focused on the display of knowledge and critical thinking.

Reports are generally:

1 professional documents reporting on situations, issues or research, using headings and sub-headings to separate topics, marking sections with the use of bullet points and numbers; graphs, tables and diagrams may be included in the text, or in an appendix, to illustrate findings or the analysis of the data;

2 commonly used in business and the professions, with analysis and evaluation of particular events or situations;

3 focused on what happened, and the findings from the investigation.

Essays

An essay is basically a long piece of writing about a topic, usually in answer to a question, or to address a number of issues in a set task.

EXAMPLE

A typical academic essay 'question':

> Discuss the importance of online shopping for retailers. What are the advantages and the disadvantages to retailers and consumers? Is it possible for a modern business to ignore online shopping trends?

Notice that the question actually asks you to address one task and two related questions in your answer:

Task: Discuss the importance of online shopping for retailers.

Question 1: What are the advantages and the disadvantages to retailers and consumers?

Question 2: Is it possible for a modern business to ignore online shopping trends?

The task also asks you to 'discuss'. 'Discuss', in this type of task, usually means to describe trends, use actual examples of what retailers and customers are actually doing in relation to online shopping, and link to theory. The theory that you use in your answer should be the theory that you have learnt from the module lectures and books. For example, in this case, the theory might be about how businesses maintain competitive advantage, and how consumers make purchasing choices. 'Discuss' usually means to critically evaluate, as well as to describe important trends. You are also expected to give your own opinion, both in the conclusion, where you make sure that you answer the two questions, and in your comments throughout the essay, on what the 'experts' are saying about the issues. Your comments should be in the form of:

It appears from the evidence presented, that if certain types of business do not have an online shopping facility, they will lose market share to their competitors.

Essays provide an opportunity for you to show your knowledge and understanding of your subject, your ability to apply the knowledge in a given context, as well as your ability to analyse, synthesise and critically evaluate.

Essays don't normally have sub-headings for each topic, like reports. The only heading which appears in an academic essay is the heading for the final reference list – called 'References'. There is no heading for the 'introduction', 'discussion' and 'conclusion' part, and these words should not appear in the essay. However, the first paragraph is always an 'introduction' and the last paragraph is normally a 'conclusion'. The text in the middle is the main 'discussion', which consists of several paragraphs with linked topics. However, each tutor might have different requirements, so please check with your institution or tutor for any specific requirements. The basic structure of an academic essay is shown below.

TABLE 4.8 Typical essay structure

Introduction

1) A first sentence introducing the topic:

This essay will investigate the issue of...

2) A brief description of the main issues:

Surname (year) has suggested that... However, Surname (year) has questioned this view, stating that...

(Continued)

TABLE 4.8   *(Continued)*

---

3) A definition or definitions that you are going to use, and why you are going to use that particular definition:

Surname (year) has defined X as Y. This definition is widely used by many researchers (e.g., Surname, year; Surname, year).

4) A brief statement about the structure and direction of the essay:

The essay will firstly consider the issues of... It will then discuss the current strategies used by UK companies... Finally, the essay will make a conclusion in relation to the question of...

Discussion

This section of the essay is where you put your main research for the essay and your critical evaluation. It is organised in a similar way to the 'critical sandwich' which we introduced to you in Chapter 3.

Surname (year) states that... However, Surname (year) appears to disagree with this view because he (or she) suggests that...

Conclusion

This is where you finally answer the question, summarising the main evidence that influenced your final opinion.

From the evidence presented in the discussion, it appears to be the case that... It is therefore possible to conclude that it might be a useful...

References

A list of all your 'in-text' references, in alphabetical order only (no need to put into separate groups of 'books', 'websites', 'journals' etc., unless you are asked to). You might have used a 'footnote' system, in which case you put your numbered footnotes here.

Reports

A report is another basic type of assignment in the UK. As the name suggests, it 'reports' on something in a concise, formal way, using clearly defined sections, presented in a standard format, and is the formal writing-up of a practical experiment, project or research investigation. It usually contains arguments and critical evaluation to support a proposed module of action, or to evaluate an issue.

A report tells the reader what you did, why and how you did it, and what you found, and is written in a way that assumes the reader knows nothing about the experiment or research. It is usually written more concisely than an essay, with headings and sub-headings and perhaps bullet-point recommendations. Since it is reporting on what happened, it is mainly written using past tense, except for the referenced evidence.

Different tutors will have their own particular requirements for assignment reports. There are different types of reports, so check what your tutor expects. Most reports include some of the sections below. Some types of research report (e.g. a dissertation) will probably have all of them.

1. Title page
2. Abstract *or* executive summary (check if required, and which type you require)
3. Table of contents
4. Terms of reference (check if required)
5. Introduction
6. Literature review (check if required)
7. Methodology (check if required)
8. Results/findings
9. Discussion and analysis
10. Conclusions
11. Recommendations (check if required)
12. References
13. Appendices (check if required)

TABLE 4.9   Typical report structure

Front page

The front page should show your own student details, the title of the report, and perhaps an eye-catching photo or design related to the topic.

Abstract (for research reports) or executive summary (for management reports)

This is a paragraph which usually includes the following things:

A statement of the report topic and why it is important

A statement about what your report will do

A statement of the report conclusions

Table of contents

You can produce this automatically in most word-processing programs, or you can do it by hand if your report is not very long. Your report will have headings and sub-headings, and these are shown in the table of contents.

Introduction

This is a paragraph outlining the issue investigated and why it is important.

Discussion

This section contains your discussion, evaluation and argumentation.

(Continued)

TABLE 4.9 *(Continued)*

Conclusion and recommendations

This section summarises the main conclusions on the basis of your discussion, and directly addresses the report question or what you were asked to do (sometimes called the 'terms of reference'). In longer reports, you might have to put the 'terms of reference' in a separate section.

References

This section contains ALL the references to all the sources that you used and cited in the report text.

Appendices

This section can contain accompanying data that is necessary for the report. However, it must be referred to in the main report text by using a 'cross-reference', e.g., '(see Appendix A)'.

EXAMPLE

TABLE 4.10 Report structure with examples

Title page

This should be short and precise. It should tell the reader what the report is about, e.g. *A report into the feasibility of establishing a student-run catering service at the college.*

An investigation into...

Title of the report

Author(s) and ID number(s)

Submission date

Module

Module name and number

Module tutor

Word count

Abstract or executive summary (Check that your tutor wants this part)

The abstract is a self-contained summary of the whole of your report – it summarises what the report does (as opposed to the purpose, which goes in the 'terms of reference' section). It should therefore be written last and is usually limited to one paragraph. The term 'executive summary' is normally used if it is a business report, and the term 'abstract' if it is an academic report. It should contain an outline of what you investigated (as stated in your title).

- The issue being investigated, with brief reference to other relevant research if you are writing a research report.
- A brief summary of the method of investigation.
- Main findings (and how these relate to the research question if you are writing a research report).
- A conclusion which may include a suggestion for further research (research report) or recommendations (recommendation report).

EXAMPLE

The ABC company has recently been advised to change its accounting system from outsourced to 'in house'. This would bring it into line not only with current accounting theory, but also with the current practice of many modern large corporations which have seen major advantages in establishing a management accounts function within the business. However, because ABC is a relatively young and medium-sized enterprise, there are issues concerning both the structural changes required and the cost effectiveness of implementing such a system. This report examines these issues in detail, utilising academic and practitioner secondary sources. The report concludes that the original recommendation for a transition to such a system should be implemented. Such a transition would supply ABC with enhanced operating information which would improve profitability and the efficiency of the accounting process. Recommendations concerning the implementation are also given.

Table of contents

Include all headings and sub-headings used in the report and their page numbers (do this last).

Terms of reference (Check that your tutor wants this part – it is often left out because it can be placed in the introduction)

This outlines concisely the purpose/aim of the report.

EXAMPLE

This report will investigate whether the ABC company would benefit from establishing a management accounts system rather than continue with the present system of outsourcing accounts. The report will cover European and UK operations for the period (date) to (date). The report is required to supply statistical evidence and recommendations.

Introduction

The Introduction 'sets the scene' for your report; it does this in two ways:

- By introducing the reader in more detail to the subject area you are dealing with.
- Through presenting your objectives (and hypotheses in a research report).

You should explain the background to the problem, with reference to previous work conducted in the area (i.e. a literature review). Ensure you only include studies that have direct relevance to your research.

(Continued)

TABLE 4.10 *(Continued)*

Briefly discuss the findings of other researchers or the experiences of other practitioners, and how these connect with your study. Finally, state your aims or hypothesis.

Your introduction should have the following parts:

- a topic sentence to set the general context;
- specific background and context;
- what is the basic issue?
- why is the issue important?
- what will you be able to conclude after your investigation?
- a 'signpost' to lead us into the next step.

EXAMPLE

Many companies are considering whether or not to establish a management accounts function within the company management structure (Surname, year). The ABC company is a fast-growing IT company with operations in Europe as well as the UK. ABC started operations on a small scale in 2000 as an information technology solutions provider. In (year), the company moved into its present premises in Cambridge in the UK, and began focusing on web-based technologies and computer networking for small, medium and large businesses including government and municipalities. With consolidation and expansion, management has found that their current accounting practice of outsourcing the accounts leads to problems related to issues of information effectiveness. After completion of a recent consultancy-based review, they have been advised to consider establishing an integrated management accounts function within the business itself in order to handle their internal audit, financial accounting and management accounting functions. Since they are beginning a further period of expansion, ABC management requires a more comprehensive and effective database for company strategic planning.

Literature review

This is a review of all relevant sources, such as a comparison of academic theories plus government/company reports.

EXAMPLE

There have been many research studies on the issue of organisational strategic planning (e.g., Surname, year; Surname, year; Surname, year)…

Methodology (Does your tutor want this part?)

The methodology section should describe every step of *how* you carried out your research in sufficient detail so that the reader could replicate your procedure exactly if they wanted to. Information on your experimental design, sampling methods, participants (if any), any special equipment and the overall procedure employed should be clearly specified.

This information is usually presented under the following sub-headings:

Participants (if there were any): State how many participants or items were included. Why and how were they selected? What were their defining characteristics?

Design: State what your research method was (e.g. primary/secondary research, questionnaire survey, etc.) and why you chose this method. What was your design, e.g. how you chose your samples.

Procedure: A step-by-step description of what you, or you and your group, did.

EXAMPLE

The research was conducted during Semester B, year, using secondary data from...

Results/findings

Your results/findings section should clearly and concisely convey the findings on which you will base your discussion/analysis, so the reader needs to be certain of what you found.

Describe what the results were; do not offer interpretations of them. Present them in a logical order. Those that link most directly to your hypothesis or research issue or question should be given first.

Do not present the same data in more than two ways, i.e. use *either* a table or graph/figure, and explain in the text.

Remember that a graph/table should be understandable independently of any text, but you may accompany each with a description if necessary.

Use clear, concise titles for each and label the axes of graphs. Say which variables the graph/table compares.

Describe what the graph/table shows, and then check that this really is what it shows. If it is not, you need to amend it/your description.

Remember, you might need to put all graphical and statistical information in an appendix – check with the assignment guidance you were given.

Present data in a summarised form (e.g. means and standard deviations).

Raw data (e.g. individual recordings taken during the research) should be included in the appendices.

Statistical analysis

If you conducted a statistical analysis of your results, state which statistical test you used (e.g. chi-square, t-test) and briefly explain why you chose that particular statistical test, if this was your own choice.

Show how your results were analysed, and any calculations you used.

Clearly state the results of the analysis.

Discussion and analysis

The discussion/analysis section is probably the most important and longest section of your report. It helps the reader to understand the relevance of your research to other research, past and present, in the subject area. This is your chance to discuss, analyse and interpret your results in relation to all the information you have collected. It relates and links to the introduction and to the results/findings section. It should contain the following:

(Continued)

153

TABLE 4.10   *(Continued)*

1) An overview of the main results of your work.
2) Interpretation of these results in relation to your aim and objectives. You should compare your results with those of other researchers that you mentioned in your introduction and your literature review.
3) Consideration of the broader implications of your findings. What do they suggest for future research in the area? If your results contradict previous findings, what does this suggest about your work or the work of others? What should be studied next?
4) Discussion of any limitations or problems with your research method(s) or experimental design, and practical suggestions of how these might be avoided if the study was conducted again.

Analyse each issue:

- Break down the issues identified in your findings into parts, e.g. X, Y and Z. State the relationships between these parts and what effects X has on Y; Y has on Z; Z has on X, etc. Consider every possible aspect of each issue. This is often made easier by asking yourself as many questions as possible, such as who?, why?, what?, where?, when?, which?, how? Your analysis will contain these answers.
- Identify and analyse the key patterns. Follow the report brief and if appropriate, evaluate which parts are having the greatest effects.

Evaluate each issue:

- Assess how valuable or otherwise each part (factor) is in terms of its effects on each issue.
- Judge the strengths and weaknesses of, for example, ABC's current situation.
- Compare with other possible theoretical solutions suggested by academic theory and by other expert practitioners.

Conclusions

Summarise the key points already made and the main issues arising from your report.

EXAMPLE

Findings from this research indicate that a suitable strategy for the company might be...

Recommendations (Check that your tutor wants this part)

Recommendations always follow the conclusions. Only after you have assessed the strengths and weaknesses is it possible to offer your recommendations. Some carefully considered ideas for further research in the area would help clarify or take forward your own findings.

For example, suggest what the ABC Company should do, by whom, when and how, so that there is a sense of priority. This can be done in bullet points, as below:

EXAMPLE

- *The ABC Company should accept the recommendation of the consultants to implement a management accounting system.*
- *The ABC Company should action the Finance Director to recruit and establish a new management accounts unit by the end of the year.*
- *Recruitment should start as soon as possible with advertisements in local newspapers.*
- *The ABC Company should establish a realistic timeframe for the transition. This might be nine months by the time the selected candidates are in place. If not...*

References

Give details of work by all other authors who you have referred to in your report.

Appendices

Appendices should only be used for material that is relevant to your report but not essential to the main discussion, e.g. statistical tables, calculations, examples of questionnaires, a glossary of terms, etc. All appendices should be clearly labelled and referred to in the main text (e.g. 'See Appendix 2'. This signals to the reader that Appendix 2 contains all the research method details).

EXAMPLE

Appendix 1: Organisational Structure

Appendix 2: The Financial Situation

Appendix 3: Current Accounting Procedures

THINK 4.1

From what you have learnt, and what you have experienced in China, how are essays and reports in the UK different from those you had to write in China? If you don't think there are so many differences, then tell us how they are similar. Write some notes here.

Critiques and critical reviews

Sometimes you may be asked to write a 'critique'. A 'critique' is a critically evaluative 'review' of a single article, book chapter or research paper. To 'review' means to 'look again' at the article, and tell us what you find in it.

When asked to write a critique, you are generally required to firstly describe what the article is about – what is the author's main argument? You then have to weigh up the strengths and weaknesses of the article or paper – firstly as other experts have indicated, and then as you see them, on the basis of your evaluation in relation to other independent experts.

So a good formula to use would be the DASEY formula we have described earlier:

D = General description of the article and the main arguments.

A = Analysis – how does the author organise his or her article?

S = Synthesis – what does your analysis information tell you?

E = Evaluation – use independent expert ideas and your own to make your own conclusions about the article.

Y= Your own voice – finally make some personal conclusions about the article and the arguments.

Remember that to evaluate an article (judge how useful or relevant it is) you need to 'analyse' the article first (identify the different factors or parts). This requires taking apart ('deconstructing' or 'unpacking') an idea or statement and examining the parts to see how they might be interrelated. Analysis means considering the answers to questions such as what?, who?, when?, why?, where?, which? and how? These need to be considered in depth, to develop a line of argument and reach a conclusion to your narrative.

You may be required to critique an academic journal article or business article in an assignment structure format. A critical review requires you to examine critically and judge carefully all aspects of an academic or business article, focusing on one aspect at a time. Your lecturer may ask you to review an article, firstly get you to carefully read the article, and then, to check if you have really understood the article and the wider implications of the points the author(s) make.

So firstly read the article objectively, and then evaluate the reading: the completeness of its data, the strengths and weaknesses of the article, in relation to other theorists and the current situation, etc., before presenting your own viewpoint.

How to write a critical review

A critical review is usually written like an assignment and begins with an overview, stated in your introduction, outlining and explaining the purpose of the article. It includes a concise summary of the author's point of view/ suggested purpose of the article within its context, containing the following:

a. a brief statement of the author's main idea (i.e. thesis or theme);
b. an outline of important points and lines of reasoning that the author uses to support the main idea;
c. a summary of the author's explicit or implied values and their importance;
d. a brief presentation of the author's conclusion or suggestions for action.

Following this, your critique of the article should include:

a. an analysis of the points presented on the basis of their relevance and accuracy;
b. an assessment of its limitations, logic and possible omissions;
c. an evaluation or judgement of the consistency of the author's arguments;
d. an appraisal of the author's arguments, in comparison to other authors' works and also in consideration of your knowledge, understanding and experience.

Examples of criteria used for evaluating and reviewing a research article

(However, remember that they will not all be relevant for all articles.)

- What is the logic of the view presented?
- What is the validity of the evidence?
- What theoretical framework is used? Is it valid? And applied appropriately?
- What is the methodology?
- Is the methodology appropriate?
- Is the methodological approach explained clearly?
- Does the methodological approach have any weaknesses?
- Is the research sufficiently comprehensive and thorough?
- Is anything important omitted in the research?
- Are the findings presented and described clearly and fully?
- Do the findings seem correct in relation to the information presented?
- Could the data be interpreted in another way?
- Does the author account for everything in the data or ignore something important?
- Is the analysis of the topic thorough?
- How does its value compare to other articles on the topic?
- How effective does it seem to be in relation to the needs of a specific user/audience?

Remember that a critique is still academic writing, so you need to make sure that you do the following things:

- Provide more than just a summary list of what critics have written about the author or the article. You must also evaluate and include your own opinion.

- The assignment must use an appropriate objective tone (which is usually formal). Write in the passive mode wherever possible and avoid the first person.
- Check that your assignment is free of grammatical and spelling errors. Get a friend with good English to proofread it for you, after you have done this yourself.
- Vary the types of sentences you use. For example:

According to Surname (year), China's economic growth is sustainable in the long term.

It has been argued (Surname, year) that China's growth is sustainable in the long term.

Research (Surname, year) **indicates** that China's growth is sustainable in the long term.

- Remember that 'criticism' does not mean that you have to attack the work or the author, or be negative about it. It means you should think critically about it, exploring it and discussing your findings in relation to how useful these findings are to your task.

Persuasive and creative writing

Another type of writing which you might have to do is the type of writing which tries to persuade somebody to do something. This is quite common in marketing, advertising and journalism – for example, to persuade customers to buy a particular product or service.

In fact, all writing is persuasive to some extent. Even the 'objective' academic essays that we have described require that you 'persuade' your reader that your own final answer to the question is a good one, based on the evidence that you have supplied. There are no right or wrong answers to any of the issues that you will have to research and write about, so there is always an element of persuasion that your own research and opinion has produced the best answer to the problem or issue.

Creative writing

Creativity is a skill which requires you to use your existing knowledge and to apply it in new and potentially effective ways, to produce and market a new product for example. If you are studying marketing and advertising, you may have to prepare a marketing 'brief' which persuades your readers that your own ideas are going to produce the best outcome. This is where you might have to be especially 'creative' in your thinking and writing. The creative skill is one which is greatly valued, and you may find that some of your assignments require you to be creative in the way that you answer the assignment question or task.

EXAMPLE

This type of writing is often required in response to a group project which involves producing a 'creative brief'. For example, here is a typical task you might have to complete:

> You are the marketing agency for the ABC company. Write a creative brief for a marketing mix campaign which induces a trial for a new product (gets new customers to try it). ABC already produces cosmetic products for young people. They want to extend their product range. Your creative brief should have the following sections.

TABLE 4.11   Typical creative-brief structure

Background	Why you are doing this. The business case for introducing a new product. The competitive environment of the company. The business case for the introduction of this particular new product. Details of the new product.
Campaign objective	The objective is to induce a trial – to get existing customers to try the new product, and to also create a new customer base.
Target audience	Details of the target market demographic.
Strapline	Your strapline is your advertising slogan. The group needs to create a short, memorable group of words used in advertising campaigns. The words must draw attention to the most distinctive feature of your new product, to project a particular image for your target market.
Features and details of your product or service	You need to create features and details for the new product that set it apart from other similar products on the market.
Key message	What your target audience should think about the new product, what they should do after your campaign, and why they should do it.
Logistics	Practical details of the campaign, timing and marketing mix to be employed etc.

This type of writing has different features from evidence-based academic writing. You are basically trying to get new customers to try your product. Although you will be required to provide evidence for your new product and marketing suggestions, because the assignment requires you to act as a creative group, you can use a mix of first and third person, with phrases such as:

> We (the group) suggest that…
>
> We (the group) think that…
>
> From market research, it seems evident that…
>
> The new product should…

Case studies

An important type of writing that you may have to both read and write is the case study, so we have explained it in detail in this next section. Many Chinese students come to the UK to study business, and case studies have a long history in business education. They are also used extensively in engineering, health sciences and the social sciences.

A case study presents students with an account of what happened to a real business, organisation or industry, over a period of time. It can also be a case study of an issue, wider events or specific situations. A business case study includes the events that managers and employees had to deal with, such as changes in the competitive environment, and the case study records the organisational response. Cases are valuable for two main reasons:

1. They provide students with practitioner experience of 'real-world' organisational problems that they probably would not have the opportunity to experience directly.
2. Case studies illustrate the theories and models which students study in their academic modules. The meaning of academic theories is made clearer when they are applied in practice, or when you can see how other people have actually applied them in practice. The theory and concepts help show what is happening in the organisations studied, and allow students to critically analyse and evaluate the solutions that specific organisations have adopted in order to solve these problems.

Typically, information is presented about a company's products, markets, competition, financial structure, sales volumes, management, employees and other factors affecting the company's success. Or it might be the way that an organisation like a medical service responded to particular patient issues.

When you analyse these case studies, you work like a detective, gathering relevant data and then synthesising the evidence to enable you to make conclusions and recommendations.

Importantly, case study projects often provide you with the opportunity to participate in group work, and to gain experience in presenting your ideas to others. This is a very important part of your skills development. Your tutor may ask you to research particular module issues, and to critically evaluate the theory and practice in relation to the issues, plus identify possible solutions to problems.

You will have to organise your views and conclusions so that you can present them to your group and then perhaps to the class. Your group members may analyse the issues differently from you, so you need to argue your points to persuade them to accept your views.

Tutors may also assign an individual, but more commonly a group, to analyse a case during a seminar. The individual or group will probably be responsible for a 20–30-minute presentation of the case to the class. Presentations usually cover the issues involved and specific problems, and they might also require a series of recommendations for resolving the problems. The discussion may then be opened to the class, and you may need to defend your ideas. Through such discussions and presentations, you will develop your communication skills and self-confidence, which will be very good for your future career.

Case studies are therefore a very valuable way to learn. They provide you with experience of organisational problems that you probably have not gained for yourself. They give you a chance to understand the scope and type of problems faced in the real world outside education. They help you apply your theoretical knowledge, and improve your understanding of current issues. The assignment could be individual or group work, and involve a presentation, but most often, a written report is required.

Case studies often require you to think (reflect) about the case, and answer questions. Case studies require students to think deeply about the issues raised by the case and ask their own questions about the case. Many tutors will show you videos of real cases and you will be expected to critically evaluate the case and suggest solutions to the issues and problems raised.

Types of case study

Case study designs could focus on a single case – perhaps a critique of a company – or an extreme or unique case, or a particularly successful case.

Alternatively, multiple case studies might look at several cases across a particular industry or commercial sector.

Cases can be based on hypothetical (imagined) or empirical (real) situations. Hypothetical cases present you with fictitious company information and fictitious personnel but the hypothetical case will be based on real-world examples. Empirical (real-world) cases are based on real companies, real events and real people.

Applying theory to cases

Cases illustrate what you have learnt from your module theory, so it is important that you can demonstrate that you understand the theory by being able to apply it to case studies. When you analyse cases, you are trying to find out the causes of the problems under investigation. There will be no 'right' answers, just effective or ineffective solutions to these problems. Every problem solved can also be another problem created, so keep that in mind when you make your case study recommendations.

What does applying theory to the case mean? There are two main ways in which you might do this:

1. Comparing 'reality' to theory

   How do organisations and people behave in the real world, and how does their behaviour compare with the academic theories you have learnt from your studies?

2. Comparing theory to reality

   What does the academic theory predict will happen in the real world? Are there any examples of organisations that have used the theory, and what happened when they did?

Group-work case studies

If you work in groups to analyse case studies, you will experience the group process involved in working as a team. As we discussed in Chapter 3, when people work in groups, it is often difficult to schedule meeting times, and allocate responsibility for the compilation of the case study. There are always going to be some group members who work harder than others. This is another aspect of the authentic nature of team work. You need to assign group roles, organise your time, arrange group meetings and decide on ways to make group members take full responsibility for each agreed part of the process. Agreeing roles in the case study process before you start is helpful, and often required in order to complete a 'group log', itemising what each group member was responsible for doing.

TABLE 4.12   Example group log for a case study

Student	Research responsibility	Writing responsibility
Student A	The history and development of the organisation or issue	Title page, contents and binding. Introduction Contributor log Proofreading
Student B	The external environment – political, economic, social and technological impacts	Strategic analysis: SWOT, PEST Proofreading – final compilation
Student C	Existing strategies employed to solve problems Proposed new strategies to solve problems	Conclusions and recommendations Proofreading
Student D	The resources required to implement strategies and logistical problems which will have to be solved	References: in-text citations and references list Appendices Proofreading

Stages of case-study report writing

If you need to submit an individual or a group report, use a similar writing plan to the one outlined below. Check your assignment instructions and your module handbook carefully to make sure you follow your tutor's guidelines. If you are not given specific guidance, use the following general guidelines. Obviously, your structure will have to be carefully shaped to fit the individual case that you are considering. Some business cases are about companies or organisations experiencing very few or no problems. In these cases you should focus on analysing why the company is doing well, and you might be required to give recommendations.

TABLE 4.13   Typical case study structure

Introduction

Case studies begin with an introduction to the case. In the introduction, you usually outline briefly what the oganisation does, how it developed historically and its current situation. Beyond this brief introduction, you must avoid being too descriptive. Use signposting to show how you are going to approach the task you have been given. Do this sequentially by writing, for example, 'First, the report will identify the environment of X... Next, the report will analyse X's strategy... Lastly, the report will provide recommendations for X to address the issue of...'

Critical analysis and evaluation

Avoid too much description because analysis and critical evaluation always get higher marks. Do not repeat large pieces of factual information from the case because your tutor already knows the case very well. Check if your tutor allows you to include any appendices. Use relevant evidence from academic and practitioner sources as the basis for your analysis and your critical evaluation.

(Continued)

TABLE 4.13   *(Continued)*

You need to analyse first before you can evaluate. This analysis is often done using a combination of descriptive theoretical models such as SWOT or PESTLE. These theoretical 'tools' can provide you with an 'organising principle' which shapes the way that you write the case study. For example, basic SWOT and PESTLE models enable you to consider the strengths and weaknesses of organisational strategy in relation to relevant theory and practice regarding the specific issues the organisation is addressing.

You should use clear headings and sub-headings throughout this section to structure your analysis and evaluation. The actual headings and sub-headings you use will depend on the specific case issues.

Here are some general suggestions of what you might need to do – obviously, your actual task requirements will be more specific:

1. Analyse the organisation's history, development and growth, and its position in a macro-economic context. The macro-economic context is the wider industry and global context of the organisation's operations. Investigate how an organisation's past strategies affect its operations now. Identify the critical incidents in its history. These are the events which had the biggest impact on the organisation. You can use a PESTLE analysis for this, as in the example on the next page.

2. Identify the organisation's *internal* strengths and weaknesses (the microeconomic context). Use the incidents you identify to develop an account of the organisation's strengths and weaknesses. Identify where the organisation is currently strong and where it is currently weak. You can use a SWOT analysis for this, for example:

Typical SWOT analysis factors

Strengths	Weaknesses
• Strategic advantages • Current capabilities • Unique selling points • Resources • Employee experience, knowledge • Financial situation • Innovation and creativity • Pricing, value, quality • Accreditation • IT systems • Communications	• Competitive strength • Reputation • Investment in R&D • Specific problems • Cash flow • Supply chain issues • Media issues • Planning • Employee morale • Online purchasing facility
Opportunities	**Threats**
• Global influences • Market developments • Emerging markets • Competitors' vulnerabilities • Industry or lifestyle trends • Technological affordances, developments and innovation	• Competitors • Market demands • Political/economic impacts • Legislative impacts • Environmental effects and requirements • IT developments • New technologies, services, trends

---

Typical PESTLE analysis factors (political, economic, social, technological, legal and environmental)

Political factors	Economic factors
• Political situation • Government's economic policy • Culture and religion • Trade agreements • Tax policy	• Interest rates • Inflation • Employment • Economic health • Asset and taxation issues
Socio-cultural factors	**Technological factors**
• Culture • Globalisation • Language and communication • Leisure and lifestyles • Gender issues • Population issues • Ageing populations • Rich and poor • Social expectations • Security issues – identity protection	• Affordances (opportunities from new technology) • Internet • New products • Consumer expectations of products and service • Security issues
Legal factors	**Environmental factors**
• Government legislation • Organisational policies • Local laws and policies	• Environmental directives • Recycling/pollution directives • Sustainability issues • Community issues

---

3. Evaluate your analysis. Having identified the company's external opportunities and threats (for example, from your PESTLE analysis) as well as its internal strengths and weaknesses (from your SWOT analysis), consider what your findings mean and critically evaluate them, i.e. compare strengths and weaknesses with opportunities and threats. Some of the questions you might ask are:

   • Is the organisation in a strong position? Why? Why not?
   • Can it continue to pursue its current strategy? Why? Why not?
   • What can it do to turn weaknesses into strengths and threats into opportunities?
   • Can it change to be more effective in relation to its goals?

4. Analyse macro-level strategy. To analyse an organisation's strategy, you need to firstly define the organisation's mission and goals. Sometimes the mission and goals are stated explicitly in the case, but at other times you will have to find them by looking at how the organisation actually operates.

(Continued)

TABLE 4.13   *(Continued)*

Conclusions

In your conclusion, you cannot present any new information. Summarise the main issues you have discussed and your conclusions in relation to them. Remember also that you have a recommendation section to follow your conclusions, so make sure you do not recommend things in the conclusion itself (unless your tutor requires this). Your conclusions should be in line with your previous analysis so that your analysis, conclusions and recommendations fit together 'coherently' and move logically from one to the next.

Recommendations

The recommendations section is very important because your tutor will be able to see how much work you put into the case study from the quality and realism of your recommendations. They should be clearly linked to your critical analysis and should generally centre on the specific issues that the task requires you to address. The recommendations will be specific to each case to provide solutions to whatever strategic problems the organisation is facing, which you have already identified and critically evaluated. You will need to show creativity and independent thought in this section.

Try to ensure that your recommendations are consistent with your findings and the case study brief.

- You can use bullet points. The recommendations might also contain a timetable that sequences the actions for changing the organisation's strategy, or implementing a new service etc.

- Use modal verbs such as 'should' to strongly suggest, or 'might consider' or 'could consider' to make less assertive recommendations, perhaps where the situation was not clear. There might be alternative recommendations, conditional on other things. In this case, you might need to use the conditional tense and write:

  If the organisation did X, then Y might result [or]
  If the complaints from customers continue, then the organisation might consider outsourcing its customer service facility.

- Finally, check very carefully for grammatical, spelling and referencing errors. Case study reports are important communication documents in the professional world so it is extremely important to always proofread and edit your work.

Reflective and self-evaluative writing

In the UK, 'reflection' is considered to be a very important skill for students to develop. This is because it is a powerful way to learn – to reflect back on what you have done and think about how you can improve. Many people do not have this ability naturally. They always think that everything they do is OK. However, in order to advance your learning, you always need to reflect on what you have done, and how you can improve.

All learning in UK Higher Education requires that you develop this reflective ability. You can develop this reflective thinking ability very effectively, and you will often be required to use it in your academic writing. You may be asked, for example, to write a reflective essay on what you have learnt from a module.

'Reflecting' means to think back to something you have done. You must ask yourself two important questions:

What did I learn from that experience?

How could I have learnt more?

Chinese students may not be used to this style of thinking or writing. However, reflection is a natural process – we all reflect every day on our current and past experiences and also on our hopes for the future (reflection also involves looking forwards as well as backwards).

Additionally, most employers want their employees to become 'reflective practitioners' in the workplace. Reflective practice is a component of continuing professional development (CPD), required by all professional organisations in the UK.

Reflecting on your learning at university is the start of becoming a reflective practitioner and gaining a skill you can continue to use throughout your career through appraisals and annual reviews. There are two basic skills which you need to develop in order to write reflective essays and reports:

1. The ability to be self-reflective. This is not always a natural skill for everyone, particularly if you come from a culture where self-reflection has not been encouraged. When reflecting, you need to be 'honest' with yourself and talk about your weaknesses and strengths, as you personally see them.
2. Knowing how to write reflectively. There are certain format requirements which you need to observe, in order to record reflections appropriately.

You may be asked to produce one or more of the following:

TABLE 4.14   Writing reflective essays and reports

Method of reflection	Content
Self-reflective log/blog	You may be asked to keep an ongoing record of a task or group work you are involved in.
Reflective essay	This involves an analysis and evaluation of you/your group's experience rather than a description of it.
Reflective portfolio	You may be required to provide evidence of what you learnt on a work placement or internship, writing about what experiences you had, and what you learnt from these experiences.
Reflective report	You may be asked to do this at the end of a module. Do not just describe the things that you did, but evaluate your performance and the learning experiences you had.

General steps for reflective writing

1. Keep a diary, a journal or a log. This will provide you with your data for your reflection; otherwise you will forget exactly what you did, and how you felt at the time.
2. Be specific rather than general. Use your personal data to focus on specific situations that you can reflect and learn from. This is better than writing generally about the whole experience, although you might want to finish with a general conclusion.
3. Your writing should always be positive, and aim at improvement. Choose situations or tasks that were difficult. Think about what caused the problems you experienced, and how you could change your response to achieve a better outcome next time.
4. It is very important that you take responsibility for your own actions, and don't try to blame other people in your reflective writing, even if you are personally convinced that they caused your problem. You could have reacted differently, so focus on your own performance and how you can improve. If you are writing about a group exercise, and you feel that certain team members did not work as hard as you, discuss how the team could be better organised next time to ensure a fairer distribution of team tasks.
5. Evaluate – don't just describe. Reflection involves analysing the situation objectively and then evaluating your own, or the group's, performance. Do not just describe what happened, but weigh up strengths and weaknesses, costs and benefits, and decisions and outcomes.

EXAMPLE

Example of a reflective diary, which is critically evaluative rather than just negatively critical or overly descriptive:

Today was a good day. I realised that I often leave my assignments until the deadline and then I get very stressed because I have not left enough time. But this is a time-wasting method and it does not produce good work. It also makes me very anxious about the quality of my work. I realise that I am the kind of person who needs someone to push me to do things and I need to develop more self-motivation. So now I am trying to stick to a definite plan, and write my draft essay with plenty of time before the deadline. In this way, I can feel less stressed and I will have more time to make any changes I need to, and this will also make me feel more in control of my own work.

If the student had not written a good reflection, it might have looked like this:

Today was another bad day. I often 'put off' assignments until the last minute when it's no longer possible to put things off and I have to do it. I am quite depressed about the quality of my work and I wish I could motivate myself more. I don't know what to do. My friends don't help either – they all leave things to the last minute, but they always seem to get better marks than me.

It is self-critical, but does not take personal responsibility, and has no evaluation or suggestions about ways to improve.

Other types of reflective writing assignments might involve reflecting on a module or group work. The following sections offer some suggested questions you will need to answer for each of these two types of reflection.

Reflection on module learning outcomes

- Why did you choose your programme/module: what were your aims and objectives?
- Have these changed since starting the programme/module?
- In what ways and for what reasons?
- What were you expecting from the programme/module?
- What did you expect from yourself?
- What led you to form these expectations?
- What are the learning outcomes for the module(s) you have taken so far?
- What skills development is linked to the module(s) you have taken?
- How do these outcomes and skills correspond to your own aims and goals?
- How does your reflection link with theories about reflection and learning?

Reflection on group work

- What contribution did you make?
- What went well and why?

- What strengths did you identify?
- When did the group utilise your strengths?
- What did you learn from others?
- What did the other members learn from you?
- What went badly and why?
- How did you solve any problems?
- What weaknesses did you identify?
- How did you and the group address them?
- Did you improve on your weaknesses?
- What do you plan to do in future about the weaknesses you have identified?
- What would you do differently next time?
- How does this link with the theories on successful group work?
- How does your reflection link with theories about reflection and learning?

When you are reflecting on group work, start by giving a clear account of who did what and when, and what problems or difficulties you and the group encountered. Analyse the group activities by answering questions like these:

- What was the group trying to achieve?
- What were the different views and misunderstandings?
- What was left unsaid?
- How were decisions made?
- How did you feel about this?
- How did the others react?
- What might they have felt?
- What was the group motivation like?
- Did anything unexpected happen?

Identify group contributions, but remember not to personalise and criticise. Outline the difficulties the group and you personally faced. Assess strengths, weaknesses and critical points, for example, when decisions changed the direction of the group which allowed breakthroughs to be made.

EXAMPLE

Example: Reflection on group work

Overall we worked effectively as a team and fulfilled our main objective. However, in the future I would want to do more work as a team rather than individually. We mostly worked individually after we had agreed our team roles. Working individually meant that it was sometimes difficult to make decisions. Another solution could be to find out more about each other's contributions during team meetings before moving onto the next stages. If we had to do this again, it would be necessary to organise group meetings better. Sometimes, even though they had clear objectives, our meetings lacked structure. In addition, I think we should have had more group meetings to discuss how the work was going.

Example: Reflection on professional performance from work experience

I felt that my second assessment was a big improvement on the first one because I showed improvement in all areas that were assessed. Following my first report, I worked hard to ensure that I improved in all areas, particularly areas where I received a D grade in the first report. The second report showed that I had not only improved in the work I was doing, but had also developed in terms of my professional attitude by continuing to improve my working and social relationships with other colleagues.

I was especially pleased with my grades for 'decision making' and 'organisational skills' because in the first six months of my industry placement I had been given many projects to work on simultaneously, many of which I was solely responsible for. The two B grades I received for these areas showed that I was managing and taking control of the projects to a good standard. Another area of the report I was delighted with was my supervisor's written comment. He said he felt that I was a valued member of the team and played a key role in team activities. He also had a positive attitude towards my continued development. I think the modules I did in the first and second years at the university helped me achieve this comment, as I was able to apply some of the theory to my work and made improved contributions to the team.

Reflective writing is always more personal and subjective than academic writing. Here are some useful words and phrases you can use:

This made me aware that…

I identified this as a strength, so…

I found this important because…

I used my previous experience to…

This meant that I should have…

I know that I need to develop…

I realise that because of this, I…

This changed because…

With hindsight (looking back) I would not…

Looking back, I should…

I learnt that…

The next time I shall…

At this point I realised…

This is a priority because…

Because I had practised…

I made a decision that…

Following this experience, I…

This may have happened because…

This relates to my experience of…

Despite the setbacks, I…

Next time I could…

In the future I must improve…

My presentation skills were enhanced because…

Unfortunately, I did not understand, so…

Evidence from my reflective journal shows that I…

I need to improve my interpersonal skills because…

This was a significant milestone (important point) because…

This feedback was useful because…

Taking responsibility has meant that I…

I became aware that I do not always…

Things to leave out of your reflective writing

Things you should avoid in your reflective writing are:

- Being dishonest
- Making excuses
- Criticising, blaming other people, and being negative
- Putting in very personal information and very private material
- Unnecessary examples
- Too much description rather than analysis and evaluation
- Repetitive or irrelevant material
- Materials or content produced by other people (plagiarism)
- Casual, colloquial, conversational language, emotively expressed.

Using the advice above about writing reflectively, and using some of the words and phrases for reflective writing, write a reflective paragraph answering the following questions:

- What is my main impression of student life in the UK so far?
- What are my main achievements so far?
- What are the main problems I have experienced so far?
- What can I do to improve my student experience in the UK?

Use the space provided in the Appendix.

Portfolios

Portfolios are collections of different types of documents. They might consist of essays, reports, reflective writing, group presentation slides etc. You might be required to keep a portfolio of your work in relation to specific learning outcomes, for example employability and how your academic work might relate to your future career. This might include the following specific documents which you have written and compiled over the complete period of your degree or further studies:

Work experience reports and reflections.

Module reflective writing.

An assessment of your skills development during your academic studies and work experience.

Action plan to further develop your skills.

Curriculum vitae (CV) (your past and current work and academic achievements).

Future career plans and an action plan to develop specific career-related skills.

Portfolios are often submitted via module VLEs, and kept there for continued development and for relevant staff to access in order to make comments to help your development.

Oral presentations

One very important study skill for students is oral presentation, whether individually or as a project team. Presenting your research and ideas to

other students and tutors is an important part of academic life. It is also a vital skill in your career after you finish your studies.

This section gives advice about the best ways to plan and organise an effective presentation, with special reference to language issues which might arise. When preparing a group presentation, it is important to work as a team to present your topic. To do this, you need to have regular meetings at the planning stage and you will need to practise the presentation as a group. It will be quite obvious to the audience and your tutor whether the group prepared and practised the presentation together or not. Also refer to the sections on effective group work, in Chapter 3 and in this chapter.

Public speaking and presentations

An important type of speaking that you will have to do during your studies is 'public speaking' – presenting information to other people in meetings and educational situations such as tutorials and seminars. You might also have to take part in class debates, where you will have to stand up and speak about an issue.

Most professionals need to be able to communicate effectively with others by speaking in meetings, presentations and interviews, so this is a very important part of your education which will also be highly valuable for your future career. A good opportunity to practise will be any time you need to explain how something works, or any time you need to tell someone how to do something – for example, giving help on a piece of software that you are familiar with.

It is very important to always take opportunities to develop your English speaking skill. Speaking will be very important in your studies. You will be expected to ask questions in lectures, take part in group discussions and present your ideas in seminars. You will also have to give formal presentations.

Public speaking uses different skills to those we use in general conversation. Here are some good tips:

1. You need to project your voice by increasing the loudness of your voice, and making sure you pronounce key words correctly and clearly. Check key-word pronunciation with your tutor or a fellow student.
2. You should make sure that everyone can hear what you are saying, and maintain that volume throughout.
3. You should emphasise key points, but take care not to shout, or to appear aggressive.
4. Speaking too quickly or too slowly are also problems for good communication. Speaking too quickly is often caused by nerves, and too slowly by a need to stick closely to a 'script' which you will be tempted to read. If you read from a script, you will quickly bore your audience.
5. A good tip is to record yourself speaking so you can see what you sound like, or ask for feedback from a friend. If they say that you were speaking too quickly, then try to relax and slow down.
6. Try to breathe slowly and naturally. Since English is not your first language, you will naturally be nervous on the day of your speech. The way to control your nerves is to plan the speech very well, and rehearse the speech.
7. You should record your rehearsal to check what it sounds like and to check your pronunciation of key words. Practise in front of a mirror to check your body language.

Giving a presentation

Students often have to give presentations during their studies. This means that you will have to stand up before an audience and either by yourself, or in a small team, report on a project you had to complete. It might be some research you had to do for an assignment. Presentations can be very difficult for many students because you will worry about feeling embarrassed if you say something 'incorrectly' in front of your audience.

Tips for a good presentation:

- Prepare exactly what you want to say, and prepare the visuals (slides, charts etc.) that you are going to use in the presentation. Make sure that your visuals do not contain too much information and that your audience will all be able to read them clearly.
- Rehearse your speech. At this stage, you can read it from your notes, but you must not do this for the final presentation.
- If you are presenting in a team, practise your introductions and 'change-overs': 'And now John will summarise…'
- If you can, rehearse your presentation with someone who can give you feedback. Check the timing during your rehearsal.

- Speak clearly and try to look at everyone in the audience (eye contact) during your presentation – you do not have to look directly at them, but in their direction, so that they feel you are talking to them.
- NEVER read from notes.
- Keep good timing and leave time for questions at the end of the presentation.
- Speak at a normal speed, varying the pitch of your voice as you speak. Keep telling yourself to slow down as you present.
- Use correct grammar and vocabulary, ensuring you can pronounce all the words.
- Use simple and plain words if possible.
- Pause often for the audience so they can think about the information you are presenting and avoid information overload.

Planning your presentation

The first step is to 'brainstorm' your proposed presentation. If it is a group presentation, meet with your group members and write down your thoughts and ideas on the presentation topic. Look at the topic from different points of view. Research the topic to find out the latest information. Get statistics, illustrations, references and quotations to back up your points.

However, be careful not to collect 'too much' information, as this will risk taking too much time. If it is a group presentation, normally, you will be quite limited in the amount of time you have – often only around five minutes. As a team, you need to decide on what each member will do. Usually each student completes some research and talks about this as part of the presentation. Ensure your research is relevant and ties in with the topic given. Plan several group meetings to check that the content is not repetitive. Check that you all have the same style and practise clear hand-over points where the next group member moves the presentation on to the next speaker.

Decide if you will involve the audience in your presentation – it is often a good idea to do this. You can ask particular questions at certain stages in the presentation to make the audience feel more involved. This can help to hold the audience's interest and keep them focused on your presentation.

Consider ways to create a 'rapport' (good relationship; pronounced with a silent 't') with your audience. Anticipate likely questions or counter-arguments that may arise from your presentation, and prepare outline responses for a question-and-answer (Q&A) session.

Preparing your presentation

Structure your points on index cards or slides, using headings and bullet points. Select the materials you will use according to the aim and objectives of your talk and the audience. It is better to say too little, but with a clear message, than to say too much and run out of time.

Organise your material into a beginning, middle and an end so that it flows. Begin by preparing the middle, e.g. give the best evidence to support your case and anticipate likely objections. You can then add the introduction and the conclusion after you have decided on your main arguments. Ensure that one piece of information links to the next one, using signposting and markers to help the audience.

Being specific and relevant

Do not overwhelm the audience with too much information. Explain key terms clearly. Technical terms and statistical information may be better referred to or presented graphically rather than talked through. You could use a supporting visual aid or handout for numerical information. Think of practical examples and your own experiences to get your points across clearly. This will also make your presentation more credible and more interesting.

It is only when you have organised the main part that you can think of the introduction and the conclusion to your presentation. The conclusion should flow naturally from the main section. It will summarise the main points you made, and end on either a conclusive or challenging note, in accordance with the purpose of your presentation. Leave the audience with something to think about. The introduction should be the last part you prepare. This section involves introducing yourself (and your group) and the subject of your talk. This is followed by setting the subject in context and stating the objectives of your presentation.

Using visual aids

Use appropriate visual aids – slides, photos, flip charts etc. – for your presentation. This will enhance your presentation and keep the audience's attention. Importantly, it also means that you won't forget what you are going to

say, because the information is already on your slides or your flip chart etc.

All visual aids should be legible and clear for the audience. Do not stand in front of the visual aid, blocking the audience from seeing it. If you use handouts, do not hand them out too soon, as the audience will begin reading them and stop listening to your presentation. It is often better to provide handouts at the end of your talk. Check any equipment in advance – not just before you present – and have a backup plan in case the equipment fails on the day.

Do not present too much visual information, and check that everyone in the audience will be able to read it – even from the back of the room. Do not read your visual aids, as you will risk boring the audience. Do not rush through, as the audience will need some time to absorb the visual information. It is also a good idea to have a paper copy of your visuals so you can use these in case there is an equipment failure.

Using graphs and charts

Make sure that the audience knows what your diagrams, charts and figures mean. For example, if you are going to use graphs, clearly label the axes and indicate the unit of measurement being used. Ensure the scale is as large as possible, so it will be easy for the audience to read. You must indicate the source of the data, using correct referencing.

Using notes

Never read your presentation from notes. Notes are used to remind you of the things you need to say, not to read from during your talk, so only use headings and bullet points. Put your notes on index cards. Number the cards or tie them together so they do not get mixed up. When you give the presentation, point to important things on your visual aids, but also make sure that you turn and look at the audience as much as you can.

Practice and nerves

It is always a good idea to practise delivering your presentation to the rest of the group and time the length of it precisely. Every presenter is nervous, and for Chinese students, the main worry will be using English in a very public environment. However, if you have practised delivering the presentation many times, you will be fine. The best way to deal with the inevitable nerves you will feel is to be very well organised and to have rehearsed the presentation several times.

Body language

When you practise your presentation you need to be aware of your nonverbal communication, or 'body language'. This means your physical appearance, eye contact and body language such as gestures, facial expressions and the way you stand or move around. The audience can be distracted if you are not 'natural' in front of them.

- Try to stay close to the audience, avoiding barriers such as tables, and make sure the audience can see you.
- Keep your head up when you speak, otherwise your voice will be projected into the floor, which makes it inaudible. By not standing straight, shoulders back, you will not be making direct eye contact with the audience and you will not appear confident.
- Avoid fixing your eyes on one person, i.e. the tutor – and ignoring the rest of the audience. This will cause the audience to lose interest since they will feel you are not speaking to them.
- Make sure you glance across the audience occasionally. Be careful that you do not end up looking at your slides and ignoring the audience.

Question time

Question time often opens up the topic and allows for a wider discussion to occur. The audience can show their understanding of the topic, clarifications can be made, and misunderstandings can be cleared up by the presenter. If the audience do not ask questions, you can initiate the dialogue by asking the audience a question yourself. Listen carefully to the questions the audience ask you. It is important to repeat each question so that everyone knows what is being answered and you can ensure you interpreted it correctly. Have your pre-prepared answers in mind.

If you do not hear the question, ask the person to repeat it or rephrase it, e.g. 'I'm sorry, I didn't quite hear that – are you asking me whether or not...?' or 'I'm sorry – could you repeat that question please?'

If someone makes a comment, without asking a question, listen to what they have to say and then move on to the next question. If a questioner is hostile or negative, remain composed without getting into an argument with him/her.

Presentation assessment

The following aspects of your presentation will normally be assessed by your tutor:

- **Content and quality of argument** – accuracy and relevance; clarity of argumentation/ explanation; currency of information; level of interest; level of independent research.
- **Planning/organisation of the material** – evidence of prior planning; logical order of the content; introduction/summary/conclusion.
- **Linkage/signposting** – the use of signposting and frames; explicit linking between different parts of the presentation.
- **Use of language** – Was the language grammatical, well expressed and understandable by others? Could everybody hear the presentation?
- **Use of body language** – appropriate use of gestures; facial expressions; eye contact; posture; personal appearance).
- **Support materials** – How appropriate were the materials for supporting the delivery of the content? How well were they used?
- **Use of time** – How well was the presentation timed and paced?
- **Group functioning** – how well were the roles defined and executed? How cohesive and co-ordinated does the group appear to be?
- **Audience** – Was there good interaction with the audience? How well was the audience's interest held?
- **Response to questions** – How well did the presenter respond to questions put to him/her?
- **Overall impression** – How did the entire presentation link together?

THINK 4.2

Reflect on any presentation you might have given as a student, either in China or in the UK. What were the most difficult things about the presentation? Using what you have learnt from this section on presentations, write a reflective paragraph in the space provided in the Appendix, answering the following questions:

- What went well about the presentation?
- What could have been improved about the presentation?
- How could I improve my future presentations?

Module assignment feedback

Getting feedback on your performance is very important to all students, but particularly international students, working in unfamiliar academic environments.

Your assignments will normally be marked by a group of tutors who teach on the same module or modules. Feedback is often written, and can consist of 'generic' feedback which gives you a general idea of what was good or bad about your assignment. The feedback might also be specific, and give you detailed comment on what you have written. You should also ask to see your tutor personally about your assignment if you do not understand any of the feedback.

Assignments are marked according to marking criteria which are designed to assess how well you have achieved the module learning outcomes. Typical criteria for academic assignments would include all the important aspects of your learning such as knowledge of the module; the ability to analyse, synthesise and evaluate information, and so on.

How to use feedback to improve

EXAMPLE

TABLE 4.15   Typical feedback comments from tutors and suggested response

Tutor comment	Suggested response to feedback
Too descriptive	Make sure that you include more critical evaluation next time. This means that you not only describe the issue but also compare and contrast the different 'expert' views.
Your argument isn't clear	Make sure that you understand the various arguments concerning the issue. Check with your tutor if you don't. Make sure that you present the arguments clearly, using 'signposts' in your writing ('Next', 'finally' etc.)
The writing is often disorganised and incoherent	Coherence refers to how the points you make are logically joined together. Make sure you have used signposts, and introduced each point, followed by the reasons why you think the point is relevant and important, and say how it links with the next point etc.
The writing is not cohesive; many grammar mistakes; too assertive, without adequate evidence; poor referencing and lack of academic style	Cohesion refers to your grammar and vocabulary. Use the proofreading tips in Chapter 2 to help you find grammar mistakes. Ask a friend to read through your assignment and also check for you. Use a spell-check program on your computer. Use the information in this book to make sure that you are using the correct academic style. Make sure that your referencing is complete and correct and in the right style for your module.

(Continued)

(Continued)

Tutor comment	Suggested response to feedback
Not enough critical evaluation	Make sure you compare and contrast the different expert views, indicating strengths and weaknesses as seen by the experts and yourself.
So what?	Make sure that you indicate to the reader why you have included a particular expert view or a particular argument. What do you see as the possible implications and consequences of the arguments?

Examinations

This section gives advice about effective exam preparation and strategies for successful exam completion. UK institutions use many different forms of exam assessment, including:

- closed examinations, where you are not allowed to refer to books or notes, and have a specific time to complete a certain number of questions;
- open examinations, where you can refer to books and notes and may even be able to take the question paper away and return it by a certain time;
- assessed assignments, individual projects and dissertations;
- group work projects;
- portfolios (a collection of work);
- presentations to a tutor;
- a display or performance of work (for example, an art show or music performance);
- practical assessments (for example, in laboratories or on hospital wards).

Some modules are 'continuously assessed', meaning that instead of examinations at the end of the year, your progress is assessed on your coursework performance throughout the semester.

Exam techniques

Pre-exam preparation

Chinese students are normally very used to traditional closed exams. Many modules still have quite a heavy assessment weighting with regard to the final exam, so it is worth being highly organised and preparing well for exams. The first issue is revision.

Organise your revision time

Organise your revision well before the actual exam. Firstly, check the exam date, time and venue. It's also a good idea to actually visit the room before the exam day, so you know its exact location and layout. Then make yourself a revision timetable like the one below.

EXAMPLE

TABLE 4.16 A typical exam revision timetable for a business student

Monday	Tuesday	Wednesday	Thursday	Friday	Saturday	Sunday
			Morning			
English exam revision	Module lectures	Business exam revision	Module tutorials	Economics exam revision	Statistics exam revision	Marketing exam revision
			Afternoon			
Human resources exam revision	Business exam revision	Module lectures	Module lectures	Module tutorials	Economics exam revision	English exam revision
			Evening			
Statistics exam revision	Management theory exam revision	Marketing exam revision	Strategy exam revision	Strategy exam revision	Break	Break

Preparation

- Look at past exam papers if available.
- Look at your module handbook and identify learning outcomes being tested and any grading criteria given – perhaps list the items being tested, to give you a clearer picture of what you need to research.
- Go over all lecture and seminar topics, ensuring you have covered everything listed, including topics that were briefly covered or mentioned during the module.
- Use the reading list in the module guide to begin your research. Read more than is on the list – to get a good grade you need to show you have read widely and beyond the list given. Using one module text alone will not get you a good grade.
- Thoroughly research the area identified using books, journals, databases, newspapers, websites, magazines, etc. Ensure your sources are as recent as possible.

- Make a revision timetable and discipline yourself to use it.
- Practise your handwriting – exams put a lot of strain on your hand, and if you have only been using a keyboard before the exam, you need to make sure that you practise your handwriting before the exam so that it is neat and clear.

For open book exams, because you can bring textbooks/notes into your exam, you need to follow these tips:

- Look at your module handbook and learning outcomes to see what you are expected to know. Identify themes and issues that could be raised as exam questions.
- Look at past exam papers if available.
- Make yourself a revision timetable. You should be very familiar with your textbooks – you should to be writing, not searching or reading, in the exam. Time will pass very quickly.
- Organise your file or folder by topic or by learning outcome using section dividers. Set up a table of contents for your notes.
- Note section numbers, paragraph numbers, lecture numbers – in order to reference theory and case evidence in the exam.
- Highlight key points and annotate the resources you will be allowed to take into the exam, e.g. textbook, case study or folder. Place markers in the book, case study or folder – use index cards, sticky notes, tabs, highlight pens, use colour coding, mind-maps and cross-referencing to clearly mark summaries, headings and sections.
- Prepare brief, concise notes on ideas and concepts that could be tested. Include your own commentary on each topic as it can strengthen your argument and demonstrate that you have thought it through.
- Do some further reading on the subject in question. Carry out analysis so that you can use the outcomes of that analysis in your answers.

Prepare yourself the night before your exam so that you do not get too stressed, although some stress will be natural. Set your alarm clock, and also have a backup alarm. Make sure you have your student identity card ready, and any other items such as your candidate number and any equipment you will need. Make sure you take two of each piece of equipment, like pens and pencils. If you will need a calculator, make sure it is approved by your college or university. Make sure you know which room the exam will be held in. Go there and check the day before to make sure that you know how to get there on time.

You can also work out timings for the number of questions you must answer. If you are going to do a two-hour exam and you are required to answer three questions, this means that you have 120 minutes for three questions. However, if you also allow 5–10 minutes at the beginning to read, select and plan the questions, and you allow 5–10 minutes at the end to edit and complete unfinished answers, you will only have approximately 100 minutes to answer the 3 questions.

Starting the exam

- Listen carefully to the invigilator's instructions.
- Allow up to 10 minutes to read all the questions carefully. Check if you have any compulsory questions (i.e. ones you must answer) and what the instructions are. Select the questions you will answer. Cross out ones you will not do.
- Check the number of questions to be answered and how much time you will allocate to each one. Note down the timings next to the questions you will answer.
- Re-read the paper to decode the questions. Read the questions and make sure you focus on the exact question set. What exactly are the questions asking you? Highlight key terms in the question such as 'evaluate' or 'to what extent'.
- Start with familiar, well-known topics. If there is a multiple-choice section, it might be a good idea to start there. Multiple-choice questions help remind you of vocabulary and familiarise you with the topic.
- Quickly plan your answers and perhaps note down a quick structure at the top of the paper, making sure the structure will answer the question, addressing the focus of the question. Use brainstorming or mindmaps to generate ideas. Make quick notes to help unlock your mind and provide you with well-thought-out and structured answers. Note any formulae or laws you may need to include.
- Finally, don't just sit there – start to write. Use a general sentence to get you into the answer. Your time is limited, so you need to be well organised to quickly find the data, quotes, examples and arguments that you use in your answers. Leave a space after any questions which you think you could write more on later. However, don't forget to come back to the questions.
- Provide relevant evidence from the case study, textbook or lecture notes – not only what you underlined. Models, tools and frameworks may be referred to but don't just describe them. Write concise, accurate, thoughtful answers based on evidence. Do not use quotations – paraphrase all the information into your own words. It is your words and your argument that count. In open book exams, do not copy out long quotations: use your own argument, referring to the material.
- You don't normally need to reference in exams, unless it is an open book exam. However, it is always good to reference all important theory, even if you can only remember the name of the theorist.
- Keep an eye on the time during the exam. Leave your watch on the desk, so you are aware of the time.
- Keep checking back to ensure you are answering the exact question, not just writing everything you know. Try to write as neatly as you can so that your answers will be easy for the person who marks your exam to read. Write neatly and number answers clearly, starting each on a new page.
- Aim to allow sufficient time to check and proofread your work, and finish off any parts that you left, before the deadline.
- Ensure you answer all the questions required of you.

Open book exams

Increasingly, you will find that modules in the UK use 'open book' exams, rather than the traditional exam where you have to memorise a lot of information. This is because many students are not good at memorising and if they are just memorising things for the exam, they are probably not really understanding the issues and theories.

Open book exams are exams where you are given the materials and resources that you will need for the exam – perhaps a case study, or a chapter from a book, or specific questions which you will need to research on the day of the exam. So you use specified resources, either in the actual exam, or in preparation for it. This type of exam involves applying your module knowledge, and showing understanding of the module content. This also involves problem solving and critical evaluation skills.

Another type of open book exam involves a tutor giving you a task, case study or question in advance to research and prepare for a prescribed date. This could be to complete a task or questions under general ('closed book') exam conditions, or under various open book exam conditions set by your tutor. Check that you know what you need to do, which resources you can use, and which resources you need to bring to the exam venue.

For an open book exam, you can bring resources which you have prepared into the exam room. Your tutor will tell you in advance whether to bring your notes, a textbook, a folder, a case study, etc. You will be tested on your understanding and application of the material, so you can consult the allowed resources during the exam. You discuss and research the material before the exam but you do not know the actual exam task(s) until you see them in the exam paper.

For example, students with a case study are usually expected to:

1. Apply theoretical knowledge to situations in the case study.
2. Analyse elements and relationships in the case study.
3. Evaluate with supporting evidence, include using the materials.
4. Solve problems and suggest alternative solutions.
5. Draw on any additional reading around the case study and/or subject.
6. Reference sources of information.

Scenarios

In this situation, you will be given a brief about the area to be tested in advance. You will be given a 'scenario' – a situation based on the real world – and you need to carry out secondary research on the topic before the exam date using materials you consider appropriate.

On the exam day you will be given a task to complete in an allocated time scale, e.g. a critically evaluative report, in a time frame of a few hours, and in a secure room. This type of exam may be given to you in an exam room or sent to you electronically (sometimes called an 'online' exam).

Chapter 4: Key words and concepts – English and Chinese

abstract – 概要

analysis – 分析

assessment – 评估

assignment – 作业

critical – 评判性的

discussion – 讨论

draft – 草稿

evaluate – 评估

executive – 执行的

feedback – 反馈

flow – 流畅

flowing – 流畅的

function – 功能

investigation – 调查

linked – 联系的

log – 记录

nerves – 神经

online – 线上/网上

outcome – 结果

persuasive – 有说服力的

portfolio – 学习记录文件夹

relevant – 相关的

review – 回顾复习

scope – 范围

specific – 特别的

structure – 构架

summary – 总结

threats – 威胁

visual aid – 视觉焦距

CHAPTER 4: TEST YOURSELF

Put an ✘ for an incorrect statement and a ✓ for a correct statement. Check your answers in the Appendix.

1 'Analyse' means to break a topic, issues, concept etc. into the main parts. .... ☐

2 'Evaluate' means the same as 'analyse'. .... ☐

3 'Discuss' just means to talk about something. .... ☐

4 Reflective writing should always be positive and aim at improvement. .... ☐

5 It is best not to rehearse oral presentations, so that your presentation will be fresh and interesting. .... ☐

(Continued)

(Continued)

6 You should read your presentation from notes so that you don't forget what you want to say. ☐

7 It is essential to make a revision timetable before an exam. ☐

8 Open book exams require the answers to be referenced. ☐

9 It is important to read the module guide to make sure that your assignments show that you are achieving the module learning outcomes. ☐

10 If your tutor writes 'So what?' on your assignment, it means that you did not make it clear why you have included this particular information, or what the consequences might be. ☐

Chapter 4: Reflection box

Write some notes below about what is the same and what is different about assignments and assessments in the UK and in China:

Assignments in China

Assignments in the UK

Assessments in China

Assessments in the UK

5

Research and dissertations

Introduction

Since research is so fundamental to academic activity, we have devoted this last chapter entirely to that subject.

All students in the UK have to learn how to research. Every time you have to write an assignment, you will need to know how to find the best information – where to find it and how to evaluate the information. This is often

called 'secondary' research – using other researchers' information. You may also have to engage in what is called 'primary' research sometimes. This means getting the information yourself by interviewing people or sending out questionnaires, for example. For both undergraduate and postgraduate programmes, you may have to do a longer research project, and write a long research report called a dissertation.

However, we have often found that students can be very confused by the enormous amount of research-method information available. Chinese students, and other students whose first language is not English, have particular problems with the difficult words and concepts, and the different and often complex philosophical approaches to research methodology. This chapter is not a substitute for your research methods course, or other more comprehensive research methods books. It is essentially a simple guide which clearly explains the basic information you need to understand in order to complete successful research projects in UK Higher Education.

Many Chinese students are still attracted to the UK for postgraduate study, despite the growth of trans-national campuses set up by UK universities in China. Many postgraduate students are very unsure about 'research' and what a research degree is. This chapter will provide you with important information about research, and what is required for successful completion of research-based qualifications.

Chapter 5: Xiangping's study tips

毕业论文或者毕业设计是学习中最重要的一部分，它不仅象征着大学学习的一个总结，更是大学毕业后的一个起点。所以，选择毕业论文/设计的课题至关重要。

- **课题选择**：你要知道作毕业论文/设计与平时学习中的作业有很大的不同，最重要的一点就是，平时的作业和报告一般都是老师给你指定的题目。而在你的毕业论文/设计中，你有很大的自由和空间，可以自己选择自己喜欢的课题，彰显自己的创造力、创新力。
- **时间把握**：在做毕业论文/设计的过程中，时间是你自己的，一般没有固定的论文课程，所以你要自己把握时间进行写作。你会和你的导师联系，不过导师是引导左右，一般会给你意见和建议，但是不会告诉你应该怎么办。
- **管理关系**：你和被分派给你的导师的关系很重要。在做论文/设计的过程你，你要自己采取主动：主动联系老师，修改老师给你的反馈，安排论文辅导。

- **掌握信息**：每个学校和学院对论文/设计的要求不同，所以你一定要对学校的论文要求要仔细阅读掌握，了解详细的要求、规定、截至日期。如果你没能很好地了解信息，你所做的可能不合乎学校的规定。

一般论文的结构如下：

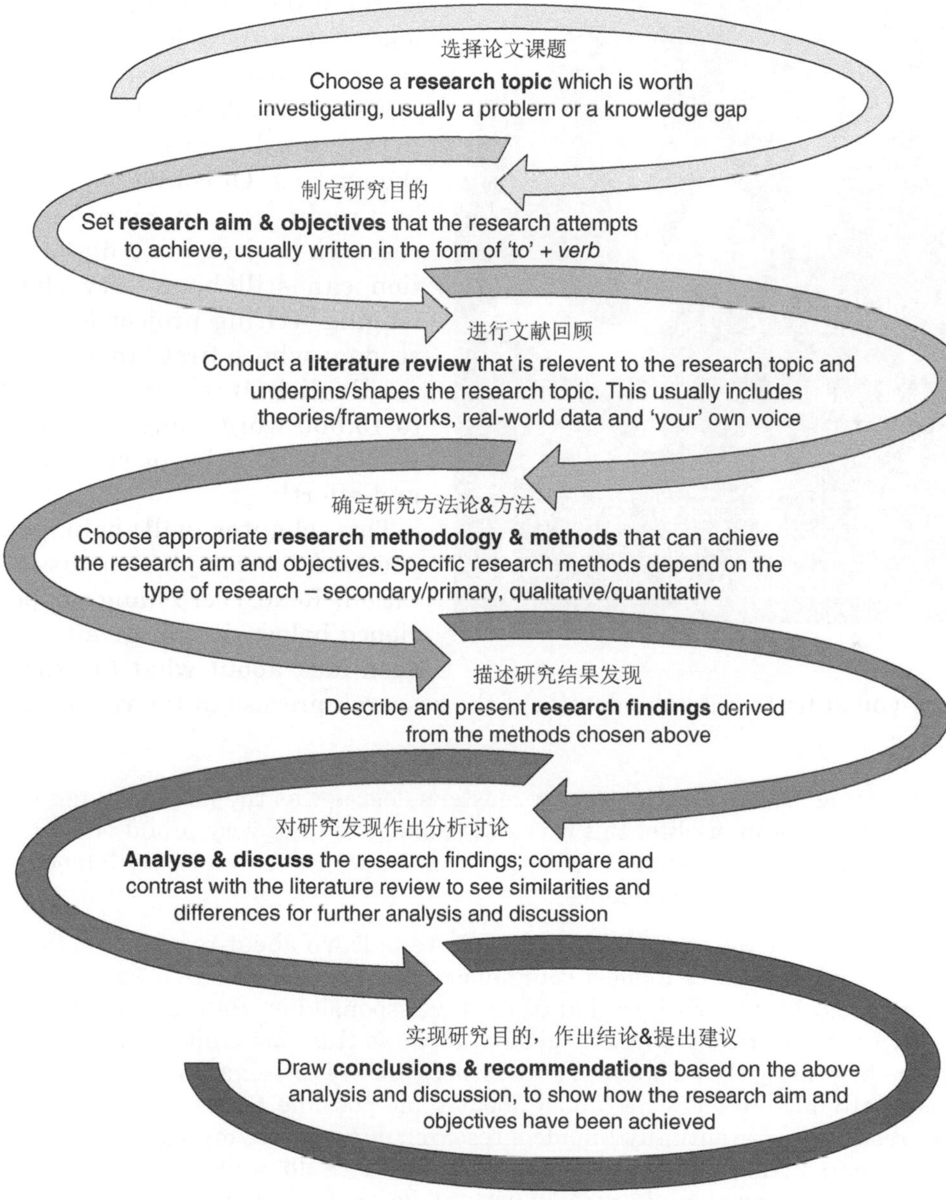

选择论文课题
Choose a **research topic** which is worth investigating, usually a problem or a knowledge gap

制定研究目的
Set **research aim & objectives** that the research attempts to achieve, usually written in the form of 'to' + *verb*

进行文献回顾
Conduct a **literature review** that is relevent to the research topic and underpins/shapes the research topic. This usually includes theories/frameworks, real-world data and 'your' own voice

确定研究方法论&方法
Choose appropriate **research methodology & methods** that can achieve the research aim and objectives. Specific research methods depend on the type of research – secondary/primary, qualitative/quantitative

描述研究结果发现
Describe and present **research findings** derived from the methods chosen above

对研究发现作出分析讨论
Analyse & discuss the research findings; compare and contrast with the literature review to see similarities and differences for further analysis and discussion

实现研究目的，作出结论&提出建议
Draw **conclusions & recommendations** based on the above analysis and discussion, to show how the research aim and objectives have been achieved

FIGURE 5.1

Dissertations

Many Chinese students who come to the UK will have to complete a 'dissertation' as part of their degree programme. A dissertation is a long research report, based on a research project which students are expected to propose, design and complete themselves. Of course, you will be taught how to carry out a research project, but a dissertation can still be a very challenging writing project for any student whose first language is not English. It is usually 10,000 to 15,000 words long, and so it will take up a lot of your time and effort!

This chapter will help you successfully complete a dissertation. Read Cici Zhang's experience below. It will give you a good idea about what to expect before you start to read the details of the research process in the rest of the chapter.

Completing my dissertation for my master's degree was the hardest thing I have ever done in my life! But it is also something I am very proud of. The dissertation process taught me so much and gave me so much confidence and increased my independence.

When you start your master's, you will have to learn about research methods. You will also have to meet your supervisor to talk about what you want to research. I was surprised that it was my responsibility to find a research topic. I thought that I would be given a topic, so this was a bit hard for me in the beginning. But I was very lucky because my dissertation supervisor was really nice to me. She talked about some possible topics I might find interesting, and eventually I made a research question for myself, and then my research aim and objectives, and finally I could write my research proposal. The proposal is very important because it is the plan of your research. She helped me a lot during this first part of the dissertation. She also helped me a lot during my research, but she was only supposed to have a fixed number of meetings with me during my master's programme. I know from talking to my friends that the most important thing about your supervisor is that he or she is able to make you feel happy about what you are doing, because doing dissertation research can sometimes be very stressful.

Sometimes, I felt very scared because I did not know if I was doing the right things, but I knew that I could not keep asking my supervisor about everything. I did not want to trouble her too much. I thought she would think that I was not a good student because she told me that I was expected to be independent. I was not used to this because, in China, our teachers always told us what to do. But gradually, I learnt to find things out for myself. There are lots of books about research in the library, and also other students and tutors who you can ask if you are not sure about something. Another problem was my English. It took me a long time to read some of the things I needed to read for my research. You have to make a proposal for your research, saying what you want to research and why you think it is important. To do this, you have to write a literature review. This means that you need to read what other researchers have already found out about your topic. Research journals can give you the best information for this, but they were hard for me to understand because they are written in academic language, with many ideas and words I did not understand at first. I was worried that my reading was too slow.

I often got scared if I asked my friends what they had already completed. It always seemed that they had done much more than me. Sometimes, I did not know if I was working hard enough. Sometimes I got a bit depressed and worried. I could not fail! I could not go back to China and face my family and friends if I failed! Unfortunately, this thought gave me a lot of pressure. I remember that for some weeks, I couldn't sleep or eat properly because I was always thinking about my dissertation. I never had time for anything else and did not go out with friends. Maybe I should have allowed myself to relax more, and look after myself more, but always I had this thought about what would happen if I failed!

You will not really know if you have passed the dissertation until it has been marked at the end of your programme. But your supervisor will normally tell you if they think that you need to work harder or if you need to change things. My supervisor was able to help me make a timetable of the things I needed to do, and the time period that I needed to do them in. This helped me organise my time. I know that some of my friends who failed the dissertation did so because they did not organise themselves well. Some of them went back to China for holidays, and left everything until they got back. Then they could not catch up.

Not long before the final deadline, I lost my confidence again, and felt that my dissertation was not good enough. I found writing it quite hard, and I knew that I had many grammar mistakes. Supervisors will not normally correct your work for you, so I asked an English friend if he would help me correct my English. Luckily, he wanted to learn some Chinese, so we made a good deal! After this, I felt better and worked very hard to finish it. I made sure I left enough time to get my dissertation properly printed and bound, and when I submitted it on time, I felt very relieved. I still had to wait for some weeks for the result, and I was already back in China when the result was published. It was the happiest day of my life when I found out that I had passed!

Cici Zhang

What is research?

The word 'research' can refer to just getting information for your undergraduate assignment, or it can refer to finding out information for an undergraduate or postgraduate 'dissertation'. A dissertation is a long research report – usually from 10,000 to 15,000 words, although it can be much longer.

Research basically means investigating an area of interest to answer a question. It is actually what you do if you want to buy anything – say, a new mobile phone. You start off with an inductive guess (hypothesis), for example that the new smartphone will be the best one for your needs. You then go on to visit phone shops and gather deductive (detective work) and empirical (real-world) evidence to support or not support (but never 'prove') your original hypothesis. How many shops do you need to visit? Ideally, include the largest evidence base you can. What other data sources do you need to consult? Ideally, these should not be biased (subjective) sources like smartphone salespeople, but authoritative and refereed communications journals (checked by expert editors) and independent practitioner (trade) sources, such as consumer magazines for example. Research always involves finding out new things and evaluating information. There are many ways to do this.

Both undergraduate and postgraduate Chinese students will be involved in research to some extent, and postgraduate degrees are purely research degrees. Research for a research-based module or degree programme consists of:

1. agreeing a research topic with your tutor (often called a 'research supervisor');
2. finding out what other researchers have said about the topic from their research (secondary research evidence);

3. completing your own research into the topic (primary research evidence);
4. finally compiling a research report on the basis of your evidence, which is 'balanced' (includes many different academic and professional views on the topic).

Research is **NOT**:

1. finding out about a topic and writing everything you have found out;
2. finding out about a topic to confirm your previous ideas about the topic;
3. finding out about 'famous' brands and companies, popular products, hobbies, travel destinations etc.
4. trying to solve major global problems and advising governments how to do this.

It is also important to realise that research never 'proves' anything. In the academic world, we use the word 'prove' in a different way from the way we normally use the word. You can never prove anything with research, because it is always possible for other researchers to find new evidence to change the way that we think about all topics. Research finds evidence, using reliable evidence collection methods, to provide a reasonable answer to your initial research question.

THINK 5.1

Think about your own research experience and answer the following questions. You may have more research experience than you think!

Have you ever done any research before?

What did you research and why?

What kind of research was it?

Was your research successful?

How do you know?

Evidence-based research

All research requires you to gather information, either from experiment or observation, or by discovering relevant information. This information is your 'evidence' which is relevant to the issue you are researching. Students will often be expected to conduct not only their own secondary research of other

researchers' findings and publications, but also their own primary research in the form of questionnaires and interviews etc. This is fundamental to 'an evidence-based approach' to learning.

However, Chinese students have often come from a mainly 'fact-based' education in China, where the belief is that what academics say is to be learnt and not to be seriously questioned. Consequently, you might think that 'research' for assignments or dissertations is finding out as much as possible about a subject and then presenting this as a relatively detailed, unquestioning description. Unfortunately, this approach to research is contrary to UK research methodology, which relies on finding out both supporting and non-supporting 'evidence' and then evaluating the evidence to make conclusions.

There is also another problem that we have often found – that in Chinese research perceptions, there is a tendency to only use supporting evidence. You might not want to use any information that does not seem to agree with your own ideas about the issue. You might see this as weakening your own research. It is always a great temptation to only use information which seems to support your own ideas, particularly because 'arguments' in the Chinese tradition are normally 'won' by constant repetition of evidence which appears to support the initial research assumption. However, this would not be regarded as 'balanced' research.

All research starts with an inductive 'guess' (hypothesis) about possible connections between things. However, it is normally only science or engineering students who use hypotheses to research a possible relationship between issues or events. A hypothesis is generally only appropriate for 'scientific' research because this type of research process is designed to 'test' the hypothesis.

Actually, as you can see in the next section, it usually tests three types of hypotheses concerning the possible relationship between two 'variables' X and Y (variables are parts of the issue, or problem things which 'vary' or change). You cannot easily or ethically experiment on humans, so in the social sciences, this kind of scientific or 'positivist' research is not normally feasible; but you might use this type of research if you are studying engineering, finance, chemistry etc. – any subject which involves a lot of numbers and quantification.

Scientific research

Scientific or 'positivist' research is research which 'tests' things – usually under controlled laboratory conditions. It was originally thought to be the best and most objective type of research, precisely because it appeared to control the things which might change in the research situation (the variables). However, even scientists realised that when they studied things under laboratory conditions, they also had an effect on what was being studied. So they realised they could not be as objective as they thought.

With this type of scientific (positivist) research, you usually set up three types of hypothesis, then gather data (evidence), and finally 'test' the hypotheses to see which hypothesis is more likely to be acceptable:

1. Hypothesis type 1: There is a measurable positive relation between X and Y (positive hypothesis).
2. Hypothesis type 2: There is no measurable relationship between X and Y (null hypothesis).
3. Hypothesis type 3: There is a measurable negative relationship between X and Y (negative hypothesis).

For example, if you are an economics student, your positive hypothesis might be that the variation in bank interest rates over a period of time has a relationship with the inflation rate. You might guess (hypothesise) that lower interest rates put more borrowing power in the hands of consumers so that they spend more. When consumers spend more, the economy grows, creating inflation. You can gather inflation rate data and interest rate data over a period of time in different economies to test this hypothesis, and finally conclude which one of the three above is supported by your results.

Grounded research and structured research

There are generally two types of approach to research in UK Higher Education institutions: grounded research and structured research.

With grounded research, you take a long and detailed look at the issues first. You carry out preliminary investigations of the topic and you look for 'gaps' in what is already known about the issue from other research. Then you find existing theories which might help you to construct your own research investigation and which will help you explain your data. If you are a PhD student, you might also be expected to create your own theory on the basis of other theories. If you have time, this is probably the best type of research and is called 'grounded' research, but it is usually only practical for PhD programmes which are longer than a year, and where you are expected to produce your own theory.

The grounded theory method is a research method which is actually the opposite of the usual method of undergraduate and master's research. You don't start with a hypothesis or research aim, but with your data collection. This data forms the basis for your own theory.

Most student research in the UK uses what we can call a 'structured' approach because of time limitations.

Structured research starts with a research question which is then investigated using established theories. This is the most common type of undergraduate and postgraduate research in UK Higher Education. The structure of the research process is clearly defined from the proposal to the dissertation. It always involves a literature search where relevant theory is found first, and this is then evaluated against the student's actual research findings (i.e. do your findings support what the theory says should happen?). The process has to be well defined in order to fit into the tight timeframe of an undergraduate final year or a postgraduate year.

Primary and secondary research and triangulation

Primary research is research that involves collecting first-hand primary data. Primary data is data you get yourself, usually by interviewing people, sending out questionnaires, etc.

Secondary research is research that contains data that other researchers have already obtained, such as the literature in your literature review. It is possible to do a research project just using secondary data.

However, it is better if data can be collected from at least three sources so that it is 'triangulated'. The term 'triangulation' is taken from navigation, where a location is 'fixed' by taking directional data from three points. A fix from three points is more accurate than a fix from two. The same principle is applied to research data. If you have three sources of data for your research, the resulting description is likely to be more accurate.

Quantitative, qualitative and interpretive research designs

In very simple terms, quantitative methods are used with data which you can 'count' such as numbers. Statistical data is quantitative.

Qualitative data is data that you cannot count (such as interview data) but it can be used to discover patterns and trends, and add 'depth' to existing descriptions of a phenomenon. In practice, you also have to make qualitative data quantitative by 'coding' it so that you can organise the data for your analysis and put it into categories to help reveal patterns, trends and themes.

Because you need to 'interpret' the patterns you find from qualitative data, it is sometimes called 'interpretive', and qualitative research designs are therefore sometimes called 'interpretive' research designs.

Mixed and creative research designs

In practice, most research designs are actually 'mixed' – they will have some quantitative and some qualitative data. Some researchers think that such designs are confusing, but generally, researchers see mixed designs as advantageous because they help to look at data in different and complementary ways. Most research designs you will be involved in will be mixed.

Depending on your institution and your subject, your research project could just include the standard qualitative and quantitative methods we have outlined, or it might include more creative research designs, incorporating video, diaries, photographs, and collecting people's stories and experiences, feelings and ideas etc. Whatever the methods you finally use, the basic principles we have outlined in this chapter will apply, and your data – qualitative or quantitative – will need to be collected and analysed, and finally reported on, using the same basic research principles. Check with your tutor or your supervisor about more creative research formats if your institution allows.

Research topic

If you have to complete a research project as part of your degree programme, how do you start to choose your topic? What do you actually want to research and why? Generally, students are expected to develop their own topic after some detailed reading of a general topic area. Do not expect your supervisor to define your topic.

You should make sure that you have a strong interest in the topic yourself, and the topic must also be clearly related in some way to your modules. Be prepared to put your own ideas forward, but accept that your supervisor has far more experience than you, so don't be surprised if he or she suggests that you change your ideas.

Firstly, think about possible topics. Start with what really interests you. It is no good choosing a topic that you will be bored with, or that you will find difficult to research because there is not much data available. Once you have decided on general areas, do some research to find which of these areas is already well researched so that there is a lot of 'expert' data already available. For a master's, you should generally look for areas where there has already been a lot of research by expert researchers. This will make your research aims and objectives and your literature review much easier. It is different if you are doing a PhD. This is the highest research degree, and with a PhD you are expected to make an original contribution to knowledge, so you will actually be looking for 'gaps' in current knowledge, where there is currently not much information.

General 'tips' for choosing a research area are:

1. Choose an area/issue that you are motivated by and preferably already know something about.
2. Think about researching a topic that might be connected with your future career – this can be very useful at future career interviews.
3. Check the library and databases and make sure there is plenty of relevant current data that you can use. Do not pick a topic that is not researchable – one that you cannot get good data for.
4. Be realistic: do not try to do a PhD thesis for an undergraduate dissertation! You do not have to produce knowledge breakthroughs with your dissertation – just demonstrate that you can undertake and complete a modest and extended piece of academic research in the correct academic way.

The formal requirements of the dissertation will impose some limitations on the choice of subject. It has to be your own work, so do not choose something that someone else has already researched unless your approach will be very different. Draw up a shortlist of possible topics using the following guide:

- Is there something that you have come across in your modules that you did not have time to explore properly and would like to?
- What is currently happening in your field of study?

- Has a new data source become available? Do you have contacts with a business which could give you the basis for a dissertation? (Good for the business and good for you.)
- Has someone published a case study which it would be interesting to replicate in a different context?
- Is there some literature in your field that you are critical of, or a train of thought you would like to follow? Do you feel you have something important to contribute to the debate?
- Do you have some personal experience that you would like to draw on? For example, maybe you have experienced bad customer service which has set you thinking about how to improve customer relations in general.

Avoid very big subjects set in the future, such as 'What will be the impact of current Chinese government policy on the Chinese economy?' This is not only far too broad, but there will not be enough reliable data, and too much speculation on your part will be involved.

THINK 5.2

What do you want to do when you finish your study in the UK? What type of career do you want?

If you have the chance to do some original research as part of your study programme, think about a research topic that you would like to research which might be beneficial for your future career. Make some notes in the reflection box at the end of this chapter. Using the chapter information, include some ideas about how you might research the topic.

Topic focus

Once you have decided your topic, you then need to 'focus' it – narrow it down to a specific issue in a specific location. Ask yourself these questions

- Is this subject specific enough?
- Is this subject narrow enough?
- Do I have a clear aim – a clear question to answer?
- Do I have a feasible approach to the subject?
- Is there enough substance in the topic to make a complete dissertation or is this looking like only a piece of market research?
- Am I enthusiastic about this subject?

The research question

Your preliminary choice of topic and the reading for your preliminary literature review should have given you a good idea of the main issues in your chosen topic area, and perhaps the issues that still appear to be under-researched. This should lead you to making a preliminary research question.

After you have agreed a research question with your tutor, you can then start to decide on which research methodology and research methods you might use. Research questions which lead to qualitative research design and qualitative data collection methods normally involve further questions of the following types:

Definitional: What are the defining features?

Descriptive: How can we classify the issue(s)?

Interpretive: What causes the issue? How has it developed?

EXAMPLE

Cici was interested in consumer purchasing theory. Were people always motivated by the price, or were other things such as the brand, how the product looked, what features the product had, and the perceived quality of the product also important?

She decided to base her research on investigating this issue, using the various purchasing theories she had learnt about in her marketing module, as a basis for the research. She decided to focus her research by only looking at a particular market – students – and one particular product that all students used – computers.

This then gave her a **research question**:

What criteria do students use when they buy computers?

And it provided a **research aim**, based on this question:

To investigate the rank order of purchasing criteria used by students at the university when they purchase computers for their studies.

And this also gave her some research objectives – how she was going to achieve this aim:

> **Research objectives**
>
> 1. To investigate consumer purchasing behaviour theory.
> 2. To investigate what other researchers have found in relation to consumer purchasing behaviour through secondary-research content analysis. (This, together with the results from (1), formed the basis of her literature review.)
> 3. To investigate the purchasing criteria students at her university actually used. (This could be done with primary research questionnaires, interviews and focus groups, using a selected sample of students.)
>
> Having three research objectives enabled her to 'triangulate' her data – get information from three sources, to get a better final answer to her research question.

Research methodology and methods

The following guidance is intended to supplement the information you should receive from your programme with regard to research methods. This guidance is very basic, and you should also take the time to study research methods books which are specifically written for your subject.

There is a difference between research methodology and research methods. Your research methodology is the approach that you take to the research – is it scientific, or is it descriptive and interpretive? Your research methods are the specific 'tools' that you use once you have established your methodology.

However, we have often found that students can be very confused because there is a lot of very complicated research method information, often written in difficult academic English. Students whose first language is not English might have particular problems understanding these complicated philosophical approaches to research questions.

When you write a 'methodology' section for your research proposal or your research report, you will need to include a discussion of the research methodology and research methods ('tools') that you intend to use. It could typically be a mix from the following list:

- Primary research: Do your own research, for example interviews/survey.
- Secondary research: Find out what other 'experts' have already researched in your topic area. This is often called 'content', 'desk' or 'library' research.
- Quantitative analysis: Statistical analysis of your data.

- Qualitative analysis: Your interpretation of your data, particularly if it is qualitative data from interviews, for example.
- Case study: A more detailed study of a particular country, industry, company, incident, etc.
- Mixed design: Primary/secondary, qualitative/quantitative research.

A discussion of the limitations and problems associated with the work, as far as you can predict at this point, also needs to be included.

Survey questionnaires

Questionnaires are a popular method for students to find data for their research. 'Survey' is a term applied to any research that involves investigating a specific sample of people. Questions of sample size and sample type then become important, as explained below.

We have included the following advice about questionnaire construction because, from our experience, it is a particularly difficult area for most students who are new to research, and particularly Chinese students, working in a second language. Questionnaire writing needs to be accurate and precise in order to get useful data.

You will often need to design and complete effective questionnaires and surveys for your primary research data. You can ask people directly to complete paper questionnaires, and you can collect them after they have finished so that you don't lose them. You can also complete the questionnaire for them by asking them the questions and recording their answers. You can send the questionnaires out online too, if you have permission to use the recipients' email addresses.

Additionally, there are commercial online survey facilities you can use which allow you to create questions, view and test them, and then have an email sent to your potential respondents which will invite them to click on a link which takes them directly to your survey.

The key steps to designing a questionnaire are:

- Decide on what information you need.
- Decide on the wording of the questions and the questionnaire instructions.
- Decide on which order you are going to ask the questions.
- Write a short introduction, telling people about your research, and how the questionnaire will be used.
- VERY IMPORTANT: Test the questionnaire with a small representative sample (this is called a 'pilot').
- Revise your questionnaire if the pilot results show any problems.

- Finally check and print the questionnaire if you need to.
- Decide how you are going to collect the completed questionnaires.

Qualitative and quantitative questions

When you are designing your questionnaire, you need to ask yourself what you really need to find out. Your questions can be either 'open ended' (people can answer in any way they like) or 'closed' (people can select from a fixed choice of answers). These can involve qualitative or quantitative questions, or both.

Open and closed questions

Use short simple sentences for your questions, even if you offer many possible answer choices. Questionnaires can be structured by using 'closed questions'. For example, closed questions design 'yes' or 'no' as answers, or numerical choices, or picking from multiple choices so there is a limited choice of responses, as shown below.

1. Was the skills book useful for your assignments?		
Yes: ☐	No: ☐	Not sure: ☐

FIGURE 5.2   Example of a closed question

In this way you can offer response suggestions, but remember to include categories such as 'not sure' or 'other' for an unexpected response. When you use the word 'other' to invite another response, make sure that you include a place where the respondent can give more details. Closed questions are easiest to analyse statistically but limit the responses. An example of a closed, limited response would be groups of ages, e.g. under 18, 19–25, 26–30, 31–35, 36–40, 41+. Make sure you do not allow responses to overlap, e.g. 36–40, 40+.

'Open' questions allow space for any answer, inviting the respondent's own views and feelings. As opinions can be difficult to report quantitatively, limit your open questions to topics that you want to get people's individual feelings about. Otherwise, you will get too much material to analyse. The example below illustrates a prescribed choice of answers; you can instruct the respondents to tick all answers that apply, or set a limit.

TABLE 5.1   Example open questions for a questionnaire

2. What do you think about the skills book? Tick all that apply to you.

I find it very useful
It is important to learn about different methods
It is very detailed
It has lots of general information
It is easy to find what I need
It includes many useful examples
I like to read the personal experience of other students
It is very supportive
It is easy to understand
It helped me to think differently
It is essential for me to do well

'Additional comments' often come after the closed questions, as open questions usually take longer to complete. An example of 'additional comments' is shown below.

TABLE 5.2   Example additional comments box for a questionnaire

10. Please write any comments you wish to make about the skills book, in the box below.

We welcome
your opinions

Likert-scaled questions

For questions that require more detail or more opinion, 'Likert'-scaled responses ask respondents to make a choice to indicate the degree of their feeling or agreement – where their opinion is located, e.g. from 1 to 6, or from 'very much' to 'not at all'. If you have several questions using a Likert scale, try to make the style consistent. Always put high numbers/positive/strong responses on the same side, e.g. on the right. Decide how many points you need in your scale. Some people design an odd number of choices with 'neutral' or 'don't know' in the middle. However, an even number of choices is better practice as it will force respondents towards one side or the other, which can be very useful. A scaled example is shown below.

1   Please rate your satisfaction with the following statements.
2   Give an answer on a scale of 1 to 10 where 1 = strongly disagree, 5 = neutral, and 10 = strongly agree:

TABLE 5.3   Example Likert scale

	1	2	3	4	5	6	7	8	9	10
Education is the most important thing in life	○	○	○	○	○	○	○	◉	○	○
If you do not have a good master's degree, you cannot get a good job in China	○	○	○	○	○	◉	○	○	○	○
A degree from the UK is worth more than a degree from China	○	○	○	○	○	◉	○	○	○	○
Working experience is more valuable than a good degree if you want to get a good job	○	○	○	○	○	○	◉	○	○	○

Questionnaire wording

Choose the words you use very carefully so that everyone can understand the questionnaire in the same way. Generally avoid informal words, slang, abbreviations and subjective words. Sometimes you might need to define terms so that they are understood in the same way by everyone, e.g. 'success' or 'failure' mean different things to different people.

Avoid questions that can mislead or have a bias. For example: 'When did you last read a text book?' might be answered very differently by respondents. What does *when* mean? If this is an open question, an answer might be a date, a day of the week, a time, even 'in the rain, last summer'! So it might be better to ask 'How often...?' as part of a closed question. What does *read* mean? It might be understood as when did you read it completely? If you read or used only some of it, does this mean that you read it? What is a *text* book? Is it one on the module reading list or a book in a local library? Does it include e-books?

Avoid 'leading' questions – questions which already assume too much. For example, the question 'When did you realise that your time management was poor?' assumes that the respondent has actually had poor time management before.

Order of questions

Place the questions in a logical order so that the flow of ideas serves your purpose and so that it is not difficult or threatening to respondents.

Start with an introductory section, saying who you are, why you are doing the research, and how the results will be used. Say how much time the questionnaire should take and the number of questions. Insert your ethics number (if you have one)... and don't forget to say 'Thank you for your valuable help' at the end.

EXAMPLE

Here is an example of an introduction to a survey about what criteria students use when they buy computers.

Welcome to the survey. The purpose of this survey is to find out what features students look for when they buy a computer for their studies.

The survey is completed anonymously and should take less than 10 minutes to complete.

All data collected in this survey will be held anonymously and securely. No personal data is asked for or retained.

Survey results and feedback will only be reviewed within the university and not published. Data may be retained for future surveys. This research has been approved by the university ethics committee.

Questionnaire checklist

Check that your questions are effective:

- Will your questions address your research aim and objectives?
- Will you discover enough data?
- Are all the questions written clearly and are they easy to understand?
- Are they all necessary? For example, do you really need to ask about age or gender?
- Are your questions neutral? Try to avoid leading questions, i.e. those giving the impression that you want a particular response.
- Have you covered all possibilities, especially when you use pre-set categories, and multiple choices? Always include 'other' as a possible answer; there might always be a different response.
- Can the respondent explain further? Include extra answer boxes, e.g. for 'please state', 'specify' or 'why?' to fill if they wish.
- Can these results be analysed in an appropriate way?
- Have you carried out a pilot survey to test the questionnaire on a small group of people to identify any problem areas completing or understanding it? This is always good research practice.
- Is it easy to complete? Make sure it is not too difficult, too personal or takes too long to complete, as it may discourage people to complete it and produce a low response rate.
- Is the timing appropriate for getting the respondents that you need? Send it out at a selected time and then send a prompt shortly before your deadline, to try to improve the response rate.
- If you have to use a postal survey, give respondents an address or a stamped addressed envelope. Give your contact telephone or email for them to contact you if they are interested or need more information.

Remember that the reason for completing primary research is that you are able to define your own questions and do some original research. Therefore, take time to design the most appropriate, relevant questionnaire possible to assist your research task.

Interviews

An interview is another commonly used data collection method, which is mainly used to collect qualitative data. Interviews can be structured or unstructured, or a mixture of both. This is called a semi-structured interview. Structured interviews use a fixed set of questions for each person being interviewed. This ensures consistency, but can be too restrictive in terms of exploring the issues. Unstructured interviews don't have a prior set of questions and are essentially an exploratory conversation with respondents. A good interview will have a mixture of set questions and more open-ended questions. You can record interviews to take notes after the interview, but you must make sure that you have the written permission of your interviewee to do this. You must also use the same reassurances about the restrictions on data use that you would use for a questionnaire.

The interviewer effect

No two interviewers are alike and the same person may provide different answers to different interviewers. The manner in which a question is asked is important in terms of the response. Interviewees might provide false answers to particular questions asked in the 'wrong' way. For example, if someone asks you how much money you earn from your job, you might tell them you earn more than you actually do, in order to make your job look more important.

The respondent effect

Respondents might also give incorrect answers to impress, either on a returned questionnaire, or during an interview. They may intend to impress either the interviewer or a third party, such as their boss, particularly if they think that the interview or questionnaire data might be seen by these people. This is another reason why the interviewee must be assured that the interview data will be totally confidential. It is also vital that the respondent is aware of the purpose of the study.

Focus groups

A focus group is like a group discussion, but is 'focused' on a particular discussion topic. It is a qualitative research method – often used in marketing – which involves asking a selected group of people about their perceptions, opinions, beliefs, and attitudes towards a product, service, concept, advertisement or idea. It is an effective way of collecting qualitative data.

The role of the researcher

The researcher is also referred to as the 'facilitator' who asks 'prompt' questions, designed to get the group talking. The role of the facilitator is to encourage everyone participating in the discussion and ensure an interactive process for the ultimate outcome. Shy group members can be gently brought into the group by asking them directly about their opinions.

The normal group size is between four and six people – any more than this and people can feel too reticent to offer uninhibited responses. Focus groups are particularly used in business and marketing to obtain feedback about new products. In marketing, focus groups are usually used in the early stages of product or concept development, in order to make sure that the final product will be one that people will want to buy. Participants are recruited for the focus group on the basis of similar demographics, psychographics, buying attitudes or behaviour.

Pilot studies

It is always good research practice to make a small 'pilot' study first to test out your research techniques – particularly your questionnaire. This helps you to be sure that the answers you get will give you the information you think you need. Give the questionnaire to a small group of people who might be representative of your target demographic, and be prepared to change the questionnaire when you see the results.

Sampling

A lot of research involves questionnaires and surveys and focus groups. These can be qualitative or quantitative, or both, in terms of the methodology. The one thing they all have in common is that you will need to choose a sample of people for each of these methods.

A sample is a finite (fixed) section of a statistical population whose properties are studied to gain information about the whole population. In other words, a sample is chosen to 'represent' a certain population (a larger group in society). Therefore, a population is a group of individuals, persons, objects, or items from which samples are taken for measurement, for example, a sample of students who all use the university or college restaurant. These students are your research 'subjects'.

Bias and errors in sampling

A sample is expected to accurately 'represent' the population from which it comes. However, there is clearly going to be no guarantee that any sample will be precisely representative of the population from which it comes. There may be a number of untypical observations being made – the students interviewed about the restaurant may only have been using it because another campus restaurant was closed. In practice, it is often impossible to know if your sample is 'representative', so normally, researchers are reduced to reporting in the methodology that the sample may not have been representative, or using statistical 'confidence levels'.

Selecting the sample

The chance component (sometimes called random error) exists no matter how carefully the following sample selection procedures are implemented, and the only way to minimise the chance that sampling errors exist is to firstly select a sufficiently large sample (sample size is an important consideration discussed below) and to carefully trial (pilot) questionnaires and interview questions etc. to make sure that you are getting reasonably 'unbiased' responses.

Sample size

This is an important area to consider. Obviously there are practical constraints, but statistically you would need at least 100 returned questionnaires, for example, before your questionnaire data becomes what statistically would be regarded as 'significant', i.e. reasonably reliable conclusions can be made from it. This figure can be calculated from a statistical formula.

In practice, with most student research, it is often not possible to achieve more than approximately 30–50 completed questionnaires, ten interviews and two focus groups. In this case, the data obtained will not be statistically significant or allow you to make generalisations. In addition, you will have to admit this in the 'limitations' section of your methodology chapter. However, the research will still give the required 'deeper description' of your research topic and show that you have learnt how to use basic research techniques.

Common types of samples

There are four basic types of samples which students tend to use for their research. The most common one is probably the convenience sample, and then there is the quota sample, the judgement sample and the random sample. They differ in the manner in which the basic units are chosen, as we explain below.

The convenience sample

This is probably the most common sampling type used by student researchers. It basically means using people for your research who were available at the time, without any consideration about other factors. For example, if you want to do research on which airlines people use when they travel, you might just ask the students on your module who live outside the UK, and therefore often have to fly. This can give you a useful description, but there is no possibility of 'representation' of a wider population.

Quota sample

This is a common type of sampling in market research, when you select an amount (quota) of research subjects (or respondents) on the basis of pre-established criteria. For example, you might want to make sure that you interview 50 per cent of males and 50 per cent of females who use a particular product.

Judgement sample

A judgement sample is obtained according to the advice of someone who is very familiar with the relevant characteristics of the population. For example, you might ask an employer if you could interview a number of people who had recently received training by the company. The employer would know which people to direct you to in order for you to ask their permission.

Simple random sample

This may be the most important type of sample and is probably the one that is most often confused with the convenience sample. Statistically speaking, a random sample allows a known probability that each elementary unit will be chosen. For this reason, it is sometimes referred to as a probability sample. This is the type of sampling that is used in lotteries and raffles. For example, if you want to randomly select ten students from a wider population of 100 undergraduates, you would need to write down all their names on separate pieces of paper, put them into a box and then pick out ten without looking at the names first. In this case, every name has an equal chance of being picked.

Quantitative analysis methods

If your research involves quantitative analysis, perhaps because you have a lot of numerical data, or you have a positivist design, you might need to use statistical software for your analysis. Statistical analysis details are out of the scope of this book, but your institution will have statistical experts who can advise you. Unless you have studied statistics before you started your programme in the UK, it is a good idea to check with a statistician any statistical assumptions that your research will be making, as well as checking on the best type of statistics to use in order to address your research aim.

Content analysis

This is analysis of the data content – usually from research by other researchers (secondary research). For example, you might make a content analysis of all the articles on a particular topic in a specific business journal, over a fixed time period. Content analysis looks for themes and patterns in the research literature, or in your qualitative data results.

One of the biggest problems with qualitative data is the amount of it – usually very large amounts of descriptive data from interview transcripts, questionnaire open-ended question results etc. You will need to make decisions about this data in order to organise it. You will need to 'code' the data into similar categories so that you can then make more quantitative assessments about the number of respondents who had similar responses etc.

Research projects and dissertations

As Cici described at the beginning of this chapter, the first step to beginning a research project is to write a research 'proposal'. The proposal sets out in detail what you intend to research, why you think that the topic is important, and how you intend to complete the research. Research projects are usually for the purpose of writing a dissertation. Undergraduate and postgraduate degree programmes in the UK often use a 'dissertation' for your final assessment. There might be other assessment options, but certainly for a postgraduate master's degree, a dissertation, or extended research report, is usually required.

Producing a dissertation enables you to:

- choose your own area of interest;
- explore this area in depth;
- establish your own research question;
- experience a complete research process;
- manage a research project;
- use all the communication, data management and intellectual skills which you have developed during your education.

Research proposal

There are various different formats for research proposals, so always do what your tutor or supervisor suggests. A research proposal normally has the following parts:

1. Provisional title of your dissertation e.g. *An investigation into the...*
2. Introduction: Brief background to the proposed subject area; your reasons for choosing the work.
3. Aims and Objectives: A clear indication of aims and objectives to be achieved, plus either your dissertation question(s) or specific research hypotheses if these are appropriate. The aim is what you are trying to achieve, and the objectives are how you intend to achieve the aim.
4. Literature review: An initial and brief literature review, highlighting the main theoretical areas that underpin the work. This must be correctly referenced and the reference list included as an appendix.
5. Methodology and methods: A discussion of the research methodology and research methods you will be employing to achieve your research aim, and the reasons why you are choosing these particular methods.
6. A recognition of any problems or opportunities that could arise, and limitations in the work/scope of the work.
7. A timetable showing the things you will have to do to complete the research, and the deadlines that you must meet.
8. A list of references of the sources of information you have used for the proposal, specifically the literature review and the research methodology theory you intend to use.

The structure of a dissertation

Dissertations generally follow a standard order of sections, as indicated below. However, different institutions may have different conventions and requirements.

Title page

If the dissertation contains confidential information, this should be indicated by the student on the title page. The title should be relevant to your research and clearly focused. It has to be accurate as markers will assess your dissertation against this title.

Dissertation title

Your research question can be converted into a statement which can be developed to form your research title. For example, if you are a marketing student in a business school, your initial research question might be:

What purchasing criteria do Chinese consumers use when they are shopping for luxury-branded goods in the UK?

Put this into a statement – for example:

Chinese consumers' purchasing criteria when they are shopping for luxury-branded goods in the UK

Then you can refine it to a more 'academic research' project title such as:

An investigation of Chinese consumers' purchasing criteria of luxury brands in the UK

Normally, titles can have one, two or three parts. For example:

- An investigation of the impact of Chinese buyers on the London property market
- Agricultural machinery trade between China and Europe: A case study analysis over the past three years
- Has the role of HRM changed in China? A critical analysis with a focus on Chinese multinational companies
- Internal marketing as a change management tool; an evaluation of whether internal market segmentation theory really benefits companies: The case of ABC Corporation

Research titles are important, but do not worry about getting it exactly right: you can always refine it later. Choose an initial title that is not too restrictive so that it can accommodate small changes in direction if you need to make them later in the dissertation process.

Resist the temptation to make a long and very 'inclusive' title, for example:

An investigation into the Hong Kong tourist market with specific reference to the issue of sustainability in relation to a growing global awareness of the impact of tourism on environmental issues such as the use of scarce water resources

Avoid 'catchy' or 'journalistic' titles which show unacceptable bias, e.g.:

Customer service problems in a UK company: how the ABC company can improve its customer relations

This title assumes that there are problems and that the company should improve. Academic research should always try to be neutral and objective, at least until the research is completed.

Remember that a dissertation is not a piece of investigative journalism which has already decided who is guilty and why. It is evidence-based research written in report format and appropriate academic style.

Acknowledgements

It is usual practice to acknowledge the help and guidance of your supervisor, and any other supportive staff. You can also mention people who have personally supported you during the research process, such as family members.

Abstract

The abstract must be written last, when you have completed the whole dissertation. It is a brief overview of the dissertation and its findings. A common mistake in this section is to write too much about methodology and none on outcomes. Your abstract should contain the following elements, in this order:

- Brief statement of the issue
- Brief statement of why the issue is important, and your topic's relevance and interest value
- Brief statement of methodology
- Brief statement of findings, analysis and outcomes
- Brief statements of conclusions and recommendations

Table of contents

This should be compiled using an automatic table of contents (ToC) facility on your computer.

Chapter 1: Introduction

A good introduction is more than just the first section of the dissertation: it tells the reader what the dissertation is intended to provide, in an interesting way. The introduction sets the scene and puts the whole inquiry into its proper context. It includes a clear statement of the aim and objectives, the terms of reference, the sources of information on which the dissertation is based, and how it was collected. It includes an outline of the research methodology. The topic/problem to be investigated is defined and explained, linked with a statement of the management issues involved and how the topic and issues changed as the work evolved. The reasons for the research are stated and the significance of related work on the topic is made clear. Chapter 1 is very important and usually addresses the following questions:

- What is the problem or issue? (A 'topic' is not enough.)
- Why does it need research?
- What is the main aim of the study and the objectives to achieve this?
- What is your hypothesis (your initial guess about what is happening)?
- In what sense will your contribution add to what is already known? Who might benefit?
- What are your dissertation objectives or hypotheses?
- What are your steps to solve the problem, e.g. collect data, analyse data?
- What methods will be used to get research data, e.g. primary research, case study approach, etc?
- What are the constraints or limitations of the study?

You should include your dissertation aim and objectives in the introduction. Follow the advice of your supervisor. Remember that you are not setting out to 'prove' anything, only to gather good evidence to help you evaluate the issue(s) and provide evidence 'for and against', to support or not. If your evidence finally does not offer much support to your main argument, then you will need to be honest about this and discuss the possible reasons why, in your findings and analysis chapter and in your conclusion. It might be that your research methods were not comprehensive enough, or that your original hypothesis did not reflect the reality of the situation. It is perfectly OK to find this out, and this represents balanced and honest research.

Chapter 2: Literature review

This is probably the most important part of your dissertation, so we have provided a lot of guidance in this section. Students tend to find that it is difficult to write because it cannot just be a list of every relevant piece of research you can find. It has to be critically evaluative, and focus on theory and concepts, as well as what other researchers have found. It is a review of what is already known about your topic and issues.

You should evaluate the usefulness of past research, studies, articles from relevant journals, books, newspapers, etc. Summarise and review the literature of other researchers who have published around the theme of your research. Because of this, precise referencing becomes very important in this section. It is vital that you acknowledge the authorship of all other people's theories and ideas.

The literature chapter should be drafted early in the dissertation process. As you find relevant literature and read it, reference it and write draft notes on any relevant data you find. Your literature review should critically evaluate other research by indicating not only the relevance of it to your own study, but also any weaknesses in the research that other researchers have pointed out. Do not just make your literature review a description of material, or a 'list' of any relevant research you found. Instead judge the following:

- What are the main general arguments and themes in the subject area?
- How much is relevant?
- Who are the main authorities In the field?
- What are the major research findings?
- Are there significant gaps that the dissertation attempts to address?
- Can you apply some lessons to your work?
- What relevant theories, models and conceptual frameworks are used?
- What research methods are commonly used?
- How do they apply to this dissertation?

Writing the literature review

The 'literature' means all the relevant books and research reports about your topic area. A 'review' is an inspection of the literature to try to find out what experts are saying about your topic. In simple terms, a literature review is a review of what the 'experts' (academics and practitioners) have written and said about your chosen topic that is more complete than the one you wrote for your proposal. The literature review is the foundation of your research.

You should start with the basic literature review you compiled for your proposal, and this will give you a basis for producing a more comprehensive literature review.

The initial literature review for your proposal highlights the main theoretical areas that underpin the work. Ask yourself: 'What is there in the literature that is relevant to my dissertation, and which provides me with a starting point and something to build on?' You need to highlight elements of the literature that you are actually going to use or refer to later.

- Include the main expected 'expert' literature plus additional sources.
- Use module reading lists from the module handbooks.
- Make full use of the library, the VLE and databases for your subject.
- Find out about specialist sources for your subject.
- Identify the most relevant journals and company publications.
- Use the internet to research the latest issues and debates in relation to your topic.

Start compiling an accurate bibliography in the preferred referencing style for your subject, as soon as you start reading. The bibliography is the place where you record all your background reading, although you might not use all the sources in the bibliography when you compile your final reference list. However, it is much easier to find them again if you need to, if you put them in a bibliography now. Accurately record all the details of each publication you use at this stage, and keep this habit. Be very strict about this because it will make life a lot easier when you later need to compile your separate list of references of all the sources you actually referred to.

Critically evaluate the literature

A literature review has a dual purpose; it shows that you have done appropriate reading as a basis for your research, and it provides you with a data bank of ideas and information to direct your research, and inform your discussion and analysis later in your dissertation.

The literature review is not just a list of all the relevant theories and researchers. In your literature review, you should tell us about current research in your topic area, and any important debates there are about the research and the concepts in relation to your topic area. You should critically evaluate the literature. This means that you should present literature that shows the many sides of the arguments and issues in your research area; for example:

> Surname (year) suggests that the issue of globalisation has been overstated. However, a more recent and more extensive study by Surnames (year) reveals that the general influence of this factor may still be crucial. However, as Surname (year) states, in a related study, more research is necessary into the effect that micro-factors have on the situation.

This kind of description of the positions and arguments is the only type of description you should supply. Notice that the writer is also actually revealing his or her opinions (evaluation), using terms such as 'however' to indicate a possible problem, and the term 'more recent' to imply that perhaps the original study was outdated in some way. Your literature review should consist of this kind of writing, where you describe things and evaluate them at the same time.

So, avoid a review that is too descriptive and not evaluative enough, and is just a list of what each author says. For example, **avoid this kind of 'list':**

> Surname (year) suggests that the issue of globalisation has been overstated. Another study by Surnames (year) states that the influence of micro-factors may also be important. Another study by Surname (year) states that more research is necessary.

You should critically review and judge the worth of the evidence you choose in relation to the main issues and problems that you will address. You are, in effect, providing the groundwork and source of evidential support for your later critical discussion. You are also showing your supervisor that you are reading relevant sources of evidence for your particular area of enquiry. During this process you must identify appropriate academic theories, models and conceptual ideas. You need to compare and contrast the differing views that will later link to your analysis and discussion section.

The literature review forms one important chapter of your dissertation, usually Chapter 2, and is called *Literature Review*. (The word 'literature' is already plural, so do not use the word 'literatures'.)

Steps to writing a literature review

Step 1: Read and record

Firstly, get the 'big picture' by reading widely around your topic to find out the general overall picture. Read general articles before you read specific articles. A good place to start is the list of references or bibliography of a recent article or book on the topic. Then use other bibliographic resources, including abstracts, electronic databases and the internet.

Step 2: Establish the sections

Establish each of the sections of your review. The way you do this will depend on your material. You could organise them chronologically, by theory, by topic, by company, etc. Whichever organising principle you select, you should try to make your review thematic. This means that you should organise it by themes – particular issues which you have identified as being important, and not just listing various researchers and their theories. Each section should be about one main sub-topic connected with your review and your research. The sections should reflect your reading and your research interests, and should cover all the necessary issues you will have to deal with in your research, including how other people have researched the issues, and what methodology they used.

Step 3: Write short summaries

For each section, write short summaries of the different author viewpoints in relation to the concepts and issues. Review and critically evaluate the relevance of the literature to your work, but do not draw conclusions at this stage. You will do this later in your findings and discussion chapter and your final conclusion chapter.

Step 4: Order the sections and write your introduction and conclusion

Decide the order of each section. Then write an introduction and a final conclusion to the whole literature review. In the conclusion, summarise the main points and synthesise patterns you have discovered in your reading.

Step 5: Proofreading and referencing

Your literature review should have a reference for each author or data source you introduce. Check that these are all correct, depending on which referencing style your tutor wants you to use. Check that all the 'in-text' references link to a full reference in your final list of references, which you should compile at this stage. The references section will contain all the sources you referred to in your dissertation, and the bibliography will contain all the other sources you read but did not mention in your dissertation.

Important characteristics of a literature review

Based on the above, there are important characteristics of a literature review:

1. The literature review should be organised into relevant 'themes' in relation to the topic that have emerged from your reading of the literature. It should give the reader an informed overview of your topic, with reference to both 'seminal' research (very important past research) and also the latest research in your topic area.
2. You need a clear introduction at the beginning of the chapter (written last) saying what the chapter will be about. This should link to the aims and objectives of your research.
3. Clearly signpost the separate sections in your literature review, for example 'Firstly, the issue of...'.
4. Try to give a 'balanced' review. Do not just look at authors to support preconceptions; include those who hold different views. Remember that you can never 'prove' anything. You are looking for good evidence, related to your topic, both for and against.
5. Be very specific. Avoid using the phrase 'Research shows...' (Which research? Whose? When was this research published?)
6. Generally, the present tense is used, e.g., 'Surnames (year) suggest that...'.
7. Do not start to put your findings or your conclusions or recommendations in the literature review.
8. Do not put your personal opinion directly in the literature review. Reserve this for your discussion and conclusions. However, you should indicate whether the data is valid and reliable or not. For example, you might want to qualify some of your statements: 'Unfortunately, Surnames' (year) study was based on a very small sample, so only tentative conclusions can be drawn.'

9. Do not be overly critical in your literature review. It is a critical review only in the sense that you indicate the strengths and weaknesses of opposing positions. (You can be more critical in your discussion section, where you can use your research evidence to question the positions and research methods you recorded in your literature review.)

Chapter 3: Methodology

In this important chapter, you must answer these questions:

What did I do?
How did I do it?
Why did I do it that way?

This chapter describes and evaluates in detail the methods, techniques and procedures used in the investigation which link to the scope and aims of the dissertation. It is also very important that you justify the methods used by referring to experts in research methods. You should include the ethical considerations which you complied with in your research, and any limitations of the research.

- What was the purpose of collecting and analysing the data?
- Why was this topic interesting/useful?
- Summarise in a few straightforward statements the basic questions the research set out to answer.
- What role did the findings of the literature review have in determining the data collection requirements? (Very important)
- Why did you need to collect quantitative and/or qualitative data? Or why not?

Discussion of alternative methods of data collection

- Which methods might have been appropriate for data collection (e.g. observation, questionnaire, etc.)?
- What are the advantages and disadvantages of each of these methods of data collection with reference to your own research project? (This might be best summarised as a table.)
- What reasons influenced your final choice?

Discussion of the question content and data required

- If you used a questionnaire or interviews, how were questions asked to generate the required data?
- Did you take any decisions to limit the data collection? Why? Why not?

Discussion of the format of the questionnaire(s)/interview(s)

- Why were the questions presented in your chosen order?
- How did the design of the research help or impede data collection for you as the researcher?

Discussion of the phrasing of the questions

- Why was it important to take care in phrasing the questions?
- What methods did you use to ensure that the phrasing of questions was effective in eliciting useful replies?

Discussion of the response formats

- How many different response formats did you use, and why?
- What are the advantages and disadvantages of each response format you used in your questionnaire?

Discussion of data collection method

- How were the interviews conducted/questionnaires distributed and returned?

Discussion of sample

Note that this applies if you distributed a questionnaire, conducted focus group(s) or have based your work on case studies.

- What is sampling theory?
- Why is it important to research design?
- What are the different methods of sampling?
- What are their advantages and disadvantages?
- Which sampling method did you use for this survey?
- Why did you choose this method?
- How did you determine the size of your sample?

Note on data analysis technique

- Was the collected data analysed manually or by computer?
- If analysed by computer, which package was used?

Review of the methodology used for the research

- What were the problems with the methodology implemented? (Limitations)
- How could you have avoided these problems?
- How did your methods rate for reliability?
- How did your methods rate for validity?
- If you were to run the project again what improvements would you make to the methodological approach adopted?

Data reliability and validity

You also need to comment on the reliability and the validity of your data. You need to refer to a research methods book for more detail and examples, but basically, reliability is the degree to which an assessment tool produces consistent results; validity refers to how well a test measures what it is supposed to measure.

There are different types of validity, for example construct validity, which refers to research method, and the degree to which the 'tool' you used actually measured what it was intended to measure. For example, did you use an appropriate sampling technique?

Chapter 4: Findings and analysis

(This chapter could be divided into two parts if your supervisor advises this.)

Part 1: Findings

What was observed and what was discovered/found out? Some supervisors suggest a presentation of the data first, with brief links to the analysis that follows in the second part of the chapter. You may include tables, charts, histograms, etc. Each should have an appropriate number, title and comment (referring to the figure/table, e.g. 'Figure 4.1 shows that...' or 'Table 4.1 indicates that...').

Part 2: Analysis and discussion

The key to this chapter is thorough analysis and interpretation of the findings which link to your literature review. What did you find that agrees with what other researchers found? What did you find that was different? What patterns have emerged? Discuss the differences between your findings and those of other researchers (as outlined in your literature review). This establishes an all-important link between your literature review and your analysis. Refer back to your literature review and your conceptual framework. Use the literature to evaluate your research material (point out strengths, weaknesses, limitations and criticisms by other experts). If you have hypotheses, this is where you 'test' them against your data findings to see if the positive, negative or 'null' (no correlations) hypotheses are supported.

Chapter 5: Conclusions and recommendations

Your supervisor will tell you if you need to separate the conclusion from the recommendations. Remember, you must conclude before you recommend solutions/alternatives/ways forward, etc.

Your conclusions are:

1. A summary of the main findings as a series of statements of all the key points of your dissertation.
2. Conclusions and directions for further research.

In the summary section, summarise the main findings from your research and report on whether hypotheses were supported or not. Discuss the validity and reliability of the findings. The conclusions must only be drawn from the body of evidence presented in the main sections of the dissertation. Each separate conclusion should be acknowledged – possibly by numerical sub-sections. The conclusions should be seen to flow clearly from the preceding analysis and should also indicate any problems that have been identified. Finally, there should be an account of how this section should convince the reader that the research process has met the aims and objectives of the dissertation.

Recommendations

This section flows naturally after the conclusions as it suggests ways of solving the problems or addressing the opportunities you identified in your conclusions. It may contain innovative ideas and recommend courses of action that will help to achieve further success using the aims of the dissertation. This section might include the benefits and costs of implementing the various recommendations, the programme of work required, the timescale involved, the feasibility, and resource implications. Recommendations should flow logically from the conclusions.

Chapter 6: Reflection

This chapter is not always required, although it is becoming more usual now to ask students to reflect on their research. If you are required to finish your dissertation with a reflection, it might also form part of the assessment of your management of the dissertation process. However, it may not be included in the word count of your dissertation.

It should contain an analysis and evaluation of your research process. The focus should be on your own personal reflection on your dissertation experience. You can talk about the strengths and weaknesses of your learning while you were doing the research and writing for the dissertation. You can discuss any problems or constraints you encountered and how you resolved these difficulties. In addition, you can evaluate the effectiveness of your chosen methodology and assess how you have developed your skills as a researcher. This personal reflection should link back to the relevance of your dissertation proposal. Use the advice we have given in Chapter 4 about reflective writing.

The following questions may be useful in providing a framework for this section:

- Were the dissertation objectives well defined and fulfilled?
- How did the findings compare with your initial expectations?
- Is your dissertation in line with your proposal?
- Was the research well planned and executed?
- Did any changes occur in the process of doing a dissertation, i.e. a different objective or a different research method used? Why?
- How effectively did you choose and use theory and apply it to your business context?
- What are your recommendations for improving this dissertation?
- What went well and what could you have done differently?
- What skills did you develop and what skills have you found you need to improve?
- What have you found to be your strengths?
- What would you do next time?

You should also reflect on the process of the dissertation, and how it relates to the learning objectives/outcomes from your modules.

References

Any material derived from publications (books, journals, the internet, etc.) must be referenced in the body of the dissertation, and full details provided in the references section at the end of your dissertation.

Bibliography

A bibliography contains references to all the background reading and support material you used but which was not actually referred to in the dissertation. You might find it useful to include a bibliography as well as a reference list.

Appendices

Appendices are essential where there is a lot of detailed information which, if presented in the main body, would interrupt or spoil the flow of the dissertation. Appendices include evidence of your ethics approval, your dissertation log, your proposal, detailed tables of statistics, graphs, interview questions, questionnaires, etc. Remember that really important items should be included in the text rather than requiring frequent reference to the appendices. The appendices should be referred to at appropriate points in the text.

They also need to be listed in the table of contents, and each one should be numbered and titled.

Common words and phrases for your dissertation writing

The following is a list of common ways to write the 'academic' sentences for your dissertation, depending on what you are trying to say to the reader. For example, in your introduction, you might need to tell us why the topic is important. You could start your sentence by using any of the following typical ways to do this in academic English.

Establishing the importance of your topic

X is an increasingly important area in business studies…

Central to the issue of X is the concept of…

X is critical to the analysis of…

X is an important topic in this research because…

This topic is important because…

Recent developments in X have increased the need for…

In recent years there has been an increasing interest in X because…

Recent developments in the field of X have led to a renewed interest in…

Recently, researchers (Surnames, year) have investigated…

The past decade has seen increased academic interest in…

Identifying a controversial issue in your topic

In recent years, there has been little agreement on the issue of…

Research (Surname, year) has revealed the extent of disagreement in this area with regard to…

A recent study (Surname, year) has already drawn attention to this issue…

Highlighting a lack of research in your topic area

The research to date has tended to focus on X rather than Y.

There has been very little research to date into this whole issue.

The literature reveals very little evidence in support of this argument.

According to the most recent research literature, very little is known about this issue.

Showing the focus of your research

This paper will focus on the issue of…

This essay will outline the literature of…

The objectives of this research are to determine whether…

This paper seeks to address the following questions:…

This essay critically examines the issue of…

The purpose of this report is to review recent research into the…

This essay will review the research conducted on…

This chapter reviews the literature concerning the issue of…

The aim of this paper is to examine…

The aim of this study is to evaluate and validate…

Indicating the structure of your research

The main questions addressed in this paper are…

This report has been divided into four parts. The first part deals with…

The essay has been organised in the following way:…

This essay will firstly give a brief overview of the situation…

This paper begins by… It will then go on to…

The first section of this paper will examine…

Chapter 2 begins by outlining the theoretical dimensions of the research, looking at how…

Chapter 3 describes the methodology and its justification in terms of the research aim.

Chapter 6 summarises the main conclusions from the research…

General descriptions of the relevant literature

A considerable amount of literature has been published on the issue of…

There is a large volume of published studies describing the issue of…

A large and growing body of literature has investigated…

Previous studies have reported…

Previous research findings into X have been inconsistent and contradictory…

A number of studies have found that…

The relationship between X and Y has been widely investigated…

X has been identified as a major contributing factor in the…

A significant relationship appears to exist between…

Surname (year) has recently developed a methodology for the selective introduction of…

Surname (year) published a paper in which they described…

Surname (year) demonstrated that…

Surname (year) has written extensively on this issue…

A recent study by Surname and Surname (year) involved…

In another major study, Surname (year) found that…

The effects of X were first studied by…

Surname (year) identifies the following…

Surname (year) lists three reasons why the issue has become so controversial. These are:…

Surname (year) traces the development of…

Reference to other research

TABLE 5.4   Examples of how to reference other research

Surname (year)	maintains proposes suggests states points out concludes suggests	that…
According to With reference to	Surname (year),	…

Discussing possible limitations of your research

One question that needs to be asked, however, is whether…

However, a serious weakness with this argument is that…

One of the limitations with this explanation is that it does not explain why…

One criticism of much of the literature on X is that…

The key problem with this explanation is that…

The existing research fails to resolve the contradiction between…

However, the inconsistency with this argument is…

One major criticism of Surname's work is that…

Many writers (e.g., Surname, year; Surname, year; Surname, year) have challenged Surname's (year) claim on the grounds that...

Surname's (year) analysis does not take account of... nor does she examine...

Critical evaluation

Another problem with this approach is that it fails to take X into account...

Perhaps the most serious disadvantage of this method is that...

Difficulties arise, however, when an attempt is made to implement the policy.

Nevertheless, the strategy has not escaped criticism from other researchers (Surnames, year).

One major drawback of this approach is that...

However, this method of analysis has a number of limitations.

However, approaches of this kind carry with them various well-known limitations.

However, all the studies reviewed so far (Surname, year; Surname, year; Surname, year) suffer from the omission of...

On the other hand, such explanations tend to overlook the fact that...

In contrast, one of the main disadvantages of this method appears to be that...

Writing about other authors' evaluations

However, Surname (year) points out that...

Many researchers (e.g., Surname, year; Surname, year; Surname, year) now argue that this strategy is very limited...

The government has been very critical of this policy.

This theory has been strongly challenged in recent years by a number of commentators.

Surname's (year) analysis has been criticised by a number of writers. For example...

Surname's (year) analysis has been subjected to considerable criticism.

More recent arguments against X have been summarised by Surname and Surname (year)...

Describing the characteristics of a research sample

The initial sample consisted of 100 students, although 20 did not complete the questionnaires.

All of the participants were aged between 18 and 30 at the beginning of the study...

Two groups of subjects were interviewed, namely X and Y. The first group were...

A random sample of patients with... was recruited from...

The students were divided into two groups, based on their performance on...

The research used a convenience sample of 32 first-year business studies students.

Just over half the participants (53 per cent) were female, of whom 45 per cent were...

Participants were recruited from a cluster of similar universities.

Structured interviews were conducted with ten business school lecturers who regularly flew…

A small sample was chosen because of the expected difficulty of obtaining...

The subjects were selected on the basis of a degree of homogeneity of their...

The criteria for selecting the subjects were as follows:…

Describing the research process

For the purpose of attitude measurement, subjects were asked to...

For the purpose of analysis, two segments were extracted from each...

For the estimation of motivation, a Likert scale was used.

Data management and analysis was performed using data analysis software.

The experiments were carried out over the duration of the module teaching.

Questionnaires were administered…

The mean score for the two trials was subjected to multivariate analysis of variance to determine...

The subjects were asked to pay close attention to...

The pilot interviews were conducted informally by the researcher.

Independent tests were carried out on the x- and y-scores for the four years from...

Significance levels were set at the 1 percent level using the student t-test.

A total of 100 questionnaires were returned.

The questionnaires were distributed by hand.

The interviews were conducted confidentially.

Fifteen subjects were recruited using email advertisements requesting business students from…

All the work on the computer was carried out using…

The data was recorded on a digital audio recorder and transcribed using a...

Statistical significance was analysed using analysis of variance and t-tests as appropriate.

Comparisons between the two groups were made using unrelated t-tests.

Referring to tables and figures

There are only two kinds of graphic in academic texts – tables and figures. Below is an example of a table.

TABLE 5.5   Example of a results table

A	B	C	D	E
23	56	67	24	78
12	78	45	89	45

The other is a 'figure' and is anything which is not a table, including photos, graphs, flow charts, e.g.:

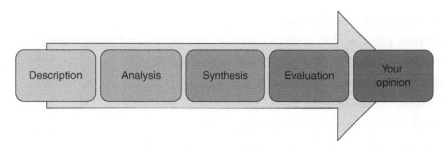

FIGURE 5.3   Critical evaluation

How to indicate figures and tables in the text

TABLE 5.6   How to indicate figures and tables in the text

Table 5.1 above Figure 5.1 below	shows compares presents provides	the experimental data on X. the results obtained from the initial analysis of X. the correlations between the parts of X.
The results obtained from the initial analysis of X	are shown can be compared are presented	in Table 4.1 above. in Figure 4.1 below.
As shown in Figure 12.1 below, Table 4.2 (above) illustrates that The data in Table 12.1 below shows that Figure 3.5 (above) highlights that	the X group reported significantly more Y than the other two groups.	
Table 4.8 below illustrates Figure 3.7 above shows		some of the main characteristics of the... the breakdown of...

Highlighting significant, interesting or surprising results

The most striking result to emerge from the data is that...

Interestingly, this correlation is related to...

The correlation between X and Y is interesting because...

The more surprising correlation is with the...

The single most striking observation to emerge from the data comparison was…

Reporting results from questionnaires and interviews

The response rate was 60 per cent.

Of the study population, 90 subjects completed and returned the questionnaire.

Of the initial cohort of 50 students, 30 were female and 20 male.

Thirty-two individuals returned the questionnaire.

The majority of respondents felt that...

Over half of those surveyed reported that...

Seventy per cent of those who were interviewed indicated that...

Almost two-thirds of the participants (40 per cent) said that...

Approximately half of those surveyed did not comment on...

A small number of those interviewed suggested that...

Only a small number of respondents indicated that...

Of the 30 staff who completed the questionnaire, just over half indicated that...

A minority of participants (10 per cent) indicated...

In response to the question about preferences, most of those surveyed indicated that...

The overall response to this question was very positive.

When the respondents were asked..., the majority commented that...

Other responses to this question included...

The overall response to this question was poor.

Some participants expressed the belief that…

One individual stated that… another commented that…

Unexpected outcomes

Surprisingly, X was found to...

Surprisingly, no differences were found in...

One unanticipated finding was that...

It is somewhat surprising that no X was noted in this condition...

What is surprising is that...

Contrary to expectations, this study did not find a significant difference between...

However, the observed difference between X and Y in this study was not significant.

However, the ANOVA (one way) showed that these results were not statistically significant.

This finding was unexpected and suggests that...

Reference to previous supporting evidence

This study produced results which corroborate the findings of a great deal of the previous work in this field.

The findings of the current study are consistent with those of Surname (year), who found...

This finding supports previous research which links X and Y.

This study confirms that X is associated with...

The present findings seem to be consistent with other research (Surname, year; Surname, year) which found that…

Reference to contradictory evidence

However, findings of the current study do not support previous research.

This study has been unable to demonstrate that...

However, this result has not previously been described.

In contrast to earlier findings, however, no evidence of X was detected.

Although these results differ from some published studies (e.g., Surname, year; Surname, year), they are consistent with those of…

Explanations for results

There are several possible explanations for this result.

These differences can be explained in part by the proximity of X and Y.

A possible explanation for this might be that...

Another possible explanation for this is that...

This result may be explained by the fact that.../by a number of different factors.

It is difficult to explain this result, but it might be related to...

It seems possible that these results are due to...

The reason for this is unclear but it may have something to do with...

It may be that these students benefited from...

This inconsistency/discrepancy may be due to...

This rather contradictory result may be due to...

Advising cautious interpretation

This data must be interpreted with caution because...

These results therefore need to be interpreted with caution.

With a small sample size, caution must be used, as the findings might not be transferable to...

These findings cannot be extrapolated to all cases.

Although exclusion of X did not reduce the effect on Y, the results should be interpreted with caution.

Giving your opinion – writing about the implications of your findings

This finding has important implications for developing...

An implication of this is the possibility that...

One of the issues that emerges from these findings is...

Some of the issues emerging from this finding relate specifically to...

These findings provide some support for the theory that...

Definitions

One definition of economics is…

Surname (year) defines marketing as…

According to Surname (year), psychology is…

Neuroscience has been defined as… (Surname, year).

In the field of management, various definitions of motivation are found.

Job satisfaction is a commonly used notion in HR, and yet it is a concept that is difficult to define precisely.

A generally accepted definition of job satisfaction is lacking.

Surname (year) identified four criteria that might need to be met in terms of job satisfaction.

The term 'post-structuralism' embodies a multitude of concepts which...

Specifying terms that are used in an essay or research study

In this essay the term 'overseas student' will be used in its broadest sense to refer to students who...

Throughout this research, the term 'business' is used to refer to both small and large organisations.

While a variety of definitions of the term 'X' have been suggested, this paper will use the definition first suggested by Surname (year), who saw it as...

In this paper, the term that will be used to describe this phenomenon is 'X'.

In this dissertation, the terms 'X' and 'Y' are used interchangeably to mean...

Referring to other definitions

Surname (year) was apparently the first to use the term...

Surname (year: page) states that valuation is: 'The attempt to...'

According to a definition provided by Surname (year: page), culture is: 'A network of beliefs and...'

The term 'culture' is used by Surname (year) to refer to...

Surname (year) uses the term 'culture' to refer to...

For Surname (year), 'capitalisation' refers to...

This policy is defined by Surname (year: page) as: 'the implementation of...'

Verbs expressing causality

TABLE 5.7   Examples of verbs expressing causality

Lack of sleep	may cause can lead to can result in	poor study habits.
Lack of skills	can give rise to	poor performance.
Much of the instability	stems from	the economic effects of the war.
Latent functionality is a characteristic	caused by resulting from stemming from	unintended consequences.

Expressing causality

The probable cause is global warming.

Another consequence of this lack of exam revision might be…

Physical activity is an important factor in maintaining fitness.

Many other types of food can contribute to high blood pressure.

Another reason why reading is considered to be very important is…

Comparison

This study was very comprehensive, whereas Surname's (year) study was very restricted.

In contrast to Surname, Surnames provide a very full picture of the issue.

Both Surname (year) and Surnames (year) deal with this issue. Similarly, they also address the point that…

Describing trends

TABLE 5.8   Describing trends

Figure 5.2 below shows that there has been a	slight gradual steady marked steep sharp	increase rise decrease fall decline drop	in the number of people admitting to this problem.

Projecting trends

TABLE 5.9   Projecting trends

The number of Xs The amount of Y The rate of Z	is projected to is expected to is likely to will probably	decline steadily drop sharply level off	after this year.

Describing fractions

Of the 100 students who completed the questionnaire, just over half indicated that…

Over half of those surveyed indicated that…

Approximately half of those surveyed did not comment on...

Nearly half of the respondents (48 per cent) agreed that...

Less than a third of those who responded (32 per cent) indicated that...

The number of first marriages in the UK fell by nearly half.

Describing percentages

Seventy per cent of those who were interviewed indicated that...

Twenty per cent of young men, and 44 per cent of young women, said that they...

The response rate was 20 per cent at 6 months and 50 per cent at 12 months.

China has the lowest proportion (10 per cent) of cities with this issue.

Chapter 5: Key words and concepts – English and Chinese

aim – 目的

bias – 偏见

biased – 有偏见的

categories – 总类

cluster – 群

code – 编码

core concept – 核心理论

criterion – 标准

deviant – 反常的

dissertation – 论文

factual – 事实的

homogeneous – 同类的

hypotheses – 假设

induced – 归纳的

intensity – 密度

jargon – 行话

judgement – 判断

limitations – 缺点

objectives – 目标

opportunistic – 机会主义的

phenomenon – 现象

population – 人口

primary data – 一手资料

probability – 可能性

purposeful – 有目的性的

qualitative – 质的

quantitative – 量的

quota – 配额

random – 随机性

research – 研究

research methodology – 研究方法

sample – 样本

scenarios – 场景

secondary data – 二手资料

snowball – 雪球

strata – 地层

survey – 调查

systematic – 系统的

themes – 主题

trends – 趋势

typical – 典型的

undermine – 低估

variables – 变量

CHAPTER 5: TEST YOURSELF

Put an ✘ for an incorrect statement and a ✔ for a correct statement. Check your answers in the Appendix.

1   You should never use 'mixed' research designs...................................... ☐

2   Research always proves things. .... ☐

3   A null hypothesis means that X has a negative effect on Y. .... ☐

4   'Research' is finding out about a topic and writing everything you have found out. .... ☐

5   A random sample just means that you choose anyone who is available to help you with your research... ☐

6   Qualitative data is sometimes called interpretive data. .... ☐

7   It's best to ask open questions at the end of a questionnaire. .... ☐

8   'Construct validity' refers to your research methods, and the degree to which they actually measure what they were intended to measure................. ☐

9   You should always pilot a questionnaire first. .... ☐

10   Likert scales give you information about what people like. .... ☐

Chapter 5: Reflection box

THINK 5.2

What do you want to do when you finish your study in the UK? What type of career do you want?

If you have the chance to do some original research as part of your study programme, think about a research topic that you would like to research which might be beneficial for your future career. Make some notes in this box (and there is more space in the Appendix). Using the chapter information, include some ideas about how you might research the topic.

Appendix

Answers to the 'Test yourself' questions

Test yourself: Chapter 1

1. Reflection means to think about what you have done, and to think about how you can do it better, and how what you are doing now will help you in the future. ✓
2. The UK is one country called the United Kingdom. ✗
3. 'British' is a word we use to describe anything that relates to the UK. ✓
4. The UK and the Republic of Ireland are also members of the European Union. ✓
5. Undergraduate degrees are called bachelor degrees because only unmarried men can study for them. ✗
6. A four-year degree is called a 'sandwich' degree. ✓
7. A high university ranking means excellent teaching. ✗
8. The VLE is a very good place for communication between students and tutors. ✓
9. You do not need to go to induction activities after you arrive in the UK. ✗
10. You will need to choose an English name when you study in the UK. ✗

Test yourself: Chapter 2

1. Language exchange is a good way to develop your academic English. ✓
2. Academic English is informal. ✗
3. Academic English uses mainly second person. ✗
4. Academic English is generally tentative. ✓
5. This is correct: 'A manager must do what he thinks is right.' ✗
6. You should generally use quotations and not paraphrase. ✗
7. A perfect verb tense is used to show that the action has completely finished. ✓
8. A colon is used before a list or an explanation. ✓

9. Semicolons can be used to separate two short sentences that are linked. ✓

10. You should use 'etc.' in academic writing to show that other things are also possible. ✗

Test yourself: Chapter 3

1. The three main academic conduct offences are cheating, collusion and plagiarism. ✓

2. It's not plagiarism as long as you give a reference. ✗

3. It's always best to use quotation and not paraphrase. ✗

4. There are two main types of academic reference systems – in-text and numeric. ✓

5. When you read an article, you must make sure you understand every word. ✗

6. You should make sure you focus on taking notes in a lecture. ✗

7. An independent learner does not need to ask the tutor about anything. ✗

8. It's a fact that London is the capital of England. ✓

9. Bloom's taxonomy shows the facts about learning. ✗

10. Theories are either right or wrong. ✗

Test yourself: Chapter 4

1. 'Analyse' means to break a topic, issues, concept etc. into the main parts. ✓

2. 'Evaluate' means the same as 'analyse'. ✗

3. 'Discuss' just means to talk about something. ✗

4. Reflective writing should always be positive and aim at improvement. ✓

5. It is best not to rehearse oral presentations, so that your presentation will be fresh and interesting. ✗

6. You should read your presentation from notes so that you don't forget what you want to say. ✗

7. It is essential to make a revision timetable before an exam. ✓

8. Open book exams require the answers to be referenced. ✓

9. It is important to read the module guide to make sure that your assignments show that you are achieving the module learning outcomes. ✓

10. If your tutor writes 'So what?' on your assignment, it means that you did not make it clear why you have included this particular information, or what the consequences might be. ✓

Test yourself: Chapter 5

1. You should never use 'mixed' research designs. ✗

2. Research always proves things. ✗

3. A null hypothesis means that X has a negative effect on Y. ✗

4. 'Research' is finding out about a topic and writing everything you have found out. ✗

5. A random sample just means that you choose anyone who is available to help you with your research. ✗

6. Qualitative data is sometimes called interpretive data. ✓

7. It's best to ask open questions at the end of a questionnaire. ✓

8. 'Construct validity' refers to your research methods, and the degree to which they actually measure what they were intended to measure. ✓

9. You should always pilot a questionnaire first. ✓

10. Likert scales give you information about what people Like. ✗

Answers to the activities

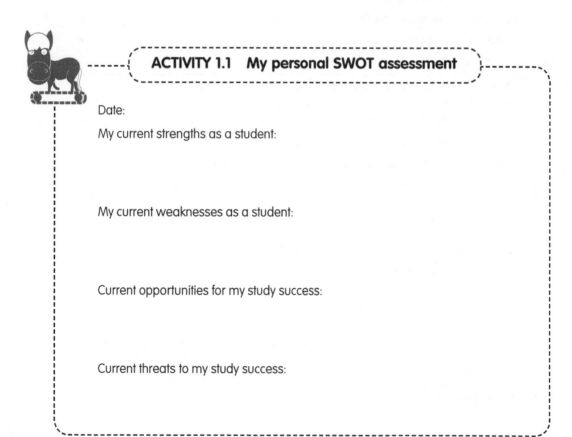

ACTIVITY 1.1   My personal SWOT assessment

Date:

My current strengths as a student:

My current weaknesses as a student:

Current opportunities for my study success:

Current threats to my study success:

ACTIVITY 2.2

Here is the meaning of the phrasal verbs:

Account for – to give a reason for something that has happened

Back up – to provide additional evidence or support

Bail out – to rescue from difficulties

Catch up – to work harder (if you 'get behind')

Deal with – to take action to solve a problem

Drop in – no appointment necessary, just go in

Fill in – to give more information

Get behind – you are working too slowly so you have missed some work

Hang out – spend time with

Head up – to lead an organisation

Roll out – to begin a new project

ACTIVITY 2.3

As we all know, online shopping is very popular and has many advantages Research shows that the number of consumers shop online has increased lately. This is because it is easier to shop online. You don't need to go to the shop only have to wait for the delivery. why would you want to go to the shop when you can have this service? It's a very convenient way to buy things! Many people are using this service nowadays. I always use this service.

Problems

Generally, the paragraph does not follow the PEEEL structure. There are also many other errors:

'As we all know' – generalisation.

No full stop after 'advantages'.

(Continued)

(Continued)

No example references after 'Research shows'.

'increased lately' – too general and therefore not accurate.

'This is because it is easier to shop online' – how do you know this is the only reason? No evidence is given.

'You don't' – short form.

'why would you…' – rhetorical question with no capital letter at the beginning of the sentence.

'It's a very convenient way to buy things' – short form and too personally assertive with an exclamation mark.

The paragraph finishes with two more generalisations and uses first person, which is not recommended for most academic work.

ACTIVITY 3.1

Which of the following statements is a 'fact'?

1. *Hong Kong was given back to China by the British in 1997*. This is a historical 'fact' or correspondence fact, because the date does correspond to the handover event.
2. *100 divided by 4 is 25*. This is a mathematical truth and therefore a fact.
3. *The best way to improve your English is to practise as much as possible*. This is only an opinion, although the theory that it represents has quite a lot of validity for most language learners. However, you cannot prove this kind of statement, only gather evidence from the experiences of successful language learners.

ACTIVITY 3.2

Think of a discussion you had recently. Perhaps your parents told you that they wanted you to study in the UK because they wanted you to have an educational advantage. Their perception is that a UK degree is 'worth more' than a degree from China. Is this 'true'?

No – it is just their opinion, which has been constructed from their own experience and from what they have heard from other people. What does the phrase 'worth more' mean anyway? This is what we call a value judgement. We know the 'value' of something that we have to pay money for – this is quantifiable. But the 'value' of education is not quantifiable: it is a qualitative judgement – an opinion.

The only 'facts' in the world are general empirical (real-world) facts such as Beijing being the capital city of 'modern' China (it wasn't always), and mathematical facts such as 2 + 2 is equal to 4. Even statistics are not facts but opinions, since their accuracy and validity depend on who calculated them, for what purpose, and on what statistical principles – which may or may not have been appropriate for the purpose of the research.

ACTIVITY 3.3

Choose a chapter or an article from one of your module textbooks and answer the following questions in the space provided (read the tips we gave you earlier about how to read an academic article):

Name of the article:	Reference:
Question	**What is your evidence from the text?**
Who do you think the article was written for?	
Why do you think the article was written?	
What is the main argument in the article?	
Are there any other arguments in the article?	
What assumptions lie behind the evidence/argument?	
Is adequate proof provided and backed up with examples of evidence?	
What are the general weaknesses of the argument/evidence?	
What are the general strengths of the argument/evidence?	
Give examples of what other expert authors have to say on the same subject	

ACTIVITY 4.1

Read the learning outcomes. Identify each of the outcomes. Are they type 1, 2 or 3?

1. To develop competency with the principles and practices that underpin marketing and marketing communications theory. (Type 1)
2. To understand the role and importance of marketing and marketing communications within organisations. (Type 1)
3. To understand key communicative and language strategies relevant to the business environment. (Type 1)
4. To develop competency with the analysis and evaluation of marketing outcomes in the light of environmental analysis. (Type 2)
5. To develop the ability to create written reports of a standard acceptable for a master's level programme and in business use. (Type 2)
6. To develop the ability to critically evaluate personal and transferable learning. (Type 3)
7. To develop the ability to conduct communication exercises based on marketing content. (Type 3)

ACTIVITY 4.2

Understanding the task. Here are the correct answers.

1. You need to make your own scenario for this task. NO
2. You need to complete this task individually. NO
3. You need to produce a management research report. YES
4. You need to write the report individually. NO
5. You need to speak for approximately 5 minutes in the presentation. YES

ACTIVITY 4.3

Referring to the assignment instruction list above, what do you have to do to answer the following questions?

1. To what extent is student life in China different from student life in the UK?

The instruction 'To what extent' means that you should estimate how much student life in China differs from student life in the UK. You would need to write about specific areas of difference – assignments, ideas about learning etc., and then make judgements which conclude that there is a big difference, a small difference, not much difference etc.

2. Discuss the problems that Chinese students might experience in the UK. Critically evaluate the advantages and disadvantages of studying in the UK.

'Discuss' means to consider from several points of view and explore the implications. You will need to put the case for and against a proposition and end with some statement of your own position. 'Discuss' usually also means that you will need to critically evaluate the issue of studying in the UK, as in the example question here.

ACTIVITY 4.4

Using the advice above about writing reflectively, and using some of the words and phrases for reflective writing, write a reflective paragraph answering the following questions:

What is my main impression of student life in the UK so far?

What are my main achievements so far?

What are the main problems I have experienced so far?

What can I do to improve my student experience in the UK?

Use the space provided below:

THINK 4.2

Reflect on any presentation you might have given as a student, either in China or in the UK. What were the most difficult things about the presentation? Using what you have

(Continued)

(Continued)

learnt from this section on presentations, write a reflective paragraph, answering the following questions:

What went well about the presentation?

What could have been improved about the presentation?

How could I improve my future presentations?

Reflection box: Chapter 4

Write some notes below about what is the same and what is different about assignments and assessments in the UK and in China:

Assignments in China

Assignments in the UK

Assessments in China

Assessments in the UK

Reflection box: Chapter 5

What do you want to do when you finish your study in the UK? What type of career do you want?

If you have the chance to do some original research as part of your study programme, think about a research topic that you would like to research which might be beneficial for your future career. Make some notes below, using the Chapter information, and include some ideas about how you might research the topic.

Index